JOURNEY THROUGH A LIGHTED ROOM

Also by Margaret Parton

LAUGHTER ON THE HILL
THE LEAF AND THE FLAME

Margaret Parton

JOURNEY THROUGH A LIGHTED ROOM

THE VIKING PRESS   NEW YORK

First published in 1973 by The Viking Press, Inc.
625 Madison Avenue, New York, N.Y. 10022
Published simultaneously in Canada by
The Macmillan Company of Canada Limited
SBN 670-40955-3
Library of Congress catalog card number: 72-9699
Printed in U.S.A. by Vail-Ballou Press, Inc.

ACKNOWLEDGMENT
E. P. Dutton & Co., Inc.:
From the book *Ungainly Things* by Robert Wallace.
Copyright, © 1968 by Robert Wallace.
Published by E. P. Dutton & Co., Inc.
and used with their permission.

For Lem

Truly and forever,
from all dimensions of space and time,
memory and love.

"Such," he said, "O King, seems to me the present life of men on earth, in comparison with that time which to us is uncertain, as if when on a winter's night you sit feasting with your ealdormen and thegns,—a single sparrow should fly swiftly into the hall, and coming in at one door, instantly fly out through another. In that time in which it is indoors it is indeed not touched by the fury of winter, but yet, this smallest space of calmness being passed almost in a flash, from winter going into winter again, it is lost to your eyes. Somewhat like this appears the life of man; but of what follows or what went before, we are utterly ignorant."

Ecclesiastical History,
THE VENERABLE BEDE

JOURNEY THROUGH A LIGHTED ROOM

1

It was a Sunday morning on the edge of spring, not very long ago. Winter logs still flamed in the stone fireplace which serves as a symbolic altar in our Rockland County Quaker Meeting House, but beyond the windows red maples were budding and birds singing.

The silence, which is our custom of worship, settled on the Meeting and, as it always does, seemed to deepen and become more intense as the minutes trickled quietly toward eternity. Finally someone spoke, as anyone may do who feels that he has a meaningful thought to communicate to other Friends. He ended with the quotation from Paul's first letter to the Corinthians: "So faith, hope, love abide, these three; but the greatest of these is love." After another silence a man seated with his wife and two young daughters began to speak. He was a white-haired man with a composed face, and I knew that he and his family were dedicated and active Quakers.

"Those words were used at our wedding," he began, "and we spoke them again when we celebrated our twenty-seventh wedding anniversary the other day. They are words we have tried to live by." He stopped for a moment and then began again. "The vegetable seeds we ordered last winter arrived the other day, and the birds have returned, the sky is blue. Once again the warm sun tempts us to remove our topcoats. It is time to look up."

Some quality in his voice as he said the last words made me turn to look at him. I saw that his wife was sitting in a straight and stony way that was unfamiliar to me; that her husband had his left arm around the younger daughter, whose head was turned against his shoulder; and that the other daughter held her bowed face in her hands and seemed to be crying quietly. How odd, I thought. How could this seemingly innocuous message have had such an effect on his family?

Again, there was silence, but this time a brief one. Then a woman spoke. "I think," she said, "that the members of the Meeting should know that last night our friends' home burned to the ground." There was a small, Quakerlike gasp, and tears came to many eyes, including my own. Then there was silence again until noon, when Meeting ended with the usual shaking of hands, and the Friends began to discuss how help could best be given.

Driving home, I marveled at the courage of these people, who had lost everything material they treasured, who had fled from the house in their nightwear, and who had yet somehow acquired clothes, and, leaving firemen still at the site, had come to Meeting to worship and to reaffirm their faith in life. I wish I had that kind of courage, I thought, and that kind of faith. I don't think I do, although some people say I am courageous.

At home, wandering aimlessly about the garden with a vodka and tonic in hand, I could not shake off the effect of the Meeting. What if *my* home had burned to the ground? What would I lose? From the end of the lawn I turned and looked at the white clapboard house, and my heart twisted with the old familiar love.

This eighteenth-century cottage on the Hudson River is the home of my childhood, my girlhood, my young womanhood; the home of my parents for seventeen happy years, their home still after I had gone off into the world and my own life, the home to which I returned in middle age. The two-acre meadow, the hundred-year-old grape arbor, the garden, and the funny little house all became for my parents, who were writers and somewhat weary radicals, a place of refuge from the battering old world outside, as it has become for me.

Walking slowly toward the house I remembered the things they did that helped to create an atmosphere of peace and love and beauty, and my mind once again conjured up all the old memories: my mother planting zinnias, my father laying the brick path, my father practicing guitar chords under the grape arbor, my mother stirring great cauldrons of spiced grapes in the old raftered kitchen, jigsaw pieces that made a pattern of lives for so many years.

These books reflect them, I thought, walking into the library; the house reflects them, and so do the myriad other things they loved and which I, too, continue to cherish. The music boxes, with their sweet tinkly tunes. The almost life-size Renaissance angel. The Chinese carvings from the early days in San Francisco. My own oil portrait, still above the living-room mantelpiece, where my parents placed it some thirty years ago. Love abideth!

My God, I realized, the whole damned house is a museum of love. And not only that of my parents for each other, for me, for books, for beauty, but also of me and my life and those people and places I have loved.

Here, for instance, are scores of my old poetry books, and if I choose to do so I can reach out my hand to find in actuality the lines which hover so often in my mind: "A thing of beauty is a joy forever. . . ." "But at my back I always hear Time's winged chariot hurrying near. . . ." "I think continually of those who were truly great. Who, from the womb, remembered the soul's history . . . the hours are suns, Endless and singing. . . . Never to allow gradually the traffic to smother With noise and fog, the flowering of the Spirit. . . ." "Nothing I cared, in the lamb white days, that time would take me. . . ." "And here above the chimney-stack the unknown constellations sway—and by what way shall I go back?"

"Lave your mind in poetry and it will sustain you all your life," my father wrote me on my eighteenth birthday. I did, it has.

On these shelves, too, was another reflection, an English anthology of modern poetry, given to me long, long ago by the one great love of my life. I took it down and looked again at the dearly familiar inscription on the flyleaf: "To Margaret, for reasons she will know and to help sometimes to keep the traffic away." Yes, Ian, I *do* know. I read Spender's poem again for perhaps the hundredth time, put the book back, and deliberately went from room to room, seeking other reflections of my life.

On the walls of the upstairs hall, framed scrolls describing awards I won during my days as a newspaper and magazine writer. Against a wall, a Nantucket schoolmaster's desk which had been handed down for generations in my husband's family. In the upstairs study, a small bronze of Shiva dancing, which symbolizes to me my five years in India. A "pear skin" lacquer box I bought during my time in Japan. A picture of Telegraph Hill in San Francisco and a photograph of my most-beloved Aunt Sara, taken at her equally loved home in Los Gatos. A huge by-line slug of type, given to me by my colleagues when I left the staff of the New York *Herald Tribune*. A big manila envelope stuffed with photographs and labeled simply: "Men and Boys."

In my son's room, I still found all the evidences of his vigorous youth: a baseball glove, a bag of golf clubs, three tennis rackets. On the bookshelves were books from my own childhood which were also part of his: Beatrix Potter, *The Wind in the Willows, Alice in Wonderland*. But also books of his own: *Mad* magazine paperbacks, biology textbooks, *An Introduction to Freud.*

The silence, the silence! And then, as I went downstairs, the voices began—the voices that my reflections so often produce in this rich silence of the house. At first they are irrelevant fragments of my life, rather like the background chattering of various radio stations when one is trying to tune into a particular broadcast: "Did you feed the cat, dear? . . ." "We find the defendant, Dr. Sam Sheppard, guilty. . . ." "Time for bed, child. . . ." "Ask not what your country can do for you, but. . . ." Finally, however, they seem to become more meaningful, although of what I can never quite decide. That Sunday they were more varied than ever, and as usual they seemed to have no relationship to each other.

My mother's voice: "What you give to life, life will give back to you."

My father: "Self-pity is the greatest vice, and courage the greatest virtue."

My eighth-grade teacher: "You can write."

The foreign editor of the *Herald Tribune*: "How would you like to go to Japan for six months?"

Ian, quoting Housman: "Clunton and Clunbury, Clungunford and Clun/Are the quietest places under the sun."

The man with whom I had my only purely sensual affair: "What a great fuck!"

Rod: "My dear, will you marry me?"

Lem: "I love you, Mother. I love you very much."

I made another drink and sat down on the living-room couch. My old yellow cat jumped onto my lap and I patted her, remembering how I had half-awakened during the night and had reached to stroke her; "I love you," I had said sleepily, and her rough little tongue had flicked out and touched my hand four times. Then my mind reverted to the jumble of voices. How the hell can I ever reconcile them? And why do I feel I must?

Restless and tired of silence and voices, I dumped the cat and went into the next room to choose a record for the phonograph. But in that mood of obsessive remembering, I could not decide between folk songs and Beethoven, Ella Fitzgerald and madrigals, Mozart and Peter, Paul, and Mary, "Stardust" and the Messiah—they had all been part of life, loved with different intensities at different times, or simultaneously. So, leaving them in their jackets, I went outside again.

My whole life is in there, I reflected. But if the house did burn to the ground and all those symbols were lost, I would still be full of memories and questions, and my life would still have been lived as it was.

But what did it all *mean*, if anything? Must one possibly have to relive all of it in order to discover a coherent whole? To find out how one got from here to there to back here again? Yes, I thought gloomily, that is probably the case.

My experience has been the opposite of those courageous Quakers, I realized. My house is untouched but I, inwardly, have burned to the ground. Yet once again, here I stand among my own ashes, an emotional phoenix with singed feathers, full of insistent memories and questions.

And so, I began.

2

For the last seven years, ever since I returned to this house, I have been excavating the past and trying to piece together the shards of what was the present, fifty or even one hundred years ago. It is all here in material form: thirty-eight years of my mother's journals and forty-two of mine; most of the letters my parents wrote each other, and all they ever wrote to me or I to them; letters written by grandparents, great-grandparents, aunts, uncles, friends. Forty letters which Clarence Darrow wrote to my mother. All of the clippings of my father's newspaper columns, and all my own clippings. All of my mother's magazine articles, and all of mine. Photographs of me at every stage of my life, and an old straw suitcase filled with smiling photographs of people who have been dead for fifty years.

For a long time I had tried to trace the flow of family reality in what seemed to me a logical order. On my mother's side: the Pilgrim ancestors; the Nantucket and Rhode Island forebears; the Quakers who befriended Indians; the Quaker great-great-grandmother, who operated a station on the Underground Railway; the gentle little grandmother who married a tyrannical Baptist; my mother, who escaped from the confines of her father's rigid Victorian home to the University of Michigan, and who became a radical labor reporter and the first honorary woman member of the Structural Steelworkers' Union. On my father's side: the Shropshire grandfather, who emigrated to America and worked as a blacksmith in Longmont, Colorado; my father, who left the thought-confining small town to attend the University of Colorado, and then became a cowboy, a gold miner, an explorer in

South America, and, finally, a newspaperman in San Francisco, where he met my mother.

But I did not find a way to make them live again, despite all the evidences of living they left behind them. So now, at last, I have learned that understanding must begin with the memories of the child and grow as the child grows. Thus, for me, it begins with the girl child who was born to Mary Field Parton and Lemuel F. Parton in San Francisco on May 22, 1915.

I cannot remember a time in my childhood when I was not surrounded by love and beauty. Sunlight and wind, clouds and fog, blue lupin on the Marin hills, the golden grasses of summertime, the blaze of California poppies, the smell of eucalyptus and acacia and of the sage and herbs at Carmel, the silence of redwood groves, the sound of foghorns at night, violins and accordions on ferryboats, the ting-ting bells of the cable cars are all tangled through the memories of my first eight years of life.

My parents were there, the way the sky is there, or air, or earth. My mother encircled me at night and sang "Baby's Boat's a Silver Moon," and sometimes a song about the nobility of coal miners, to whom we should all be grateful. Together we acted out moral dramas, like the one I called "Angel's Underwears," in which a poor person shares what she has with a starving man, and then learns that she had entertained an angel, unaware. There always seemed to be time for my mother to tell me fairy tales, and for my father to point out the constellations and to tell me the Greek myths about them. My parents were my own eternal and inextricably mingled constellation, and the skies of my life would have been unthinkable without them.

Next to my parents, I loved my mother's beautiful younger sister Sara, my fairy-godmother aunt, who lived in a big house on top of Russian Hill with a man called Pops—because, I later learned, of the sound made by his frequent opening of champagne bottles. He wore a gardenia in his buttonhole; he carried uncut moonstones, opals, and amethysts in the pockets of his gray tweed suits; he had white hair to his shoulders and a crinkly white beard in which, when I sat on his lap, I was encouraged to search for elves. Sara had a teen-aged son, Albert, whom I loved almost as much as I loved her. I remember the feeling of joy which suffused me when he appeared at our house and swept me up into his arms; I remember, too, withdrawing from the other children in the playschool I attended when I was three, sitting on a eucalyptus stump, looking up at the sky, and saying to myself, Abou is up there. Many years went by before I learned the details of Albert's death.

My parents had many friends and from them, too, came love and a feeling that I was a special person. There was a mystic who told me that I had lived before in another life and had been a princess. An Irish writer sent me a coconut from Tahiti. A newspaperwoman who visited Russia after the revolution remembered that pink was my favorite color and brought me an enormous silk scarf, all the rosy colors of sunrise. A bombastic German named Ehrenburg often tried to explain Einstein's theory of relativity to my father and assured me, to my mother's delight, that I would grow up to be a scientist; inevitably, the imaginary companion of my childhood was named "Einsein." There were other people: labor leaders who talked and laughed a great deal, painters, a reformed burglar, and sometimes men with soft black eyes and dark skins, Indian revolutionaries from Bengal.

Not only my own memories help me to relive my childhood, but also my mother's memories. She had several stories, which she told with rueful humor, illustrating my adoration of my father. At two, I would be perfectly happy with her all day long, apparently, but as soon as my father came home from work I would point a stern finger at her and give the command: "Do in de tichen and *took!*" My Aunt Sara was a prominent leader in the movement for women's suffrage (unlike my mother, who believed only a revolution could change American society) and probably for that reason at three years of age I marched with other children in a suffrage parade. At a certain point in the proceedings I was supposed to climb up on a tree stump, wave a papier-mâché hatchet, and shout: "Votes for Mommies!" As mother told it, everything went according to schedule, except that I shouted, "Votes for Daddies!"

My mother had been raised in a home of such religious strictness that she had completely revolted and thus enjoyed ridiculing the outward forms of orthodox religion and I was, alas, never taught Bible stories nor did I go to Sunday School. But she taught me a little Quaker prayer that I said every night, and the Lord's Prayer, and she was vastly amused when I ended the latter with "for Thine is the kingdom. Amen." "If God has a kingdom, he already has power and glory," I reasoned. "The child is intelligent," my father commented. I learned very early that in our family there was no higher word of praise, except, perhaps, "imaginative."

For most of my life my parents were "They"—a single unit and not the separate individuals Mary Field and Lemuel Parton. She was "Mother," not the professional magazine writer who did not marry until she was thirty-five and who, when I was born two years later, already had a fully established and successful career. It is only in middle age that I have realized how difficult the adjustment to marriage and motherhood must have been for her. Yet she did adjust to marriage and motherhood and she *did* love me, even if the love was often ambivalent, and she railed in letters about the demands of "little Maggot."

My father's love was less complex. In 1919 my mother went to Chicago on a series of labor stories and I was sent off to stay with friends in the country and brought home on weekends. He wrote in one of his daily letters to her:

When the baby was here we had a regular debauch of story telling. One night, when I thought she was falling asleep in my arms, I was stringing out a story about Agnes and Edna getting ready to run a race and Edna saying "I'll bet you one cookie," and Agnes saying "I'll see you two and raise you four," etc. I scarcely knew what I was saying and just kept this up, ad lib, "seeing and raising," just for repetition, the baby having her eyes closed. The next night she said she would tell me a story if I would tell her one, and she reeled off this whole yarn, with all the poker phraseology. . . . During the week I grow hungry for that precious, odd, intense, volcanic, little cosmic wayfarer who has joined our household. . . .

Was there too much love, I wonder? Reading the doting letters and looking over boxes of all the memorabilia my mother so carefully hoarded, the feeling of love becomes cloying, overwhelming, smothering. And yet I also reflect that it may be a case of the sundial reflecting only the sunny hours. One does not, after all, write love notes when one is in a rage. And there *were* shadows. Apparently, I had a fearsome temper and my face would darken "in that thunderstorm way." Around five, I developed asthma and had regular and quite awful attacks until we moved away from foggy San Francisco. I wet my bed until I was six. At seven, I had my tonsils out and thereafter became what my mother (who always believed me to be beautiful) insisted on calling "sturdy" and I, in retrospect and looking at old photographs, call fat.

Despite the fact that in many areas of child-raising my parents were twenty-five years ahead of their times, they made mistakes. They didn't take my overweight seriously enough, and in my adolescence it became a formative and unhappy factor in much that shaped my personality. And when at five I was found playing "patient" to a neighborhood boy's "doctor," my mother became practically hysterical and told me that I was never to play with him again. Aside from this one episode her teaching in regard to sex was admirable, if perhaps overromanticized. I cannot remember a time when I did not know exactly where babies came from or how they got there.

At a private progressive school I began first grade, learned to tell my right foot from my left, and made friends. At seven, I fell in love with a little boy named Jack and for years I treasured a tiny tin model of a firemen's hat which he gave me. I also learned to read that year and thereafter consumed books voraciously, especially fairy tales. I learned to swim, and spent happy vacations with my mother at Carmel and at Donner Lake in the Sierras. I grew.

Early in 1923 my parents decided to take the $1000 in savings they had accumulated, and to go with me to Europe for as many months as the money held out, or longer if they worked and began selling articles; 1923 was a peak year for American expatriates, and there wasn't a writer in America who didn't long to be in Paris. But I suspect that there were other, more personal reasons my parents had for wanting to leave San Francisco, and I have pieced some of them together from the memorabilia in the house. For one thing, my mother's diaries indicate that more and more she felt trapped by marriage, motherhood, and domesticity; she loathed housework and resented having to do it. She referred to my father as her "precious chum," but was, I think, often impatient with his dreaminess and lack of drive; he had not yet hit his pace professionally and money was a problem. She was unhappy, too, that she was no longer working and blamed this on the dreadful confines of marriage.

During my adolescence, when my quarrels with her were frequent and violent, my father told me that several years after their marriage he had contemplated divorce; he decided, however, that he would rather learn to adjust to her mercurial, melancholic temperament than lose her. I remember how astonished I was when he told me of those difficult early years, for never in my life had I heard my parents quarrel, nor could I recall a period when there was not a mood of harmony, affection, and love in our house.

Whatever the reasons for their decision to leave San Francisco, we sailed on June 30 on the freighter *Willsola*, with Sara and Pops and a host of other friends waving good-by from the pier. We were headed for the Panama Canal, New York, Europe, and what my mother called "The golden fleece of Adventure."

. . .

Our freighter arrived in New York harbor at sunset on July 21. Under her loose dress my mother wore a kind of rope harness from which dangled two bottles of brandy; she had rigged it so that if the revenue agents on the docks patted her during their search for contraband liquor, she could raise and lower the bottles by a kind of pulley arrangement. We got through without any trouble and headed immediately for a friend's apartment. A party was going on and I remember the great burst of laughter and applause when Mother stripped off the dress and revealed harness, bottles, and petticoat.

. . .

My parents were euphoric during the six weeks in Paris. They saw everyone—Hemingway in a boxing match, the sculptor Jo Davidson, and the muckraker Lincoln Steffens (both great friends of Mother's from her Chicago and New York days), artists, poets, newspapermen. Paris itself intoxicated them, every nuance, every flavor, every play of light and shadow. I doubt whether they ever had a happier period in their lives.

But I was miserably bored, and my unhappiness became a growing concern; as I have done ever since in times of unhappiness, I retreated to books. Despite the expense, my worried parents decided I would have to go to boarding school for the remainder of their time in Europe. Early in October, my mother took me to Lausanne, where she visited several schools and finally chose one called Montjoie, Château de Vennes. It was a good choice and I was happy there. I met boys and girls of many nationalities, played and quarreled with them, learned French fast, and saw snow for the first time in my life; all the memories of Montjoie are mixed up with winter things like the smell and feel of wet woollen gloves, the cold flagstones of the unheated little church where we were taken every Sunday, the smell and taste of the hot, black-bean soup which awaited us on our return to the Château.

For the next two months, while I was at school, my parents wandered in an ecstatic daze around Europe. But neither of them wrote or sold any articles. So in mid-December, with the money running low, my father went back to New York to job-hunt. My mother came to Lausanne to be with me over Christmas, and on January 28, 1924, we sailed from Marseilles on a Mediterranean cruise she had planned months before. We saw Alexandria, Jerusalem, the Acropolis, Naples, Gibraltar, the Azores—and on March 4 were reunited with my welcoming father in New York.

The trip had an important effect on all of us. It deepened the companionship of my parents, and their temporary separation showed my mother how much she loved and needed my father. From Paris, the night before his departure, my father wrote her: "Dearest Mary, as I begin to look back on this trip, I know that it was the wisest thing we ever did. It has given me a lot of new proportions and values, and I know you and love you as I never did before. I feel eager and assured. . . ." As for me, nothing had changed outwardly very much except that I no longer had asthma attacks. But all during my girlhood and young womanhood there lingered the memories of ships' whistles and foreign languages, the turquoise waters of Alexandria bay, the spitting camels of Jerusalem, and the purity of the Acropolis against the cobalt skies of Greece.

❦ 3 ❦

By the time my mother and I arrived in New York, my father had turned down job offers from both the *Tribune* and the *Herald* and had accepted a position as a feature writer specializing in science for the North American Newspaper Alliance. We settled down in an apartment on East 17th Street, and eventually our belongings, packed by my Aunt Sara, arrived from California: the Chinese screens, the Japanese prints, the Korean chests, the books. She also sent my beloved dollhouse—an orange crate painted green, with a little curved door covered in gold paper, which my parents had made for me the Christmas before we left California. It was always more a theater than a dollhouse and my sets and costumes changed, as I grew older, from fairyland to a *Midsummer Night's Dream* forest, and then, after my entranced discovery of *The Three Musketeers* and all the sequels, to the bedroom of the King's mistress. My first ambition in life was to be a set designer or, failing that, a costume designer. It never occurred to me that I wasn't going to be *something*.

.   .   .

In San Francisco my parents had become great friends with John and Llewelyn Powys, the English writers, who asked my mother to look up their widowed sister Marian Grey in New York. At that time Marian, one of the world's great experts on lace, had a shop on Madison Avenue and one day in early summer my mother telephoned her there. Marian invited her to lunch. As my amused mother told the story, the lunch went like this:

Mother: "Some friends showed me Sneden's Landing recently,

and they tell me you and your little boy, Peter, live there. It seems a charming community and we're looking for a summer house. Do you know if there are any for rent in Sneden's?"

Marian (veddy, veddy English): "I'm sure I haven't the slightest idea."

Mother (persisting): "Well, if you hear of any, could you let me know?"

Marian (placing her napkin firmly on the table): "Mrs. Pahton, if you persist in treating me like a real-estate agent, I'm afraid I shall have to ask you to pay for your own lunch!"

The meal was continued in silence and Mother paid for her own lunch. The next time she heard from Marian was two months later, when we were summering in a little house halfway down the Sneden's Landing hill. The phone rang at five one morning.

"Mrs. Pahton," came Marian's peremptory voice, "Petah is ill and requires an enema. Will you please procure an enema bag and come and administer it?" Mother did, and a somewhat wary friendship was established. But it was always more formal than cordial, and even after forty years Marian couldn't resist a characteristic crack. When I returned to Sneden's in 1965 she gave a little tea party for me to meet some of the new people who had come to the Landing during my absence. "Oh, here's Margaret Pahton," she trilled to the assembled guests when I arrived at the eighteenth-century cottage she occupied for fifty years. "I always thought her parents dressed her *so* unbecomingly as a child."

I remember Marian in the 1920s and early 1930s, her sturdy figure churning around the tennis court, her muscled arms slamming tennis balls with the power of a pile driver; but for the past three decades the image is one of a pink old lady with wild white hair and eagle-keen eyes, sitting in a ratty fur coat on a bench in front of her doorway and offering a glass of port and a flow of conversation to anyone who came to sit with her for a while. She mesmerized generations of young people, too, particularly today's children, and when she died recently at the age of eighty-nine, her plain pine casket was carried in and out of the church by six long-haired young men and women in blue jeans and torn sneakers. "She's the original hippie," Peter said once, with only a slight edge to his voice.

Peter and I grew up in the Landing together, and although I am some seven years older than he, we became great friends, and often exchanged the shy confidences of only and not always happy children; he remains the nearest thing I will ever have to a brother and I know that he looks upon me as a sister. We have shared too many sorrows and angers, tortures and joys to be anything else.

Today Sneden's Landing is an easy twenty-minute drive up the Palisades Parkway or Route 9W from the George Washington Bridge. But in the 1920s it was a far different matter, for the bridge, 9W, and the Parkway had not yet been built. If you had a car you could take a ferry from Manhattan to the Jersey side of the Hudson and make your way along a complicated network of back roads. If not, you could take the Hudson Tube to Hoboken, the Erie train to Tappan or Sparkill, and walk two miles (taking the local taxi cost $1 and was considered extravagant unless suitcases were involved). But from April through October there was a lovely way to come: by train from Grand Central Station to Dobbs Ferry, and by launch across the river to Sneden's. Ferries had been operating regularly between these two points for over two hundred years and until World War II a small launch chugged its way back and forth, captained in the 1920s by fiery old Captain Hill, a great curser with no respect at all for "summer folks," which is what many of us were until the Depression.

For me at nine years old and for many years after, Sneden's meant a second home in the huge chestnut tree by the tennis court, the smell of locust blossoms in June, fireworks by the river in July (on one famous Fourth, Peter, who was a devilish boy, dropped a lighted sparkler into a box full of fireworks; the ensuing scene resembled descriptions of the Marne battlefield and a number of stately dowagers made some far-from-stately dives into the water), swimming in the Hudson from the dock at high tide, fireflies in August, goldenrod and joe-pye weed in September, and every now and then a solemn funeral for a dead mouse or bird, with all the little girls wearing long white cotton nightgowns and roman-striped sashes and Sandy Vanderbilt playing dirges on his banjo. Above all delights there was the waterfall in the woods, and the dark pool into which the cascade tumbled. From the pool, steps spilled down to a marble fountain and a graveled walk that led to a white pergola covered with wild grapes; beyond the pergola was the blue river.

Much of the land in Sneden's had belonged for decades to the

Lawrence family, whose daughter Mary grew up to be a sculptress and married an Italian sculptor named François Tonetti; by the 1920s, when we first knew her, she was a redoubtable middle-aged woman who owned most of the houses in the Landing and who was largely responsible for creating the atmosphere of "controlled disorder" which so attracted the artists and writers and architects who lived there in the summer. It was Mary Tonetti and her friend Stanford White who "built" the waterfall early in the century; during the 1920s and the 1930s, anyone who lived in a Tonetti house was allowed to use the waterfall for swimming and picnics and often, on summer Sundays, processions of laughing people made their way along the half-mile trail through the woods bearing great bowls of salad, loaves of French bread, watermelons, and bottles of homemade red wine, which they cooled in the icy waters of the pool. Prohibition was never much of a problem in Sneden's.

. . .

In 1926 my father was forty-six and my mother forty-eight. The easy solutions of their early radicalism had begun to pall, the dream of Soviet Russia as the answer to man's inhumanity to man had faded, and they felt an increasing helplessness when they contemplated the pain of the world which they had hoped in some measure to alleviate. The antidote they chose was to try to create, mostly with their own labor, a small world of order, simplicity, and beauty that would provide a peaceful background for their forays into the activities of the mind and a refuge from the driving problems of mankind which had always preoccupied them. "A microcosm in the macrocosm," my father dreamed.

In those days Mary Tonetti generally refused to sell any of her houses; but in April 1926 she rather surprisingly agreed to sell to my parents a small farmhouse and two acres of land "up the hill," for $5000. (Only later did my parents discover what she knew then: that the peaceful country road a hundred yards from the house was scheduled in 1927 to become the through highway known as 9W.)

The cottage was on a small lane leading off the country road, in a setting of fields and low stone walls. The earliest part, a small kitchen with a bedroom above it which was once reached by a trap door, was said to have been built in 1729 for the hayman to the squire of The Big House across the lane. Around 1810 someone had added a small dining room, a living room with a sedate fireplace, a narrow hall with a fanlight over the front door, and a steep flight of stairs leading to two upstairs bedrooms. There were no closets, and when my father asked the farmer who had occupied the house where his wife hung her clothes, he answered, "Well, I guess she wore one and hung tother on a peg." There was no bathroom, but that first summer everyone thought the outhouse amusing. There was no running water, but the well water was pure and the bucket and pulley evocative of the rural past. There was no electricity, but oil lamps gave a lovely light. The only heating came from the fireplaces, and who needs heat in summer? But by the following summer, all amenities were installed and my parents could turn their attention to the garden.

One of their first projects was to rebuild the grape arbor with the three vines said to be eighty years old. Thin, rickety poles were replaced with red-cedar posts, soft-barked, shaggy, and sweet-smelling; the arbor was extended by twenty feet, almost to the edge of the meadow, and floored with flagstone; within a year or so the vines were producing enough grapes to enable my parents to make a hundred gallons of wine a year. All my memories of the arbor those years are interwoven with the rich smell of the purple grapes in September, with great wooden barrels hauled from the dirt-floored cellar and left to air in the fall sunlight, with talk of sugar-content and hydrometers.

The first few years of wine-making, the mid-years of Prohibition when I was still a child, I performed the first, ceremonial grape-crushing, bare-footed. Mother would scrub my feet in the bathtub, then lay a walkway of newspapers out to the arbor, where a tin tub full of fresh-cut grapes awaited my small, pink, and very clean feet. Invariably there would be crowds of adult friends on hand, all toasting "the child" with last year's wine, and exclaiming: "How charming!" "How Italian!" I don't remember that I enjoyed it very much, for I felt conspicuous and foolish as children usually do when they are required to be picturesque for the sake of elders. The grapes were cold and rather slimy between the toes, but worst of all the next Monday and days thereafter I would have to begin the school year with legs stained red to the knees.

When school began, the water and electricity were turned off and we moved back into our New York apartment, not to return to the country until the end of May. Winter life was a different world from summer life, for it centered in the various apartments in which we lived and the private schools I attended. While we were living on East 17th Street, I went to Friends' Seminary on Stuyvesant Square, a school about which I remember very little except that it was there that I acquired my lifelong hatred of arithmetic from a sadistic teacher who made me copy and recopy pages of correctly added sums because my tears kept staining the paper. In 1925 we moved to a new apartment, a top floor at 27 East 11th Street, and in the fall I entered fifth grade at the City and Country School on West 12th Street, a pioneer progressive school that encouraged creativity and independence of thought and shaped my life in many good ways.

I began keeping a diary when I was ten and a half. Most of the book recorded snowball fights, trips to the Metropolitan Museum, the installation of braces on my teeth, gifts of dolls for my orange-box theater, and the plots of fairy tales I read. But soon afterward the pages began to throb with romantic dreams involving the rosy cheeks, tangled curls, and baseball prowess of one of my classmates, and by the time I was thirteen sex was added to romance. Part of this was due to the fact that two of the girls in the class began showing up with sexy books like *Chicky* and *Bad Girl*. We all read them avidly and I remember that my parents disapproved of such "cheap stuff," but would never, of course, forbid me to read anything I wanted to read. Another reason, aside from the approach of adolescence, was my discovery that it was a delightful experience to kiss "my secret love" at spin-the-bottle and playing-post-office parties. Still, after considering the matter with great solemnity and discussing it earnestly with my best friend, Barbara, I vowed that I would remain a virgin until marriage, or anyway, never "surrender" to a man unless I truly loved him.

To judge from the diaries it would appear that during those growing years sex and romance were my total and only preoccupations. But this was not so, for City and Country was a school with many activities and I enjoyed almost all of them. Each class (which was organized by age) specialized in a craft, and so in the tens I learned carpentry, in the elevens we operated a printing press and produced the school magazine, in the twelves we studied bookbinding, and in the thirteens we learned to weave. We had rhythmics and square dancing, we wrote plays and produced them, we dipped candles and hammered out silver candlesticks, we had cooking lessons, and folk singing with Rat Tan Devi. We modeled in clay and I decided to be a sculptor rather than a stage designer.

Academically, we were excited about almost everything we studied. In the elevens we read Stephen Vincent Benét's *John Brown's Body* aloud, and studied the Civil War. In the twelves we read Elizabethan poetry, haunted the Elizabethan section of the Metropolitan Museum of Art, wrote papers about Sir Francis Drake and Queen Elizabeth, and became such devoted buffs of the era that I still feel it is "my" period. In the thirteens we were pulled abruptly into the nineteenth century and then the twentieth. Our teacher that year was Leo Huberman, a dark, intense young man whom we all adored and whom we called Huby. He was very much a left-winger and the American history he taught us that year reflected his own political and economic passions: we learned about the clay feet of our Founding Fathers, the iniquities of the reconstruction period in the South, the rape of the American Indians, the bitter history of the Negroes, the wickedness of Mr. Rockefeller, Sr., the cynical manipulations which led to World War I, and the outrage of the Versailles Treaty. We visited a steel factory, and I wrote a poem about "Mechanical men, mechanical minds . . . making a car for a rich man to ride in." Huby thought it was great, so I decided to be a poet instead of a stage designer or a sculptor. Then I did a paper on the horrors of the Immigration period and Huby wrote at the top "You can write." I decided to be a writer instead of a stage designer, sculptor, or poet.

Huby's view of United States history came as no surprise, for it was right in line with what I was hearing at home, from, among others, my parents' friends the skeptical Charles and Mary Beard. I believed it all uncritically and as I never had any other course in American history it was not until I lived overseas that I was able to evaluate my own country more clearly and later to do some reading which put the picture in better focus. As for my parents, they were ahead of me (as usual) and in 1932 when Franklin D. Roosevelt ran for the Presidency they changed from the Socialist party to the Democratic.

So at last we children were graduated and went on to our various high schools, full of odd skills, patches of information and misinformation, respect for craftsmanship and creativity, sex drives, vulgarity, nobility, and trepidation. The basic character had been formed, and what came later could only modify or expand what already existed.

4

With several City and Country School classmates I went through high school at Lincoln School of Teachers' College, now a public school but at that time a renowned coeducational private school on West 123rd Street, near Columbia University. The teaching was good, the classes were small, and in four years I managed to learn quite a lot of French and German, European history, English literature, history of art, and practically no mathematics. Creative writing (horrid phrase!) was strongly encouraged; during those years I wrote poetry in most of my spare time, and much of it was published in the school magazine. I belonged to the Library Club, and lived for the weekly meetings, discussions (Is Carl Sandburg greater than Swinburne?), and talks by people in the literary world, many of whom were friends of our wise and gentle librarian, Anne Thaxter Eaton, in whose private office we "literati" were allowed to congregate and eat chocolate cookies. It was, indeed, a privileged education.

In 1928 my parents, poor innocents, decided that the best way to assure financial security during their old age would be to buy a nineteenth-century brownstone town house at 7 Charles Street in the Village and convert it into apartments; they did so, borrowing money from Otto Kahn and Clarence Darrow. We had the entire first-floor apartment, with its high ceilings, molded cornices, and two white marble fireplaces carved with acanthus leaves. We had a dear young German maid named Lisa, whose affable attentions meant that Mother could complete a biography of her friend Mother Jones, the militant old labor leader. Meanwhile, my father was becoming nationally known as a writer on

social and economic subjects and meeting more and more interesting people, many of whom he brought home to dinner. (It interests me that my father, the most domesticated of men, never
lost his somewhat wistful interest in explorers, and often wrote
about them and brought them home. Colonel Percy Harrison
Fawcett and his son Jack spent a memorable evening with us just
before they set off on the South American expedition from which
they never returned.)

At fourteen I described a party in my journal:

Sinclair Lewis, Dorothy Thompson, a historian named Mr. Woodward and his wife, the reformed burglar Jack Black, and Mr. and
Mrs. E. B. White were here. A very amusing evening, during
which Sinclair Lewis rose from the table and carried his plate of
roast beef over to the desk where I was eating alone because
there wasn't enough room for me at the big table; he sat down on
the floor beside me and fed his roast beef to Tiggy and talked
about cats. Later Mr. Woodward came over and leaned on my
shoulder and said I was beautiful. Sinclair Lewis was so funny.
He kept getting up and starting telephone calls to Bishop Man-
ning. Very nervous I guess.

"Dinner party ruined by lovable but drunk Red Lewis," Mother's diary reports. What she didn't add was that she was furious
because, as she said afterward, he fed her expensive and delecta-
bly rare roast beef to our cat.

Clarence Darrow, whenever he came to town, was another visitor. His arrival was always an occasion of great rejoicing on the
part of my parents and particularly my mother, but I did not like
him, and all my life there has been something about his memory
which set my mind's teeth on edge. Most of it goes back to childhood, I suppose. During the year when I was ten Lincoln Steffens
never once forgot that for some peculiar reason I wanted to be
called Jane rather than Margaret. The great San Francisco newspaper editor Fremont Older solemnly invited me to join him in
swimming races. Carl Sandburg sang ballads to me on his guitar
and gave me a copy of *Smoke and Steel* inscribed "Margaret
Parton—May all the white moons of life be good to her little
feet." They were eminent men, but they could take time to notice
a child and to be kind. But with Darrow one had the impression
that he didn't care for children very much; that if you couldn't be
clever and amuse him it would be best to melt into the shadows

behind the piano. Once, I remember, I asked for his autograph and presented him with a page of my book on which Babe Ruth's name was already inscribed. Under the Babe's name, smiling, he wrote: "Clarence Darrow, Pinch Hitter." When he read this aloud everyone laughed so much that I realized it was another of their adult jokes which I didn't understand, and went away unnoticed. Somehow, with Darrow I always felt like a *thing*, an object rather than a living person who happened to be a child.

There were many other adult friends who gave much of themselves to me, and whom I loved: the sculptor Lucile Swan, who lived in China and who illuminated my imagination with the beauty of Peking on her periodic trips home; Mary Margaret McBride, who always listed sympathetically to my girlish confidences; Inez and Will Irwin, ebullient writers who made me feel that I was included in their warm love of my family; the always-*there* friends Berta and Elmer Hader, children's book artists in whose home on the Hudson we and many of these friends celebrated every Thanksgiving and Christmas for more than a quarter of a century.

Winter social life was not only my parents' parties. They took me to hear Toscanini and Fritz Kreisler, and we went almost every weekend to the theater, and sometimes twice, for it was easy to get tickets and some balcony seats cost only ninety-nine cents. For me, however, all these cultural events were whipped cream, and movies were the bread, butter, and honey of my existence. Greta Garbo, Joan Crawford, Norma Shearer, Marlene Dietrich—oh, to be like them! And beginning with Douglas Fairbanks, Sr., at the age of ten, I was regularly in love with one movie actor or another for the next eight years—Nils Asther, Robert Montgomery, Ronald Colman, Leslie Howard, Gary Cooper. In my forties I interviewed Gary Cooper, and to my amused surprise found myself drowning in those blue eyes and feeling all of sixteen again.

The movies of that period were not a good influence, I now believe, and in retrospect I agree with my concerned parents that in general they were cheap and tawdry. "But to criticize, even impersonally, is to Margaret high treason," Mother mourned in her diary. "These are her gods and goddesses."

My parents' good words were: loving, wholesome, dependable, responsible, individual, intelligent, imaginative, nonconformist, curious, intellectual, and creative. *My* good words were: flippant, fresh, teasing, insouciant, sexy, nonchalant, vivacious, flirtatious, poised, slinky, sophisticated, glamorous (none of which could even remotely have applied to me).

But the real word for the problem that lay between us during my anguished adolescence was BOYS. I was boy crazy—and unpopular. During all of high school I never had a date. During my first two years I never even talked to a boy; later I learned how to carry on a friendly conversation with one of the creatures, but I never thought of them as *people* until I was in my twenties. Once, during my junior year, I went to a dance alone and was invited to waltz by my English teacher and, later, by a boy whom I knew had been commissioned to wheel wallflowers once around the gymnasium. The memory of that evening is still so dreadful that my stomach constricts with misery when I recall it.

The great obstacle to popularity, I thought, was the fact that my mother made me dress "like a sweet, simple schoolgirl" instead of like Joan Crawford or Norma Shearer. And so there were frequent battles over high heels, lipstick, manicures, permanents, all of which my mother thought "cheap and vulgar," which was also her opinion of the pretty girls at school who had these things, including my best friend, Barbara. Her dislike of friendly, sexy little Barbara was, in fact, so intense that I could not invite her to my house, and this also became an element in the ambivalent love-hate relationship between my mother and me; once in a moment of hostile rage she struck me in the face three times. Typically, she showed up at school later in the day, weeping with contrition, and after I had comforted her we went downtown and bought theater tickets.

My father, I think, was bewildered by these perpetual conflicts, and always acted as the peacemaker. "Now, Mary," he would say when my mother was assuring me that I was damned and doomed forever, "the returns aren't all in yet," and I found the phrase immensely consoling. I remember one dreadful summer afternoon when, driven by an urge to change my schoolgirl image, I dressed up as what I thought a prostitute might look like, complete with charcoal on my eyelids, a spit curl, and a cigarette. Then, feeling magnificent and sexy, I went out on the front porch, where my father was mending a step, and, there being no other male around, tried to "vamp" him. He took one confused look and began pretending to box with me. When he went indoors I sat on the porch swing and wept until my nose ran and the charcoal got in my eyes.

The pain I was living through drove me to books, to philosophy, and into myself. I began to find that my happiest moments came when I was alone and near nature. But I communicated very little of this to my parents, for I felt that any "poetic" thoughts I might have would seem silly to what seemed to me their giant intellects. Nor did I express my longing for boys and popularity, for I was utterly confused by my mother's varying attitudes. Sex, she assured me, was very, very beautiful, and human beings are the only animals which make love while looking into each other's eyes. Sex was also an inevitable part of the vast biological drive, experienced by the mass of mankind. But the intellectual and the artist are superior to the masses, she had indicated, and one of the marks of the superior person is not to share mass interests. A equals B doesn't equal C! And so I began to hide my churning emotions behind a mask, which my mother described as "Margaret's cold, icy attitude toward people."

I sat silently at their parties, listening to the talk of economics, graft, corruption, Depression, breadlines, Russia, and what happened to all the old radicals. "Margaret, aren't you bored by all this tired radical talk?" Lincoln Steffens asked me when I was fourteen. "Oh, I understand it," I answered. "*I* was a tired radical at eleven."

To my mother, my boredom verged on the criminal. One summer we spent a week with a scientist and his wife at their remote New Hampshire home. It rained all week, they talked of science all day and all night, and I was driven to wandering alone through the dripping woods in the rain. One day I found a little overgrown graveyard with a tombstone of an eighteenth-century boy named Laben Aldrich, who had died at seventeen. After that I used to sit beside it on the damp moss, feeling closer to him than I did to any of the live adults, and with my arms around the stone, sob with loneliness.

One day that week, Mother wrote in her journal:

I wish Margaret was interested in this new environment, but there is only boredom for my poor little unimaginative, lethargic girl to whom these woods, these pines, these books, this beautiful house with its world-wide radio, its scintillating conversations offer no interest. My darling child, I should love you as one loves a poor little crippled mind, a small heart—misfortunes for which one is not to blame.

But she never voiced these harsh thoughts, and would only remark that she couldn't understand why I wasn't interested in intelligent conversation. And my parents, I now realize, knew that it was wrong for me to be continually with adults, but felt powerless to change the situation. Few of their friends had children, for intellectuals of their period had felt that it was wrong to bring more children into the world, and those few offspring who existed were older than I. Were my parents to leave Sneden's, where Peter Grey and I were now the only children? As a compromise and at a financial sacrifice to themselves, they sent me to a camp in New Hampshire the summers when I was fifteen and sixteen; I reveled in the beauty, the athletics, and the laughing companionship of girls who had never heard of dialectical materialism. I also learned a great many dirty jokes, and after that whenever I was bored at my parents' parties I used to tell them silently to myself and feel smugly superior to the adults.

"Lem and Mary were so entirely sufficient to each other, so completely one, that you always seemed a little on the outside," one of my parents' friends told me recently.

"Your mother was jealous of you," said another.

The two views seem contradictory, but contradictions can exist together. There is no doubt in my mind that my parents were absorbed in each other and totally happy in their companionship; often I would wake late on a Sunday morning, come down to breakfast in the grape arbor, and find them lingering over their fourth cup of coffee, so busy discussing the social significance of the flight of the queen bee, or some such matter, that they barely had time to say good morning. An elderly neighbor remembers that even after twenty-five years of marriage they would walk arm in arm to the bus stop, deep in eager conversation. "It's almost as hard for a child to grow up in the presence of an extremely happy marriage as it is to grow up in an unhappy home," a psychiatrist-friend once said.

On the other hand, there is also no doubt in my mind that a very special and tender love existed between my father and me, as it does between most fathers and daughters, mothers and sons. And he was, aside from being my father, a uniquely lovable human being, as the hundreds of letters we received after he died assured us. I telephoned my father once in great sadness. In the letter he sent me afterward, he wrote: "When your voice came out of the dark drizzle of rain the other night, I felt that all we can do, in this ghostly mist which is life, is to touch hands and give each other faithfully whatever of love and understanding we may have in our hearts, and this I do, my dear, with all the faith and loyalty that is in me."

Encouraged by his faith in me, I gradually began to grow up.

❧ 5 ❧

On July 1, 1932, my parents and I set out with our neighbor Bob Hyde to drive across the country to California in his Model A Ford. As he was the only one who could operate a car, my mother sat in front with him and my father and I shared the rumble seat—an open-air seat at the back, reached by two steps and considerable agility. We didn't know it at the time but Bob, who had a family in Sneden's, was on his way to another in Los Angeles.

Bob was in a hurry. He routed us out of our auto-court rooms at five in the morning, and drove fifty miles before we could stop for a cup of coffee. He begrudged time taken for meals and he himself never ordered anything in a restaurant except pineapple malted milk. Still, it was a good trip for a teen-ager. When I went to California in 1928 we traveled by train and I was too young to notice much. This time I was seventeen, and I saw the vastness and the differences of America, the variety of people, food, architecture. It was a Presidential election year and my father, good newspaperman that he was, never lost a chance to sound out opinion along the way—a lesson that was not lost on me. "Dad asks everyone what they think of Hoover," I reported in my journal, "and they hate him!"

Considering that there were no turnpikes in those days, Bob made great time: 3200 miles in seven days. And then, after a week in San Francisco, we were finally on our way to the place which became my personal paradise, and to my beloved Sara and Pops.

In 1940 Sara, a distinguished poet, wrote a short autobiography for *Twentieth Century Authors,* as did Pops. In it she describes her marriage at eighteen to a Baptist minister, their sojourn in Burma, where their son Albert was born, her horror at the suffering she witnessed, and her growing recognition of the hypocrisy of orthodox Christianity. Back in Cleveland, she continues, the process of radicalization accelerated, partly under the tutelage of my mother, who was then head of a Chicago social settlement and whose radical view of society had been deeply influenced by her close friend Clarence Darrow. When the minister and his wife became Socialists he was fired and they moved to Portland, Oregon, with Albert and their daughter, Kay, who had been born in Cleveland.

"In Portland," she writes, "introduced by Darrow, I met Charles Erskine Scott Wood. My history thereafter is largely in this association."

I enjoy the restraint and delicacy of that sentence. What it means was that Sara fell in love with a man thirty years older than herself, and he with her; that they left their families and lived together quite openly for many years before their eventual marriage became possible. When I was growing up this relationship had been going on for so long that it was completely taken for granted, but at the time I imagine the gossip must have convulsed Portland society.

At the time Sara first met Colonel Wood in or around 1910, he was not only rich but famous, with a fully lived life already behind him. After graduating from West Point he had served in the Indian campaigns of the Northwest, had made friends of the Indians, and had been accepted in their tribes. During a period in which he served as adjutant back at West Point he studied law at Columbia, and as a friend of Mark Twain was responsible for the private printing of Twain's book *1601*—considered pornographic in those days. In 1884, he resigned from the Army with the rank of colonel and began the practice of law in Portland. By the time Sara met him he was the most distinguished and picturesque attorney in the Northwest; he had not yet begun to write the satires, Indian tales, and poetry to which he later turned, but he already possessed the qualities which led *Twentieth Century Authors* to describe him as "the last of the titans."

The best description I know of these qualities was written many years later by Sara's son-in-law, James Ralston Caldwell, himself a distinguished critic and poet. His words describe the Colonel's poetry, but they apply just as well to the man Sara met and fell in love with, and the man I knew in my own youth:

He has plundered gardens, orchards, the ranges, even the desert, and he comes loaded down with blossoms, fruit, boughs, opals, a finch or a field-mouse riding his shoulder, with the smell of the sage-wind about him. Yet he holds mainly sober converse with these riches. Joyously surrounded by them, he ponders the dubious quest of man. Tenderness and pity sing beneath his gusto, something of pagan sadness in his pagan zest.

For several years, at first in Oregon and then in San Francisco where she moved with the Colonel, Sara threw herself into suffrage work, eventually becoming one of the best-known leaders in the movement. In 1915 she was one of the first three women to drive across the United States, carrying a suffrage petition with over 10,000 names, which she presented to President Wilson at the White House. They lived, in those years, in a beautiful mansion on Russian Hill where they in effect held court, entertained all the leading literary and artistic figures of San Francisco, and called each other Zeus and Sappho. Under the terms of the bitterly contested Nevada divorce which Sara finally managed to achieve, the minister (who had settled in Berkeley) retained custody of the two children during the week and she was permitted to have them on weekends. It was on Russian Hill that I first remember my cousin Albert, who at seventeen was full of laughter and outgoing love, and his shy younger sister Katherine, nine years older than I.

The accident happened in October 1918, when Albert was seventeen and Kay was twelve. Sara had learned to drive a car, and one weekend they all took the ferry to Sausalito and hired an auto for the day. Somewhere in the Marin hills the brakes failed and the car rolled backward over a cliff. The Colonel was thrown clear, Sara's leg was broken, and Albert, fatally injured, was pinned beneath the car, as was his sister Kay. "Are we going to die?" the little girl asked her mother. "I don't know," Sara answered calmly. A little later Albert did die.

Albert's death has always seemed to me to have left an empty space in the air, a space where he should be and is not. Would all our lives have been different if he had lived? Sara's? Kay's?

Kay's children and grandchildren? Mine? I have often thought so.

It was because of the tragedy, I suspect, as well as for the healthy climate of the Santa Clara Valley, that Sara and Erskine decided in the early 1920s to build a home in the high, wild hills above Los Gatos, some fifty miles south of San Francisco. It was intended to be a temple dedicated to beauty and art, with every detail crafted by artist friends, a place where the soul could rest and the ugliness of the world would not intrude; my parents had the same intention at Sneden's, but not nearly as much money.

In 1928, when I first spent a summer there, the place was still a little raw and the flat-roofed gray cinder-block house with its inset green Chinese tiles jutted from the steep hillside, unrelieved by softening vegetation. But by the summer of 1932, it had achieved the magic which made me love it then and forever afterward more than any other place in the world.

At the foot of the hill, on either side of the earthen-red road, were two seated cement cats, each about twenty feet high. Beyond them the road wound up and up, through groves of live oaks, bay, scarlet-berried toyon, wild lilac, red-barked madroña and manzanita, and skirted a golden meadow filled with wild paper-white Oriental poppies. Finally it came to an end in a large open space just above a grove of giant live oaks, where small Chinese wind-bells used to hang. Directly ahead were the steps leading up to the front door, a niche containing a large statue of Kuan Yin, goddess of peace and mercy, and to one side an apricot tree which, that July day in 1932 when we arrived at the Cats, was rich with golden fruit. At the top of the steps silver-haired Sara and Pops stood arm in arm, ready to welcome us and lead us through the great oaken front door and into a month of what was, for me, a month of enchantment.

There were many elements to the enchantment, and I think of them now with loving nostalgia. The sixty-foot-long living room, with French windows all along one side and a narrow balcony from which one looked down into Sara's "secret garden" and then out across the whole stretch of the Santa Clara Valley. The grand piano, on it an ancient bronze urn filled with white petunias; the black teakwood couch, its down cushions covered with dark blue Ming velvet and pillows made from Persian saddlebags; Sara and Erskine's bathroom, with its sunken tub of green tiles and an *ambiance* compounded of the smell of fine sponges, soaps, and colognes. Sara's big dresser in their bedroom, just as I remembered it, with the familiar oval-framed photograph of Albert. Indulgently, she let me explore it just as I used to do when I was a child, and I found the bottom drawers still filled with the most delicate of satin and silk, lace and chiffon lingerie, and nightgowns, the top drawer with strings of amethysts, moonstones, jade, opals, and amber. In her closets were capes of rare Persian brocades, chosen not because of expense but because of beauty. The attitude these choices represented was not lost upon me; it was one my parents shared, but of necessity expressed in a different way. I was deeply influenced by it, as I was by my observation that everything Sara and Erskine touched, used, or saw at the Cats was beautiful and true to its own nature; wood was wood, stone was stone, silk was silk, cotton was cotton, nothing was plastic or synthetic.

. . .

As the days went by, relatives and old friends arrived for visits. My cousin Kay and her husband Jim Caldwell came with their five-month-old baby, Sally; I fell in love with Jim's great gray eyes, his kindliness, intelligence, and wild humor, and prayed that some day I would find a husband just like him. My mother's stalwart youngest sister Marion, who had recently left Seattle and her husband and moved to San Francisco, came for a few days with her two sons, Bob and David. This was the first time I had met these cousins and I was astounded at the freedom with which Bob, who was only a few months older than I, spoke of sexual matters, for in my immediate family sex was considered so holy that there were a great many anatomical words I had never heard spoken aloud. Erskine's lovely daughter Lisa drove down from San Rafael with her exuberant husband, Kirk Smith. With them came their three children: willowy Nan, who was a year or two older than I; tomboy Katherine (always called "Tash"), who was my age; and noisy Alan, a year or so younger. I had mixed feelings about them, for I had known them since infancy, called them "cousins," and loved them dearly—yet in my withdrawn adolescence their cheerful normality made me acutely uncomfortable. "Tash and her friends make me feel like a grandmother," I wrote in my journal. "I don't think they know any poetry at *all*."

Finally, they all went home; my father returned to his job in New York; and my mother went off to Los Angeles on an assignment. At last, days at the Cats settled into the peaceful rhythm I loved.

Mornings began with fruit and toast, honey and coffee, shared with Sara and Erskine in the inner courtyard. Around the three sides of the square-U-shaped house, fluted cement pillars supported a trellis from which hung purple grapes, and white. This pergola walk, about eight feet wide, was set off from the open courtyard at the center by low beds of flowers and an occasional green-and-blue Chinese porcelain drum seat; the floor was laid with myriads of small broken tiles in all the colors of a paint box and the effect was joyous. Between two window seats set into the living-room wall was a five-foot-square mosaic of a naked god bringing fire in his cupped hands to a naked woman with outstretched arms, and in the middle of the courtyard was an oval fountain, with a blue ceramic statue by Beniamino Bufano of two small children clinging together. On the fourth, open, side of the court there was a low curved wall with a fountain decorated by a satyr's head at the center; above it four terraces rose up the hillside to a wisteria pergola on the final terrace and the wild hillside above. The edges of the terraces were massed with white petunias, warmly fragrant in the morning sunlight.

After breakfast the poets set off on a leisurely climb up the zig-zag path to their studio, and I was left to amuse myself. Sometimes I wandered through the herb garden, sweet-smelling with oregano and lavender, rosemary and thyme, passed by tall Chinese urns, blue and green and buff ceramic, spilling over with trailing pink geraniums, and climbed the hill to an immense oak under which there was a cement table and a seat inscribed: "Temples were built in the hills for the Gods. . . . This seat is for the contemplation of beauty which is true worship." Nearby was a double bust of Sara and Erskine which I always thought extremely ugly and indeed rather ferocious, but I liked the line from one of Sara's poems which was chiseled on the back of the tall cement pedestal: "Had we not clutched love flying by, where had you been? Where had I?" Beside it was one of Erskine's lines: "I know for everyone, were he but bold, surely along some starry path his soul awaits him."

So the morning would drift by while I wrote my diary in the privacy of the temple to beauty or worked on poems or short stories of my own. At noon I would hear the sound of the great Tirolean horn which only Erskine could blow, and know that he was summoning me to a lunch of salad and Monterey Jack cheese, fruit, and claret poured from an immense silver pitcher into which Erskine had earlier carefully shaved two thin slices of cucumber peel.

On the hottest days the living room was always cool and dim and, with its walls lined with books, infinitely alluring. During the afternoon I would drift for hours from Shelley to Mark Twain, from the piano to my sketchbook on the balcony; in one corner were bookshelves with locked glass doors behind which were kept a Shakespeare second folio, first editions, privately printed books, erotica, and specially bound volumes of Erskine's books: *The Poet in the Desert, Heavenly Discourse,* and all the others (and later on Sara's long narrative poem *Barabbas*). After I found where the key was hidden, I discovered exactly how bawdy eighteenth-century ballads can be, and learned the fascination of Burton's unexpurgated *Arabian Nights* in the great black and gold many-volumed edition with its eye-opening, if depressing, introduction.

In the evening there would be cocktails and hot cheese canapés in the courtyard and an excellent dinner at which Erskine regally presided, sometimes talking of General Fremont with great passion, growing angry, and pounding the table, sometimes discussing the wrongs which the white man had inflicted upon the American Indian. After dinner Sara would read us poetry, or else we sat in the courtyard, identifying constellations or admiring the glimmer of the leaves of the giant fig tree in the soft moonlight. Later I would climb the steep flight of stairs leading to the flat roof and the solarium, where I slept, and in my nightgown stroll in the darkness barefoot, look out at the vast night around me, and in my imagination walk the battlements of Elsinore, while all around I smelled the intermingled perfumes of my California: box hedge, dogs, petunias, jasmine, orange and lemon trees, eucalyptus, kittens, roses, and ripening apricots.

· · ·

One afternoon that summer I came down the stairs and heard Sara, whose voice had an unusual carrying quality, talking in the courtyard to my visiting Aunt Marion. My hand was on the knob of the screen door when I heard Sara say, "Yes, and considering that she was raised in an atmosphere of such easygoing slovenliness, isn't it surprising that Margaret keeps her fingernails clean?" My arm dropped to my side as if I had been hit by lightning from on high, and I could feel the blood draining from my face and my lungs struggling suddenly for breath. Not only was her assertion about my mother's housekeeping untrue, but this was the first time I had ever experienced the attitude of condescension toward my mother and toward me, which I eventually learned was shared by most of the members of what I called "my Western family," and which, for decades, left me hurt and—because it was mingled with elaborate expressions of love—bewildered.

Their attitude wounded me so deeply that it is only recently that I have been able to try to analyze it. It stems originally from Sara, I think, who never went to college but who was educated by Erskine in the grand tradition of a classic education in the arts and in literature. In the second generation, Kay and Jim's lives were passed in the confines of scholarly institutions—Jim on the English faculty of the University of California at Berkeley, Kay on the Art faculty at Mills College. Opposed to the sacred traditions they all shared was the world of "journalism," which they seem to have judged entirely on the notoriously sensational San Francisco journalism to which they were exposed. Apparently, without any concept that farther east there can be and are serious and objective newspapers of which any scholarly writer could be proud, they pigeonholed my parents and later me as "journalists," which meant to them people incapable of understanding or appreciating "the finer things." My father was forgiven for his profession, because they truly adored him, but my mother was not. Nor was I.

The condescension was based on ignorance, too. None of them had ever spent more than a day or so at our Sneden's house or our New York apartments; they knew almost nothing of our intellectual or aesthetic life. They retained little of what I told them of my college studies, or later of my learning experiences overseas, or even later of how I was trying to raise my son and care for my mother. It was as though they had clamped some iron mold of inferiority over me in my adolescence and never bothered again to look at what was inside.

Still, Sara was always my fairy godmother, and her gifts to me were many and meaningful. Gossamer-thin silk scarves to dance with when I was seven, and Christmas boxes with packages decorated with blue and gold and red Chinese paper butterflies; when I was in college a volume of Keats's letters, so expensive that even my dreams had not embraced it; a box of spring flowers from her garden when I was living in San Francisco. And she gave me more than material things, for she set high standards of aesthetics and would not (or did not need to) compromise. Nor would she compromise her literary standards: she encouraged my love of poetry but also helped my critical faculties by refusing to share my adolescent passion for Rupert Brooke and Sara Teasdale.

Above all, throughout my youth she gave me the feeling that she understood me, that I could confide in her as I could not in my mother, and that she would not betray me. In letter after letter she assured me that I was not popular because I was spiritually "taller" than other girls, and that if I just had faith, sooner or later I would attract a spiritually tall man, just as Kay had attracted Jim. I still felt guilty, because I kept on wanting to be popular with boys, but at least I was temporarily consoled by the thought that someone like Jim was waiting for me in the wings. This was an illusion, it turned out. So, too, was the feeling she gave me and several others of my generation: that if only we were true to art and beauty and lived a life dedicated to the spirit, we, too, would eventually live a life as precious as hers in a place as beautiful as Los Gatos.

Now, the wounds don't matter. What does matter is that I have finally balanced the sunlight against the shadow and have found that most of the memories she gave me are still bathed in the light of the high noon of love and that the others are forgotten in some dim, infrequently visited corner of the heart.

. . .

The summer went on, and I pretended I had never heard the remark about my mother's slovenly housekeeping. But life was never quite the same again, for I had learned that what is overheard is not always the same as that which is meant to be heard, and the small serpent of this knowledge rustled through my Eden.

We spent a day at the ranch home of Fremont Older, the great San Francisco newspaper editor, defender of criminals, prisoners, the poor, and the suffering and a man who often had a paroled murderer as a cook or houseboy. Afterward I wrote, with just a slight hint of the reporter I would become, "Mr. Older is a grand old sea lion. I love to watch him when someone is talking—the most interesting expressions go over his face with its fierce gray mustache." Ernst Bacon, the pianist, came one night of full moon and played the "Moonlight Sonata"; I wrote a poem beginning: "In this candlelighted room you have stopped eternity." We went on a picnic on Point Lobos, near Carmel, with Robinson Jeffers and his family; I fell in love and wrote a poem that ended: "You, unaware, thinking me a child/ I in my hidden spirit kneeling at your feet." Yehudi Menuhin, a close neighbor, played for us one evening, and I was too moved to write anything.

Mother returned from Los Angeles and made arrangements for us to return to New York by bus. Finally it was the last day and we were standing once more below the front door and the apricot tree, waving good-by to Sara and Erskine, who, arm in arm, smiled farewell from the balcony above us. As, in a sense, they stand now in my memory. And forever.

✤6✤

The Depression grew worse. As I walked to the subway every school day that winter I passed a breadline of shivering men on West 11th Street, waiting for the bowl of soup they were given daily by Saint Vincent's Hospital. Men with college degrees sold apples for five cents each on many street corners, and all the elevator operators at Macy's were said to be Ph.D.s. We sang "Brother, Can You Spare a Dime?" and "You Get No Bread with One Meatball." Mortgage repayments on our Charles Street house had been calculated on a rental basis of $90 for each of the ten two-room apartments; that autumn most of our tenants moved out and my mother waited day after empty day for new ones, but only after the rent was dropped to $45 a month did any move in. Every night my parents had to go on a hall patrol; the tenants paid for their own electricity but my parents paid for the lighting in the hall—at night tenants would sneak extension cords out into the hall fixtures. Others skipped, owing several months' rent.

In 1932 my father had started his own column, which ran in *The Sun* in New York and eventually was syndicated to 125 papers around the country. It was called *Who's News Today* and consisted of thumbnail sketches of men and women currently in the news; it was a vast success for he knew many of the people he wrote about and his style combined erudition and a kind of quiet Western-range humor which was all his own. Yet one day that bleak winter his salary was cut from $125 a week to $85. We gave up the beautiful floor-through with its marble fireplaces, and moved to the two-room fifth-floor rear, my parents sleeping on a

studio couch in the small living room while I had the little bedroom.

Early one morning in March 1933, shortly after President Roosevelt had taken his first oath of office and ordered all banks
closed, I woke to the sound of my mother's sobs, which I had
rarely heard before. In the living room, I found her in her nightgown, huddled in my father's arms, and crying desperately while
he patted her shoulders. Just before the bank closing, I learned,
Mother had taken their entire savings, $875, out of the bank and
in an effort to hide the money from potential burglars had pinned
it inside one of my wool dresses. Several days later, forgetting
about the money, she had taken the dress to the dry cleaners; this
is what she had just remembered. The money was never recovered and for many months my mother continued to berate
herself, but I never heard a word of reproach from my father.

Oddly, though, I think of that as a happy year. We ate a lot of
baked beans, hamburger (30 cents a pound), macaroni casseroles,
applesauce, and canned peaches, but my mother was a great cook
and those economy meals at the card table we were using are a
cheerful memory. (On New Year's Eve we couldn't afford to go as
usual to the theater, so I went alone to Loew's Sheridan and snif-
fled through a movie; when I came home I found my parents in
gala evening dress, with cocktails ready.)

I had several girl friends at school, I knew a few boys, and I
managed to save enough of my $3 a week allowance for occa-
sional meals at foreign restaurants and for the French, German,
and Russian art films I loved. I was doing all right in my studies,
and, to round out my growth toward contentment, in the spring
of 1933 I played the part of Mrs. Midget in the senior class pro-
duction of *Outward Bound*. A few weeks after the dazzling
triumph of the play came my eighteenth birthday. My parents
gave me the first automobile our family ever owned, a Model A
Ford roadster with a rumble seat, and enlisted the local grocery
boy to teach me how to drive. They also gave me a brown and
black half-Belgian shepherd half-Airedale puppy, whom I named
Christopher Kerry and who became my constant companion
when I was home. Chris was a dog with compassion and humor
and I loved him more than any other animal I've ever owned and
quite a lot more than many people I've known.

Shortly after my birthday came the day of our graduation. The high-school years were over and there was nothing ahead but summer and waiting to find out whether I had been admitted to Swarthmore College, which my parents had chosen for me.

When I think of summers during the Depression, I think of tennis and swimming and reading, but most of all I think of summer parties under the grape arbor. Sometimes they were small, with only ten people and homemade wine, sometimes large, with twenty or thirty friends of all ages, a $5 keg of beer and paper cups. But there was always good food, candlelight or Japanese lanterns, fireflies over the meadow, and singing, whether or not anyone had brought a guitar. Usually there was the same crowd of old friends at these parties, but one time my father brought out from town an unemployed young man he had met somewhere. The red-haired stranger had brought a guitar and at my father's suggestion he sang alone—"The Foggy Foggy Dew" and "The Lavender Cowboy." His name was Burl Ives.

It's odd, but in all those years of drinking under the grape arbor I never remember anyone being drunk. I don't know why this was, because there was always plenty of beer or wine and my parents were tolerant people. I remember one horrible night during my college years when I went to a party down the hill, and discovered that Burgess Meredith was there; he had just opened in *Winterset* and was being talked about as "the Hamlet of 1940." When he began paying attention to me, in great rapture but also in great innocence of the possible effect, I downed glasses of rum, gin, whisky, beer, and wine in rapid succession. The result was, of course, that I became violently ill, vomited, passed out, and at 4 a.m. was brought home, where I fell in bed in all my clothes and did not awaken until noon. Palsied, bleary, and horribly apprehensive of what my parents would say, I staggered downstairs and out into the arbor, where they were reading the Sunday papers. My father looked up and smiled at me. "Well, old kid," he said, "I guess this will teach you not to mix your likkers." Neither of them ever mentioned the incident again.

· · ·

The summer after I was graduated from high school I fell in love. His name was, shall we say, Michael St. George. He was twenty-four, a commercial artist, and with his elder brother, Steve, and his parents, he spent every summer for several years in Sneden's. To me, he was the most beautiful man I had ever seen, with his sun-bronzed skin, his blond hair, and his eyes which had a trick of changing from blue to gray. When he came around the corner of the grape arbor I didn't just see a man in blue shorts and a striped Brittany shirt, I saw Apollo. But that summer, and for many of those to come, he drove me nearly mad. For days on end, sometimes alone and sometimes with his brother, he would drop by our house every evening, to play croquet or just to sit in the arbor and talk, while Steve strummed the old piano in the dining room. Then he would disappear for a week or two, only to return, with no explanation, to ask me for a day's cruise in his motor boat. He never made any closer approach and only twice during that summer did he even hold my hand. I realize now that I didn't know him at all, as I have never really known most of the men I have loved. He was shy and quiet; I filled the silences with what I wanted him to be, and in my eyes he was thoughtful, intelligent, beauty-loving, humorous, honest, and noble. I don't suppose he really possessed all of those shining attributes; but I believed he did, and without a single qualm I would have abandoned all thoughts of college and a career had he, at any time during the five years I loved him, asked me to marry him.

In July the news came that I was accepted at Swarthmore. I don't suppose I would be today, for my high-school grades, aside from English, had been mediocre and my college boards were abysmal, but the year my class was admitted was the depth of the Depression and the college was desperate for students whose families could pay the $900 tuition. As for me, I was completely vague about money, and only years later realized that the reason my parents could pay for my college education was that my father took a second job writing radio commercials and eventually a third job ghosting Edwin C. Hill's columns in the *Journal American*, where he did much of his best nostalgic writing under another man's name, and that my mother sold a series of articles on successful New York career women to *McCall's*.

So the preparations began. My parents paid for ten dancing lessons at Arthur Murray's. I bought a slinky black satin evening dress with a sequin collar; my mother returned it and replaced it with a "more suitable" pink lace, which I hated. A trunk was packed with tennis socks, saddle shoes, woollen skirts, and twin set sweaters, which with the addition of a scarf or a Woolworth string of pearls was the college girl's uniform of the day. Finally,

on an appointed morning in September I took the train to Philadelphia, changed to the Media-Wawa local, and eventually arrived at the Swarthmore station full of determination "to take life
as it comes."

In the glib phrase which I suppose those of us who went there
always use in describing the place, Swarthmore is "a small coeducational college, twelve miles southwest of Philadelphia, with a
Quaker background and a high academic standing." In my day
there were around 1000 students (even now there are not many
more than 1200), and all of them were subject to a Quaker emphasis on the search for truth and to intense academic pressures.
But little of this was at first apparent to me at the beginning of
my freshman year. What I found was a welter of enchantingly
pretty girls and intimidatingly "smooth" boys; these frightening
people formed about 80 per cent of the student body and were responsible for a pervasive social atmosphere of dating and dances.
It took me quite a while to find the other 20 per cent.

I was, I suppose, a perfect example of the provincialism of the
New Yorker, plus the product of a peculiar intellectual background. I had never met a businessman, for instance. I had only
met two Republicans. As far as I knew, I had never met anyone
whose father was a member of Rotary, or the Elks, Lions, Masons,
or American Legion. Except for a few girls at camp, I had never
met anyone who went to public school. I couldn't imagine anyone
who had never been to Broadway theaters and who did not follow
theater news avidly. Since I assumed at first that everyone was
like myself, it took me a long time to learn tact.

On the train going down to college, in some new glimmering of
love and understanding of my parents, I made a resolution: that
no matter how I really felt, I would not burden them with any reflection of sadness, loneliness, or despair. So as the months went
on I wrote them about my Introduction to Philosophy course,
which was taught by dear old "Ducky" Holmes—a "Thee and
Thying" Quaker—and of how the first assignment he gave us was
to write a paper on anything we truly believed, and of how the
next day he had demolished us one by one, logically and implacably. I wrote of football pep rallies around bonfires and of football games. I wrote about girls who became my friends. I wrote,
too, of my many dates with fascinating and intelligent boys, be-

cause I knew my parents longed to think of me as a healthy, happy college girl, enjoying "normal" relations with boys. There was, of course, not a word of truth in any of these stories, for during the entire four years I never had a single date. And far from being the emotionally healthy girl I pictured in my letters, I floundered through the first two years of college in a confusion of self-pity, so ashamed of my lack of popularity that I longed to hurl myself from the window of my fourth-floor room, and only refrained because I couldn't bear to inflict that pain upon my parents.

Much of the turmoil, I suppose, was the classic identity crisis: the normal adolescent search for the answer to "Who am I?" But perhaps my turmoil was more chaotic than that of others because of the arbitrary values I had acquired from my background. It took me years to discover that girls who like to dress well and go to parties with boys do not inevitably have empty minds. I remember my astonishment when I happened to fall into a conversation with a popular girl who talked eagerly of the mysteries she was unraveling in her botany course, and in that conversation I ticked forward a few seconds toward maturity.

Another development of importance to my further growth happened during the summer following my miserable freshman year at college. I discovered that I was not unattractive to boys at home (where the competition wasn't so stiff). Michael St. George was around but as elusive as ever, so this was a particularly satisfying discovery, and brought at long last my introduction to the pleasures of necking and petting.

Bob, a tall, skinny boy, turned up in August, took me out a lot and seemed to know all the secluded corners of Rockland County where we could park. I enjoyed this, and didn't care that he was a local, noncollege boy and a Catholic, but my parents were definitely not happy. One starry night my father asked me if I'd like to go for a walk, and I said I would. I soon discovered he had something on his mind, evidently something difficult to voice.

"I wonder if you know, Margaret," he began, "that—oh, there's the Big Dipper, see?—well, that Catholic boys—see the double star in the handle?—that Catholic boys are taught—the Romans used it as a test of eyesight for their soldiers—well, they're taught that it's not a sin—and if you follow the handle you can spot Arcturus just coming up over those pines—well Catholic boys are taught thatit'snotasintoseduceaprotestantgirl! Oh, I see Altair is out now, and there's Vega!"

"Yes, Dad, I know," I said (although I didn't). I had, in any case, no intention of being seduced, much as I warmly enjoyed the sessions in the dark car parked in various lovers' lanes. I still remembered my old vow to remain a virgin, and I had, in any case, decided to stay "pure" for Michael, whom I was convinced I would eventually marry.

Near the end of the summer I discovered that it was boring to kiss someone you didn't much like, and I abandoned Bob in favor of Ted, the current young and good-looking captain of the little ferry launch which still ran across the Hudson. He lived in a small cabin by the river, and it was fun to curl on his couch in the darkness, looking out at the lights on the river, listening to "Moonglow" on the radio, and drinking a Tom Collins between kisses.

As I grew more tolerant of differences I made more friends at college, and with these friendships came a degree of contentment. For the first time in my life I belonged to "a crowd"; a group of congenial girls who mostly ate together and roomed near one another. This membership in what we all felt was an elite group gave me immense reassurance, and I particularly delighted in our frequent bull sessions, especially when we discussed life, death, sex, love, psychology, or Thomas Wolfe for half the night. I even enjoyed, rather wryly, helping them dress for dances.

At the beginning of junior year most of "our crowd" went into Honors. For the next two years we would study only three subjects: a major, in which we would have one seminar a week every semester, and two minors, with seminars in alternating semesters. I chose to major in English, much to the scorn of my mother who felt it was too easy, and minor in philosophy and French literature.

I loved the three-hour seminars, for six or seven of us would meet in the comfortable homes of various professors, read our papers, and after an hour or so break for jasmine tea (Baudelaire and Victor Hugo) or, daringly, sherry (Shakespeare). I came to know and like some of my male classmates and more and more to enjoy and understand the laughter of erudition. (Place eight kitchen matches on a table so that they spell KINI. Problem: What line from Hamlet do they represent? Answer: "A little more than kin and less than kind.")

But the seminars were intellectually demanding, too, and I found it difficult not to swell with embarrassing emotion over Keats or Lamartine, and to be instead analytical, hard-headed, and critical. Elizabeth Wright, my favorite English professor who has remained a good friend over all these years, told me once that I needed "more lemon juice" in my thinking. I knew this, and I tried to restrain all poetic impulses when writing a paper on, for instance, "The Philosophical and Aesthetic Implications of Hardy's Use of Folklore and Old Customs." Only outside the seminar work did my true nature flourish. I studied Eastern religions, tried to follow Buddha's Eightfold Path, tried self-hypnotism. I developed an interest in the occult, extrasensory perception, witchcraft, and palmistry. In the privacy of the dormitory I wore gypsy outfits and Oriental costumes.

I also broke my heart over the Spanish Civil War, and collected money for the Loyalists. Another cause I championed was the Anti-Capital Punishment League, but I found it difficult to collect much money, for Swarthmore students in those days were taught that emotionalism about a "cause" was a betrayal of scholarly objectivity. Like many in my generation (perhaps all generations) I longed for a hero, thought I had found him in President Roosevelt, and was bitterly disappointed when he failed to support the Spanish Loyalists. I longed, too, for the far places of the world and after I read Negley Farson's *The Way of a Transgressor,* decided that the life of the foreign correspondent must be the best in the world.

Of all the subjects I studied in college the one which has been of the most importance in my life was philosophy, and in particular moral philosophy, a seminar taught by that great teacher Brand Blanshard. Philosophy taught me how to think, or at least how to *try* to think; I have never been able to hear someone say, "I only live for my own pleasure," without reflecting privately: "there are three classical disproofs of hedonism, and although I may have forgotten them I know this oaf is talking through his hat." When I hear people use the words "good and evil" or "right and wrong" as easily as they usually do, I recall the intricate debates on these words by philosophers over the centuries; it is rather like knowing that the stars are in the sky even in daylight (having briefly glimpsed them) while others deny them or are ignorant of their existence.

Suddenly it was May of our senior year and I was studying ferociously twelve hours a day for the final examinations. I knew that I was only a pseudoscholar and I was badly frightened at the thought that I might let down my parents by failure. I wrote to prepare them for this possibility, and all my life I have treasured the letter my father wrote in answer to my fears. It said, in part:

If, when I handed you that little Edna St. Vincent Millay poem, you had tossed off some flip crack, or had been insensitive to its quaint Elizabethan charm, as many Phi Beta Kappas might have done, I would have flunked you in Practical and Applied Aesthetics and I would not have felt the serenity and assurance which now, I give you my word, I feel about you.

There were eight three-hour written examinations in all, covering each of the subjects we had studied during the two previous years, examinations which were set not by our own familiar professors, but by scholars from other colleges and universities. Far worse were the oral examinations conducted by these strangers and attended by our own English, French, or philosophy faculties, and any other fellow students who chose to attend. For anyone who was shy, lacking in self-confidence, and not a particularly brilliant student it was a grisly exercise in the sublimation of panic; however, the examiners were probably kinder than I deserved, and on June 7, 1937, I was graduated with Honors. Contemplating the degree back in my room, I reflected that during the four years of study it represented I hadn't learned many final answers to life—but at least I now knew some of the questions.

. . .

For several months I had been brooding about the necessity of earning a living. I couldn't go into newspaper work, I wrote home in what now seems a quaint letter, because with all due apologies to my father it was "ephemeral" and at college I had been taught to treasure the eternal verities. To go on with my English studies (which was what I wanted to do) would have meant at least two more years of dependence upon my parents, and I felt they had already done enough for me; they had finally managed to unload 7 Charles Street, but in the process they had lost their investment of a lifetime of financial savings. What else? I couldn't be a poet because I had discovered I was not a good one. I couldn't be a sculptor for the same reason. I couldn't be a stage designer because you couldn't get into the union unless you had experience, and you couldn't get experience unless you were a member of the union. Publishing, I finally decided, should be my career. But the publishers I saw in spring vacation were uniformly charming, courteous, and discouraging.

Summer came and, still jobless, I settled back into Sneden's life. In mid-June Margaret Peter, one of my closest friends at Swarthmore, was married under our grape arbor to Samuel Ashelman, a classmate of mine. It was a joyous Quaker wedding involving many college friends and has remained so in all our minds, just as Sam and Margaret have remained dear friends all of my life. A few days after the wedding they and most of my Swarthmore friends sailed for bicycle trips through Europe. As for me, I agreed glumly with my parents that the best thing to do would be to enroll in a shorthand and typing course at a secretarial school in town. But, God, how I hated that place, and how ashamed I felt to be going there after the glories of Swarthmore! So I dragged on month after dreary month without acquiring enough skills to graduate.

My only consolation was that Michael's family had rented the little "salt box" house my father had built at the other end of the meadow, and Michael dropped me off at school every day on his way to work. At the beginning of that summer I had high and happy expectations of a deepening relationship. Not much had changed between us during the four years since we met, except that Michael had kissed me on two different evenings. The first time was on the previous New Year's Eve, in the car going home from a beer party at Spitzhoff's, the local pub. I went into a state of shock for several weeks afterward, dreamed of the children we might have, and when I saw a little boy on the street who looked like Michael, started to cry. The second time was on an evening in late May, when the participants in the Sam and Margaret wedding were forgathered under the grape arbor. Michael came over for a while, and when he left I walked down to the end of the lawn with him. We looked at the stars and saw the misty red moon rising. We stood by a bush with myriads of tiny white petals, and as we gently touched the branches the petals fell on our open hands like phosphorescence. As I began to say goodnight, he drew me to him and kissed me tenderly. He kissed me again, we smiled at each other, and he went away. In the house a radio was playing "The Very Thought of You," and that song still twists my heart whenever I hear it.

No wonder I had rosy hopes for the summer. Yet despite the fact that he came over three or four evenings a week, despite Chanel Number Five, flowers in my hair, and a successful diet, despite motor-boat rides, tennis, singing, and laughter, it did not happen again. So by late June I was puzzled, by late July the doctor discovered that my heartbeat had doubled its normal rate, and by late August I was seeking consolation with someone else.

The summer before, my parents had joined a club in Alpine called Aldercress, which enabled us to go swimming in a beautiful little lake, tree-encircled and secluded. It was there that I met Greg Macdonald, as I shall call him. Greg was not much taller than I, but he was blond and had beautiful muscles and flashing white teeth. He had dropped out of college after two years, he played a jazzy guitar, and he rarely understood any of my literary allusions. The last person in the world, I would have thought, to be attracted to me. And yet he was, and also to my parents, perhaps at first more to them than to me. Sometimes he would arrive in the early evening, intending to take me to a movie, sit down for "just a few minutes" to talk to my scintillating mother or to give my father a guitar lesson—and at eleven o'clock I, not having uttered a word for hours, would say goodnight to their three suddenly guilty faces and go upstairs to bed.

But that was the summer before. This summer of 1937 it was different, for we started going swimming in the lake at night, alone with the mist rising from the edges of the lake and the stars reflected in the dark waters. From swimming in suits it was not a very difficult step to swimming naked and to wet bodies clinging together in the moonlight. It was very beautiful and exciting, but I would not concede the final point and I ended the summer still a virgin, technically speaking, and still holding out for Michael.

That autumn my parents agreed, although I was still in secretarial school, to let me take a one-room furnished apartment on West 10th Street near Hudson Street, and early in November Michael helped me to move in. After he was gone I sat down on the studio couch and stared at the unfamiliar pink walls. "I'm on my own now," I said to myself out loud, feeling mixed emotions of pride and apprehension. "I'm grown up at last. Now life can begin."

7

An intelligent wisp of a girl named Patsy lived two floors up, and through her I met a lot of Village Communists. I had long ago decided, because of my passionate belief in individual freedom that I could never join the Party. (Still, for years I felt a little guilty about not being able to believe; it was not until I read *The God That Failed* and *Darkness at Noon* that the guilt disappeared.) I liked most of Patsy's friends and enjoyed going to parties and radical theater and art shows with them, but I was often bored by their perpetual talk of factionalism and infighting, warring Party cliques and groups, Hitler's growing belligerency, Mussolini's annexation of Ethiopia, Japan's invasion of China, and Spain, Spain, Spain. My thought streams seemed to run in a different direction. I couldn't bear what was happening in the world, I didn't think I could do anything to stop it from happening (I never have), and therefore I didn't want to think about it. "And ideals or moral concepts, what place have they in the world today?" I asked myself in my journal. The day I wrote that, Italy withdrew from the League of Nations. The following day the Japanese shelled the U.S. gunboat *Panay* on the Yangtze River. I continued to think about love, and Michael.

One night the miracle I had prayed for actually happened. Michael appeared with his brother, Steve, we went up to Patsy's apartment (which had two couches), drank a lot of beer, and when it became evident that we were all feeling similar desires, Steve turned the lights out. Michael spent that night with me in my apartment, kissing me fervently between intervals of sleep but making no attempt to complete the love-making. I don't think

I've ever experienced again the sense of bliss I felt when I awoke in his arms.

This happened five more times during the winter. He never said he loved me, but once he said, "I can't decide whether or not I love you." (I was too shy to tell him how *I* felt.) We sat up until three in the morning trying to decide—between kisses— whether or not we should have an affair; he said he felt it would be wrong and therefore I said I agreed with him. After one of our nights together he would disappear for two weeks, and I found out that he was seeing other girls. He said he didn't enjoy being with them because he kept thinking of me. Early in March, when I hadn't seen him for ten days, he came to the apartment and somehow I knew before he told me that he had met a new girl. I said, as lightly as I could, "And so you fell for her?" He didn't answer, but kissed me good-by and walked out into the hall. I froze for a moment and then ran after him, put my arms around him, and kissed him again. "I have a feeling I won't see you for a long, long time," I said. He disappeared, and the image of the sun god and Galahad, which was already badly cracked, crumbled into dust—the only trouble being that it was dust I still loved.

One day in early July, when I was back living in the country, a neighbor at tea said casually, "Oh, I hear Michael St. George is finally getting married." I said, "Yes, isn't it nice?" And "Will you have some sugar?" And "Excuse me, I've just remembered an errand." And drove the car very carefully down to the river. I was so stunned and bewildered that truly I thought I would die. The following October, my then current beau and I went to a light-hearted party and afterward stopped by Michael's apartment— and met his wife. She was a pleasant, extroverted girl and I liked her. I never saw them again.

. . .

That was the year, more than any other, that I compensated for Michael and for all those lonely nights in high school and college. David, Bill, Tommy, Chris, Johnny . . . for most of the names penciled in my journal my mind produces no faces. Just a jumble of memories of parties, music, drink, hot hands pressing me back against some stranger's refrigerator or against the pillar of some friend's porch, lips on mine and mine responding, a man's voice saying, "Please, oh, please!" and mine invariably saying, "No." By this time the refusal was automatic and I enjoyed the feeling of power it gave me, as if by arousing and then denying a man I had gained revenge against Michael.

In February 1938, I dropped out of secretarial school and began working at my first nine-to-five job with the popular radio program *America's Town Meeting of the Air,* a once-a-week forum discussion on current topics. For ten cents any listener could receive a transcript of the program; for $16.50 a week it was my job to open the mail, number the letters which contained a dime (many people forgot to enclose one), and at the end of the day balance the number of dimes on hand against the numbered letters. The job sounds appalling now, but at first I thought it was glamorous to be "working in radio," and I enjoyed the office atmosphere and the varied personalities I encountered. One of them was a man from whom I had my first proposal of marriage. He sent me flowers and telegrams; he said beautiful things like "I want to fill up the hurt places in your heart," and I wanted terribly to love him in return, but I could not match the depths of his feelings. Sadly, I stopped seeing him.

The radio season ended, the program went off the air, and I got a part-time summer job with the Institute for Propaganda Analysis, near Columbia University, at $80 a month. The Institute, which had been founded a few years earlier by Columbia's Teachers College, produced reading materials for various high-school and college programs in which students were taught how to analyze and resist propaganda, particularly war propaganda. (It of course went out of business with World War II.) All the papers were written by Ph.D.s, the office was staffed by M.A.s, and with only a lowly B.A. I was treated as a mere typist, which I was. The three classical disproofs of hedonism seemed far away, and so did a life concerned with the eternal verities.

Early that summer I moved back to the country, feeling aimless and depressed. My parents scolded me for my "weak moral fiber" and my failure to develop "a positive approach to life," and I had a lot of fights with my mother. Greg Macdonald, voicing his old mating cry, blew in with his electric guitar and I went out in the moonlight and mosquitoes with him a few times; the evenings always ended in a draw. I went to the weddings of several of my friends and felt more depressed. I picked up a Jewish psychologist at the office, and for a time considered accepting an invitation to share an apartment with him, but decided against it because he was too hairy. I was still mooning over Michael.

That was the year that Hitler invaded Austria, that Czechoslovakia was partitioned, that Chamberlain and his umbrella went to Munich, the year of "appeasement" and "peace in our times." It was also the year of wrong-way Corrigan. None of these events appear in my journal, but on one occasion I complained that everyone had spent the evening talking about the crisis in Czechoslovakia.

In the fall I acquired a new suitor, a neighborhood boy I'll call Tom, who had black hair, a very white narrow face, and blazing black eyes. He persuaded me to join his little theater group and I met a lot of the nice local boys and girls I had been snooting most of my life. We walked in the late autumn to the waterfall and looked at red and yellow leaves floating on the dark waters of the pool, and our noses were cold as we kissed. We explored deserted gardens in early winter, and embraced among the frozen roses. My family stayed late at Sneden's that year, and so Tom and I wandered through the first snow, laughing, hands sharing the same frosty mitten. He was in love with me for a while and asked me to marry him. As before, I tried to respond emotionally, and almost succeeded in convincing myself that I, too, was in love. But I longed for words more than kisses, and the words he spoke were not the words I longed to hear. The relationship lingered on through the winter, which I spent with my parents at their London Terrace apartment, and into the spring of 1939. He asked me how much I thought he should be earning before we could get married, and I said $30 a week because I knew he was earning $25 and was unlikely to get a raise. A few weeks later he drifted away with some other girl and I was hurt and relieved. I was also, despite numerous times of passion, still a stubborn virgin. Most of my friends, who were either married or having affairs; were beginning to make bets on me.

I wasn't much worried at Tom's defection, for I had started to go out with a handsome sculptor who taught the evening woodcarving class in which I had enrolled. He was a talented sculptor who lived in a Village loft and had a lot of friends who were painters and sculptors; his was an *ambiance* I knew and loved. He proposed and probably I should have married him, but I didn't. There was a quality of vagueness about him, some lack of conviction which troubled me, as if he half-expected always to be a failure. After a few months, that ended, too. But I do not regret these encounters, although they led to nothing. How many lovely country walks I would have missed if I hadn't gone around for all those months with Tom; how many delightful evenings I shared with the handsome sculptor—how all the men I have known enriched my life and gave me good memories to store up like hazelnuts for my old age!

. . .

It was necessary to work, and early that winter I got a job at radio station WNEW; for $15 a week I prepared all daytime news broadcasts. I soon began to love my tiny newsroom with the clicking teletype, from which I got my news items, and the freedom I was given in choosing the content of each program. It was always exciting to hear the clanging bell on the machine which meant a "Flash" or a "Bulletin," to rip it out, edit it quickly, and rush it into whatever program was on the air. Then there were the people I met: my boss, red-haired and fatherly Larry Nixon, who was a specialist on freighter travel and who was responsible for passing that passion on to me; the slick announcers, always involved in some kind of intricate office politics; the performers who sang for free, just in order to be heard, and then trailed around the station asking everyone for *sincere* criticism—one of these was a dark-eyed young girl named Dinah Shore.

After three months I thought I deserved a raise, so I went to the station manager and asked to be raised to $18 a week. She said she'd think it over, and two days later I was fired. It was the first time this had ever happened to me, and I felt terrible. For a while I job-hunted dutifully, but even though 1939 is not thought of as a Depression year, jobs were scarce. Then summer was upon us and I moved with my parents from London Terrace back to Sneden's. I was twenty-four now.

It was a strange summer, that one. The Fascists had triumphed in Spain, the Republic of Czechoslovakia had been dissolved, and Germany and Italy had announced a military and political alliance. The Japanese were pushing into Manchukuo and the Nazis were goose-stepping in Europe. In August the Soviet Union and Germany announced a ten-year nonaggression pact, an event which strained a great many Greenwich Village friendships and also made me very glad that I had never been tempted to join the Party.

My mother had learned to drive, and in July my parents took the car to Martha's Vineyard for a month. Becky Hornbeck, a vivacious college friend, came to stay with me, and we both intended to do a lot of serious job-hunting. But we didn't—for we believed, as most people did, that war was coming to Europe. "In the fall, after the harvests are in," everyone said. So we fell under a spell of feeling that this was the last peaceful summer of our lives, and moved through it with dreamy, deliberate pleasure, playing duets on our soprano and alto recorders, or walking in the woods, singing. One night we lay on a blanket under the stars with Peter Grey, who was practically grown up by then, and played with elaborate fantasies about how we would preserve civilization when war came.

For the fourth summer Greg Macdonald appeared. "All I can offer you is fidelity," he said. While Becky was with me everything was easy, but after she left and I was alone, Greg's importunities made life difficult. The trouble was that we both understood, without exactly talking about it, that we would never marry, for we were too different in education, background, and approach to life. But I loved Greg without being in love with him, and so I was torn.

One Sunday night in July I went to a Sneden's party, and on a terraced garden overlooking the river, somewhere among the Japanese lanterns, music, wine, and fireflies, picked up a Famous Author who was visiting for a few days. That night the grizzled little man tried to convince me that it would be a Good Thing for me if we had an affair. On Monday he talked so eloquently about the beauty of sex that suddenly my problem was resolved and I sent him away, telling him I would think about what he had said. I did, but I didn't think about him.

On Tuesday night Greg and I went swimming at Aldercress, and afterward, amid the mist and moonlight, there was no longer any need to struggle. Greg has remained a lifetime friend, and recently he asked me whether I had ever regretted that night and the rest of that summer. I truthfully said no, and that far from regret I had always been grateful that it had happened that way, that night, and that summer, and with him.

My parents returned, and once more the talk in the house was of nothing but impending war. I was so concerned with my own surge of life that the world events about which the papers and the radio were clamoring seemed to have only a shadowy reality, and I felt I couldn't face the fact of war coming tomorrow, or on any tomorrows. But late in the morning of the first Sunday in September I trailed downstairs in my nightgown and found my mother seated at the desk which held the radio, listening to the news which was pouring from it. She looked at me with a face filled with pain. "It has begun," she said. Two days earlier, Hitler had invaded Poland; that Sunday, England and France had declared war on Germany.

It was a hard and bitter day for all of us. All my life I had lived in the shadow of World War I, in which my parents were pacifists, and had been influenced by the permanent sadness it threw upon them both, and my mother in particular; I had grown up hearing talk of "warmongers" and "munition-makers." It is perhaps not surprising that much as I hated fascism I equated the earlier war with this one.

But life went on, just as if catastrophe had not come burning to the world. Job-hunting seriously at last, I finally found one as assistant to the publicity director of Macfadden Publications, at $23.50 a week. I have never hated any job as much as I hated that one. I liked my boss, Joe Wiegers, who was shrewd and tough and funny, but I loathed the cheap magazines for which we were supposed to elicit publicity: *Liberty*, *True Story*, and *Master Detective*. My only hope was that for several months I had been angling for a job on *The New Yorker* through our friend and neighbor Sanderson Vanderbilt. On October 5, just when I was contemplating a jump from the eighteenth-floor windows of the dreary offices where I worked, my *deus ex machina* arrived in the form of a telephone call from William Shawn, then managing editor of *The New Yorker*. Would I join him and the nonfiction editor, Philip Wrenn, at lunch?

Mr. Shawn was little, shy, and possessed of perceptive blue eyes. Mr. Wrenn was tall, blond, and had a pronounced Boston accent. I thought them the two most glamorous men I had ever met, and the French restaurant where we lunched the most elegant I had ever seen; we drank and ate for two hours, and I didn't dare tell them that I was allowed only half an hour for lunch. Nothing was said directly about a job, but later that afternoon I had another call from Mr. Shawn, asking me to come over to *The New Yorker* offices after I had finished work; when I did so he offered me an editorial position at $25 a week. I floated home in a daze of joy.

In more than a decade of reading and loving *The New Yorker*, I had never thought of it having real offices; somehow I vaguely pictured a group of wry angels working up on a cloud somewhere. But the nineteenth floor of 25 West 43rd Street turned out to be very real, with the dirty walls of the long corridors scrawled with James Thurber drawings and miscellaneous uncompleted messages like "Kill the" and "Down with." My own office was at the far end of the corridor and I shared it with Harry Brown, an editor and poet (who later wrote *A Walk in the Sun* and disappeared into Hollywood), and Mr. Wrenn's secretary. Mr. Wrenn, my immediate boss, was in charge of all nonfiction departments—*Talk of the Town, Profiles, Wayward Press,* and so on—and occupied a small inner office. As his assistant, my job was to fine-comb every New York newspaper every day and most of the leading magazines, looking for ideas for his departments. Because of the bulk of the papers I had to work on Sundays, but I was so enamored of the job that I didn't mind.

I was dazzled by the people I met. Harold Ross, a big bear of a man, who often paced up and down the long corridor with his hands behind his back and his face thunderous, and the editors, writers, and artists who drifted in and out during each day, always very quietly and speaking in low tones. Among my favorites was Clifford (Kip) Orr, an editor with an owlish face and great horn-rimmed eyeglasses, who glided about on crepe-rubber soles. One Easter, when I thought I was alone in the office, I heard soft footsteps outside the open door. In a moment, Kip's deadpan face peered in at me. "Christ has risen and seen His shadow," he whispered. "We'll have forty more days of rain."

Becky returned to New York in early December, got a job with American Airlines, and we moved into a sunny fifth-floor rear apartment on West 8th Street which cost all of $36 a month. That winter I felt blessed by the gods with my wonderful job, the fact that I was able to support myself at last, and with what I called my "honest, clean relationship with Greg." I still longed for True Love, but nothing seemed to have any actual existence or importance outside my job, and even the thought of someone to fall in love with seemed as distracting as it did alluring.

By spring, much of the glamour had worn off and the job, although still cherished, had become pretty routine. Greg came in town from time to time, but West 8th Street wasn't Aldercress and in comparison to the suave men I was meeting at the magazine he began to seem a bit bucolic. I went out with the handsome sculptor again, then with an opinionated intellectual who scolded me for frivolity, and after that with a moist-pawed abstract painter who later became very famous. But none of it meant very much and I was beginning to long for meaning. That was the spring of Dunkirk. That was the spring that Paris fell. The headlines grew blacker, the radio broadcasts more hysterical, and ten times a day I tried to resolve the tension between my growing recognition of the need to stop Hitler and my old fear that I might be a dupe of the munition-makers and paid propagandists. It was a relief to spend my three weeks' vacation in California that summer, some of the time at Los Gatos but most of it in Carmel, where I spent an afternoon with Robinson Jeffers and his wife, Una; he took me up to the top of the tower he built above the sea and showed me a stone from the great wall of China embedded in the granite, a green one from Ireland, and a plaque which read: "Why leap ye up, high hills, when God is here?" I picked up a silver feather which one of their doves had dropped and hid it in my pocket. I still have it.

Then back to the beloved and prideful job. A new apartment on Horatio Street with Becky. Wendell Willkie running against FDR. The bombardment of London. The draft in America, and parties becoming more feverish as the boys we knew were drafted one by one. And then one day in late October, just after I had celebrated my first year on *The New Yorker* staff, Mr. Wrenn asked me to have a drink with him after work at the Algonquin.

He had never done this before, and I felt flattered as we sat in the cocktail lobby and chatted over whisky sours. When the second round arrived he told me, very gently and unhappily, that "the experiment hadn't worked out . . . they needed an older woman with more experience . . . that Mr. Ross was restless." In other words, I was fired. (Later I learned the truth: Mr. Ross wanted to hire a well-known writer, who wouldn't join the staff unless an editorial job was also found for his wife; mine was the job chosen. A few months later I also learned that she had lasted only a few weeks.)

My parents were wonderful and I felt somewhat comforted

when my father reminded me that he had warned me of Harold Ross's reputation for occasionally playing rough. But the shock was so great that I felt I couldn't bear to work anywhere else in New York. In a kind of blind passion I felt that the only thing I *could* bear to do was to go back to San Francisco and begin again. My understanding parents agreed to stake me to what my father called a "*Wanderjahr*," and for $125 I bought a ticket on the *West Notus*, a freighter sailing to San Francisco.

On November 18, 1939, with my parents waving good-by from a Norfolk dock, I sailed away from them and from the past.

8

My freighter was a working ship without frills. There was one mess hall, where the twelve passengers and the ship officers all ate good plain food, and a small pantry where anyone was free to make coffee day or night. During the day we sat on hatch covers in the sunlight, talking to whatever mates or engineers were off duty and cared to talk, and at night we walked the decks or sat in the mess hall, drinking endless cups of coffee. Captain Larsen didn't approve of liquor aboard his ship and whatever drinking went on was surreptitious.

It was easy to make friends with the deck officers and the engineers, with "Sparks," the radio operator, and "Chips," the carpenter. For the first time I came to know men totally unlike any I had ever met before, men of varied origins, personalities, and education but strong men, good at their jobs, men who were far more thoughtful about world affairs than I had believed they would be, and full of amazing and often ribald stories of their adventures in ports all over the world. Most of them were Scandinavian.

Smitty, the third mate, mesmerized me. He was a Dane, built like a rather short gorilla with twinkling brown eyes. I played Desdemona to his Othello as he ordered me to stop reading *For Whom the Bell Tolls* so that he could explain to me the elementary facts of the sea world, high- and low-pressure areas, clouds and winds and cyclones, birds and fishes. He taught me Danish folk songs and he told me fairy tales about water nymphs, princes, and mermaids. "Oh, yes, dat's true all right" he would add after each marvelous tale. Smitty, who had been at sea for twenty-five years, was one of the most widely read men I've ever met, although his pronunciation was sometimes odd. His father had been a composer and pianist, and Smitty, too, liked to "trash out" (as he called it) little waltzes in his head during his 8 p.m. to midnight watch. Late at night I sometimes went up to the bow of the ship and gazed at the tall cargo hoists swaying against the stars while I listened to Smitty, far up above me on the dark bridge, whistling his way through a new composition. Afterward I would wait for him in the mess hall, and when he came down from his watch for coffee he would talk about the laws of nature, or the wisdom of animals and their various ways of predicting weather, or any of a dozen themes on which he had been meditating.

One night I asked him how he felt about life at sea. "It's all right," he answered, and fell into a most unusual silence. I was really curious, and also not very perceptive, so I kept prodding while Smitty just sat there smoking a cigarette and grinning at me. Finally, in some irritation, I started to leave.

"It's funny," Smitty said then, "but there are some things a sailor just won't talk about. One of them is his family. I've been shipmates with men for months on end, and yet never known whether they had a wife or kids or what all. Another is what he really thinks of life at sea. You try to get it out of him and he shuts up like a clam." He took a swig of coffee and meditated for a moment.

"It's a hard life, you know," he continued. "You can't afford to be soft. You can't start talking about how you feel, or whimpering. Nope, that just wouldn't do, it wouldn't do at all."

I stammered out an apology, but he didn't seem to hear it.

"Oh, yes," he went on, "they'll tell you all about Singapore and the battle of San Juan and what they think of the unions, but they won't talk about the sea. If you want to find that out, you read William McFee." Silence again. "Well, we ought to be getting some rain soon" he said finally. "Up by the Gulf of Tehuantepec."

I agreed that, yes, it looked like rain, and crept off to my cabin, feeling like a child who has been very justly reproved for prying.

So the days and the nights slipped by, and we were sailing by the lavender mountains of Mexico. Dorothy Sebastian, a former movie star, produced a ukulele and to our amazed merriment dignified Captain Larsen descended from the remoteness of his cabin and did a tap dance. The next day he did a shimmy. And twice he even served us rum collins. The second engineer, a man with soft white arms covered with blue and red tattoos, made seductive passes at me, but I was under Smitty's spell and wouldn't give up one little song or fairy tale for any number of proffered drinks in the engineer's cozy cabin. As for Smitty, he remained mysterious and elusive to the end of the voyage.

I learned a lot on that ship, I suspect much more than passengers on today's cosseting freighters can learn; for one thing, I learned that until then I had been an appalling snob and an ignorant snob at that. I had always had an abstract concern for "the laboring man," but since I had never really known one, I had assumed that any contact beyond the perfunctory would necessarily involve condescension on my part. I had also assumed that sailors were tough, uneducated, crude, and usually drunk. What I found was more or less the opposite: most of the men I came to know were humorous, kindly, and intelligent, and if they liked to get drunk after the long, lonely weeks at sea, I didn't blame them. Above all, as they patiently explained to me the fundamental laws of the universe we all live in, I came to see how very little about it I knew, and to feel that if there were to be any condescending it should come from them and not from me.

We sailed one rosy dawn into San Francisco Bay, and I walked down the gangway and waved good-by to the *West Notus* and her crew. She was sunk in the Atlantic near the end of World War II, with I don't know what loss of life. But in my mind the dolphins and flying fish still play about her bow, and Smitty is up on the bridge, trashing out a little waltz.

. . .

I found a semi-furnished shack on Telegraph Hill, with a pocket-handkerchief garden in back and a window which looked over San Francisco Bay; the rent was $25 a month, and with my $15.72 unemployment compensation and an occasional "buy hyacinths for thy soul" check from my father I managed very well. Gradually, as the spring of 1941 washed over the California hills in a flood of yellow acacia and blue lupin, I was making friends, beginning to go to parties, flying Chinese kites up by Coit Tower, folk dancing at the William Tell Hotel, and spending weekends in Carmel. I had never had so much sheer fun in my life, and I did not job-hunt very seriously.

Four years later I published a book about that time in San

Francisco, and called it *Laughter on the Hill.* The title was appropriate, for it was a light-hearted account of my life in the shack, the delightful screwballs I met, odd bits of California history, colorful bars I frequented, part-time jobs, and boys I flirted with, including one whom I called Pete Stuart. It was a superficial book, but pleasant enough except for a few places where, with the casual callousness of youth, I hurt several people without really meaning to hurt—and the critics were kind. Still, it was not a completely honest book, for it omitted one important episode. Now, because I am determined to be honest about what life has been like, I must make myself relive it.

· · ·

Peter Stuart was the handsomest man I ever met and, despite his youth, the most accomplished seducer. His glowing black eyes would have melted the heart of Carrie Nation and the slightest touch of his hand could have shocked an electric eel. I found out eventually that he was basically uneducated, but he was a quick study and managed to memorize enough lines of poetry to convince me that we were soul mates. Pete lived around the corner with his older brother, Charles, and his recently divorced father; they were a happy-go-lucky trio, and I began spending a lot of time with them and even more time alone with Pete in my shack. I had succumbed emotionally almost from the beginning, but I kept on saying "No" until he took me for a weekend to the family's cabin at the Big Sur. There were canyons cool with great green ferns and the deep shadow of redwoods, sunny hillsides fragrant with lilac, and the smell of the sagebrush leaves that Pete crushed and rubbed against my cheek. At night we walked to the edge of the cliff, with the stars blooming in the black sky above us, and listened to the sound of the surf far below.

"There's a legend you only hear it when you're in love," Pete said. "Do you hear it?"

"Yes," I answered.

Back in San Francisco I decided I was surely a mature woman now, and should act like one. So I went to a doctor, told her I was going to be married, and was fitted for a contraceptive. It was a wonderful spring and early summer, and at least we *talked* of marriage. We walked over the San Francisco hills, we drank wine at water-front cafés, we danced to "Green Eyes" and "Amapola." On weekends we borrowed a car and with Charles and another girl drove into the Marin County mountains, walked on soft russet needles under the hushed redwoods, or ran laughing along vast and golden beaches. And at night there were the deep velvet secrets of the body.

The United States was not yet at war, but the draft law had been passed the year before and one by one our friends were called. In July Pete received his "greetings," and ten days later went off to a nearby training camp. Some little time after his departure the doctor confirmed my panicky suspicion that I was pregnant. I couldn't believe it at first, for I thought I had been faithful to her instructions. Besides, things like that happened to other people, not to *me*! But when I looked into the mirror I knew that it was true, for my face looked softer and seemed to have a glow about it. For a few moments I allowed myself to feel as I truly felt: proud and deeply happy.

I summoned Pete, he came to San Francisco, and he was angry. He was damned if he was going to get married, he said—there were still too many other girls to fuck. He knew a good abortionist to whom he had already sent three other girls, but he had no money and I would have to whistle it up for myself. I learned later that he did not believe me, and eventually I forgave him— but at the time I thought him a monster and was ashamed that I had loved him.

Those were the loneliest and most frightened days of my life. I had $7.19, counting all stray pennies, until the next check for $15.72 would arrive; the abortionist, I had discovered, would cost $80. I knew that my parents would stand by me if I called on them for help, but I felt that the knowledge of my pain would break my father's heart. As for my California relatives, I could not bear to confirm their suspicion that I was made of lesser clay than they; nor could I stand the sly taunts with which Pete's sardonic father would be sure to greet my news.

Finally, I went to a young artist who had wealthy friends and who, I knew, had helped other girls who had been in the same predicament; she managed to borrow $70, which I repaid bit by bit over the next few months. For the final $10 I appealed to an old family friend, also an artist, who happened to be visiting San Francisco. She loaned me the money and told me, greatly to my surprise, that she had had seven abortions. "The important thing," she said gently, "is not to let it make you cynical or bitter about life. And try not to think too much about the child as a person."

The night before the abortion I wrote a letter to be sent to my parents in the event of my death. The last paragraph read:

If something, by the wildest chance, should go wrong—I had to have you know . . . what? That I love you both more than anything in the world . . . and that the dearest wish of my heart has always been to give you a grandchild and to have a child of my own. I wish I could have had this child. I have such a feeling of tender cherishing—wanting to wrap my arms around my body, to care for, to protect. To love. For already I love him, and I try not to think of him, because I must lose him. But I cannot bring a child into the world, when there is no reliable father, no security. Oh my darlings, forgive me and love me, as I shall love you forever.

He was a good doctor, and although most of his face was concealed behind a gauze mask, I saw that his eyes were kind. The equipment looked modern and surgically clean and the nurses wore immaculate white uniforms. Still, I was terrified, and as they strapped me on the table and bound my arms across my chest, the terror grew. In an effort to fight it and in a final gesture of bravado, just before they put on the anesthesia mask, I said, "Hey! Let me down! I've decided to get married!" We were all laughing merrily as I sank into the dark waves of unconsciousness. Afterward the nurses led me to a bed in another room and I rested for three hours, reciting the first thirty-three lines of "Endymion"—my unfailing anodyne—and sleeping. Finally, the doctor came back, still wearing his mask, told me that I was fine, and gave me prescriptions and instructions.

"You are a benefactor to humanity," I said with some emotion. He was silent for a moment, perhaps with surprise. "I appreciate your saying that," he said quite formally. He looked as if it wasn't said to him very often. A few years later I read that he had been arrested for performing abortions and I was sorry.

I stayed in bed for three days and tried not to cry. There was no word from Pete. I tried to follow the advice of our old family friend, and I do not think I ever became cynical or bitter. And I tried, too, not to be oversentimental or sloppy. But once in a while, through the years, I've thought suddenly, He'd be fifteen now. . . . or He'd be twenty-six this month. . . . But each time I rejected the thought, as life forced me to reject him, before he ever lived.

. . .

The months went on. I worked at a series of meaningless secretarial jobs to repay my debts, went out with a series of meaningless boys, and stayed far away from double beds. My mother wrote me a long, grieving letter about my lack of interest in a serious career, my failure to consider the problem of their approaching old age, my laziness, my spendthrift ways with money, and my selfishness in not devoting more time to my California relatives. Guiltily, I started going to see my gallant Aunt Marion, who lived hell and gone on the other side of the city, and my cousin Kay and her husband Jim in Berkeley, where over many years they offered me great hospitality and much pleasure. And, of course, I went to Los Gatos to be with Sara and Pops whenever I was invited. But I was still in some kind of lotus dream which centered around life on Telegraph Hill, on my friends there, impromtu fun, and as many weekends in Carmel as could be managed. I didn't want a career, I only wanted to fall in love and get married and never be lonely or frightened or virtually penniless again.

Then it was Sunday, December 7, 1941, and the United States was at war. Nothing changed very much at first in San Francisco except for the excitement of unfamiliar blackouts. But as the months went on and moved through the grim year of 1942 most of the boys I knew disappeared into the Army, the Navy, the Air Force, or the Merchant Marine, and were replaced by smooth young lieutenants or ensigns from the East who appeared at our parties or favorite bars while waiting to be shipped out.

Even though my country was now in it, I still felt ambivalent about the war. My father wrote me about his thoughts on the subject in response to my hesitant questioning, and one of his letters particularly impressed me. He wrote in part:

With all our failures, I think the symbol is more alive here than in any country in the world. We made a brave break-away—as I said, utterly unique in all history. I believe it was the living symbol that informed and inspired this government in its beginning and I believe it is still alive. It will be kept alive not because we will have beaten our enemies in battle but because we have believed in it enough to fight for it.

If, however, we fight without believing, our victory will be Dead Sea Fruit. [As, more than thirty years after he wrote those words, it is in Viet Nam.]

I could not bring myself to join any of the women's branches of the armed services, but I went to work at a recreation center in Chinatown for GI's interested in sculpture, painting, and writing, and I also became a block leader on Telegraph Hill, ready to carry out body counts in the event of an air raid. I even applied to the Office of War Information for a job, and although my father gave me impressive references I was turned down (because of my parents' radical background, I learned many years later, which amused me, considering that it was my father who had talked me into active patriotism).

Back in San Francisco, after a brief trip home for Christmas, I started job-hunting in earnest—in the fields of publicity, radio, advertising, newspaper work, and publishing—and found that there were few nonsecretarial jobs for women. I thought I had a wonderful break when I was given a one-week tryout as a reporter on the *Call Bulletin*, but at the end of the week the city editor let me go and said doubtfully that I *might* make a good newspaperwoman some day. However, in the summer of 1942 *Mademoiselle* published an article I wrote about life on Telegraph Hill and paid me an extravagant $75. Also, I almost got married.

He was Max Wood, one of Colonel Woods's grandsons, and I met him when he was visiting Los Gatos from Portland, where he had an impressive government job. Everything about him was, at first, also impressive: his height, his girth, his energy, the Chrysler roadster he drove, the flowers he sent me, the time he spent with me in San Francisco's most expensive perfume shop, choosing fragrances most suited to my type, the elegant restaurants where we dined on Andalusian doves, and his talk of the furs and jewels he wished to buy me after we were married. For someone who had to decide every day between the drugstore's fifteen-cent and seventeen-cent (with lettuce) sandwiches, all this was dazzling.

In November I even wrote my parents about him and told them it looked serious, but that I had not yet been able to make up my mind. My father answered:

We stand aside, dear daughter, lovingly and hopefully, and trust your deeply ingrained spiritual integrity and instinctive wisdom where matters of the heart are concerned. And whatever your decision, we will be at your side as long as we live, offering whatever love and wisdom we possess.

If you do decide to marry, next June as you suggested, you will find the old place seemly and beautiful and you won't be ashamed of it. I know you won't misconstrue this as advice or urging, but the thought of seeing you "bowered in beauty" under the grape arbor, married to a good and intelligent man, has been my most iridescent dream.

(Why do I weep when I copy these words? Because I wish so much that I could have made that iridescent dream a reality for him?)

For several weeks I tried to use the wisdom and integrity my father thought I had, and came finally to the realization that I didn't love Max, and therefore could not marry him. He went back to Portland and sometime thereafter married someone else, as men usually do.

. . .

The day after Christmas 1942, my father had a heart attack and was taken to Polyclinic Hospital. For years he had been carrying two columns and that fall he had taken on a seminar at the Columbia University School of Journalism; he was proud that he had been asked to teach there, and he loved his young students and spent many extra hours preparing for lectures and assignments. Rereading his letters now I see how tired he was, how concerned he had always been about the financial security of my mother and me, and even sense a gentle weariness with Mother's parties, no matter how stimulating the conversation. Yet he was doing a tap dance and proving that at sixty-three he could still kick higher than his head when the heart attack hit.

The day he went into the hospital was the day I began my first real newspaper job, as a reporter on the *Examiner*, where he, too, had once worked. My mother assured me on the phone that he was all right and that I shouldn't come home because it would alarm him needlessly. A few days later I telephoned him at the hospital and he said not to worry, "the old ship's just in drydock for a while."

I knew he had not wanted his gentle daughter to be a newspaperwoman but I wrote him every day and the letters reflected my growing excitement at this new profession. Despite his old doubts, Mother wrote me, he was proud that I was doing well, happy that I had lasted a month and was perhaps on my way to a real profession.

At noon on January 29 a telegram from Mother was delivered to me in the city room. Dad was slipping, please come at once. Thanks to money from Aunt Sara, that night I was on my first airplane flight, headed east. During the night we landed at Reno with a defective motor and were put up in a hotel while a replacement was flown in from somewhere else. I remember the sunrise over Colorado the next morning, and that I looked down and saw Longmont, the little town where my father was raised, bathed in a glow of golden light.

We landed at La Guardia at dusk. Stella Karn, a capable old family friend, was there to meet me. Silently she led the way to the chauffeur-driven limousine she had hired. We got in and started toward the city and she still didn't say anything.

"He's dead, isn't he?" I asked.

"Yes," she said. "How did you know?"

"Your silence. And also . . . I felt it. I felt it over Longmont." Later, I found that he had died just at that sunrise moment when I was looking down at his childhood home.

Berta and Elmer Hader, twin Rocks of Gibraltar, were at the London Terrace apartment. My mother was under heavy sedation in another friend's apartment. I had to make decisions. Cremation was in his will. Did I wish to see him first? No, I wanted to remember him alive. What kind of coffin? Quakers believe in plain pine boards, so the simplest possible. Information had to be organized for the *New York Times* obituary; the next day the obit ran a column and a half and was written with the emotions of love and admiration which the whole newspaper world seemed to have felt for him.

After the obituaries appeared in papers all across the country, the flowers, the telegrams, and the condolence letters began to arrive. As is customary after a death, there was too much to do to allow time for grief, and my mother was in no condition to do anything. But she collected herself for the memorial service, which was held a few weeks later at the Quaker Meeting House on Stuyvesant Square and attended by some 200 old friends and colleagues. The Meeting was, of course, silent, but anyone was free to speak as the spirit moved them and many did. I remember particularly my father's old colleague Guy Moyston, who spoke of their early days with the Associated Press in San Francisco, and my own dear friend Margaret Ashelman, who talked of my father's playful love of her young children. The last speaker was one of the Columbia students, a shy boy who was clearly trembling with the embarrassment of speaking before strangers. But his voice gained confidence as he told of the respect and affection the class had felt for their teacher. "He was noble, and he made us feel noble too," he concluded.

Then, it was over, and there was nothing but the necessity to learn how to go on living. Mother roused from her daze enough to agree with me on a few decisions. Yes, we must keep the Sneden's house and we can bear to go back to it because we were all so happy there and he loved it so much. Yes, she would eventually return to writing or get a job. There were 300 letters to answer. "Lem was always indefeasibly himself. . . ." "I remember how Lem led us all around the garden, following the flight of a bumblebee. . . ."

I knew that I must stay with her and in a sense take my father's place in caring for her, for she was too grief-stricken to care for herself. My San Francisco interlude was over.

Early in March, when the ground was finally thawing, I took my father's ashes from the undertaker's where they had been stored, carried them on the bus out to Sneden's, and buried them in the earth he had loved so dearly.

9

It was necessary to find a job, and I was determined that it would be that of a reporter on a New York newspaper, for my father's death had changed my previously dilettante attitude toward a newspaper career into a fierce desire to do the work he had done. In normal times it was difficult for any reporter with as little experience as I had to get a job in New York, and, for a woman, almost impossible. But this was wartime and the draft was draining the male reporters from newspaper staffs; city editors were said to be hiring women.

I started with the city room of *The New York Times* and was quickly passed on to the women's department, where I was turned down, as I was at several other papers. Then one of my father's old friends sent me to see Lessing L. Engleking, city editor of the New York *Herald Tribune*. Mr. Engleking, a huge Texan with a deep voice and a gruff manner, saw me early one afternoon at the beginning of March, looked without comment through a scrapbook of my accomplishments—and told me there were no jobs available.

I went home to the apartment I shared with my mother and moped around unhappily for two hours. At four the phone rang. "Come on back up to the office," Mr. Engleking ordered. Trembling, I returned. "Started thinking over that scrapbook," he grunted. "Guess maybe we can use you. Begin next Monday, one p.m. to nine p.m. Thirty-five a week. Good-by."

. . .

On Monday, March 8, 1943, I began working as a reporter on the staff of the New York *Herald Tribune*. I also began the twelve years which were professionally the happiest of my life.

The mid-1940s were the golden period of the *Herald Tribune*, and those of us who worked there then, look back now upon that old city room as if it had been that of *The Camelot Sun*. White-law Reid, the owner, was determined to produce a good and objective paper and so was his diminutive but powerful wife, Helen Rogers Reid. Although the Reids were Republicans, never in all my time on the paper was it even faintly suggested that I should slant a story in any particular way except the way in which I saw it. The paper had many notable foreign correspondents, prize-winning photographers, about sixty reporters on the city staff, and a great city editor to drive us to accuracy and to arouse in us a craving for originality and a passionate determination to beat the *Times* on every story in terms of facts and good writing. There was a fine library (or "morgue," as some other papers call it), where everything could be checked and damned well was. Above all, there was enough space in the paper to allow room for humor, pathos, satire, or whatever else was needed to make a feature story outstanding. And if it wasn't, a topnotch bank of rewrite men could doctor it into a masterpiece.

But I didn't know anything about all this on that first day, and I was frightened as I walked into the city room on the fifth floor, for it was far bigger and noisier than the *Examiner*'s and people seemed to rush around more. The city desk, where Mr. Engleking sat with his assistant, Dick West, was at the center of the room; the horseshoe-shaped copy desk was nearby, and over the head of the chief copy reader, who sat "inside the rim," a large cowbell hung suspended from a light fixture, to be rung only when one of the enemy belligerents surrendered or the war was won.

Ranks of reporters' desks were lined against a far wall, and Mr. Engleking led me over to the one that was to be mine and introduced me to the nearest reporters, among them Virginia Clemmer, another girl reporter and a real pro, and Herbert Kubly, who was almost as new as I was; they became my first real friends on the paper and with their helpful hints saved me often from the wrath of the Zeus whom everyone called Engle.

Because of wartime egg shortages, the city had just lifted its ban on raising poultry in city limits, and that morning Macy's department store had advertised a sale of live hens and roosters. My first assignment was to go down to Macy's and find out how the

sale was going and what kind of people were buying the fowl. I
did, but back at the office and seated at the typewriter I felt para-
lyzed and couldn't think of how to begin. "Help me, Dad, help
me please!" I whispered. Suddenly I felt a wave of confidence
flow through me and I began to write. The story was cut, but at
least it ran. I made the same appeal successfully a few more
times, but I felt I shouldn't do it too often and gradually I began
to depend on myself alone.

I had two guidelines for my behavior in this essentially masculine world. One was a letter my father had written me when I
began the tryout on the *Call Bulletin*, warning me against in-
volvement in office politics and suggesting that a degree of formality in relationships with co-workers and editors was a good
idea, at least at first. I heeded these cautions and found them
wise. My other guide was the book *City Editor*, by Stanley
Walker, who for many years had been city editor of the *Tribune*
and who was still to be seen downstairs at Bleeck's (the former
speakeasy next door which was frequented by the *Trib*'s editorial
staff) playing the match game with Lucius Beebe. Mr. Walker's
book had a chapter on women in the city room, a subject on
which he had mixed opinions. Following his rules for female behavior, I never sat on desks and I avoided any romantic entangle-
ments with the staff or discussion of my personal affairs. I never
expressed shock at rough language but I didn't use it myself. And
as a deliberate policy I never complained about assignments or
hours. I found that Walker was right, for newspapermen are old-
fashioned romantics: if a woman *must* work on a paper they want
her to work like a man but to remain "a lady."

There were a number of other women on the staff, and they set
good examples: woman's page editor Dorothy Dunbar Bromley,
crisp and intelligent; dear Emma Bugbee, who had joined the
staff before World War I and who still chugged along indefatiga-
bly, no matter how difficult the assignment; diplomatic Marie
McGowan, the star girl reporter whom we all envied because she
was assigned to travel across the United States with Mme.
Chiang Kai-shek; and Marguerite Higgins, who had come to the
paper the year before I did. Maggie, who became a very famous
foreign correspondent, was still a cub, with carbon splotches on
her lovely face and a pencil stuck into her disheveled blond curls
—but she was one of the most ferociously thorough and concen-

trated reporters I ever met. There are a lot of male foreign correspondents around the world who would add the word "unscrupulous," but I have always suspected that many of them were
jealous of her courage and ingenuity.

As the war went on, more women joined the staff: India McIn-
tosh, Marguerite Young, Betty Graham, Jo-Ann Price, Jean Now-
ell, and shy little Judy Crist, who worked for the woman's page
and wasn't nearly as glamorous as she is today. Like the older
members of the staff, they were all professional, which is my
highest word of praise. So too were the girls I met on various assignments who worked for other papers or wire services—
especially my lifelong friend Lucy Freeman, who at that time was
a topnotch reporter with the *Times* and who taught me many
techniques of the craft.

Yes, there were a lot of us around in those days, and I don't remember that any of us felt that the men discriminated against us,
except in the case of a sudden big local news break requiring fast
action—fires, floods, sensational murders, and riots. On these occasions excited editors completely forget there are women on the
staff, but this happened rarely and we accepted it with philosphi-
cal amusement as part of nature's law.

. . .

It was a long, very hot summer and the local news was slow. I
covered occasional dog shows, Boy Scout meetings, war-bond rallies in the far reaches of Queens. The rest of the time I sat at my
typewriter with the sweat pouring down my face and my hands
grimy from carbon paper, writing obituaries and dreaming of San
Francisco wind and fog. But I didn't want to go back, I decided,
not when I had a by-line and discovered how powerfully life can
be spiced by ambition. Besides, my mother still needed me, although she had made a gallant effort to recover and was working
part time at the Planned Parenthood offices and also doing library research on tropical diseases for the United Fruit Lines.

Gradually, Engle taught me my trade. "*Write* this," he would
command, handing me back a piece I had written in a pedestrian
manner. Or, "Put some imagination into it." Somehow I would
know what he meant and rewrite it so that there was a sparkle to
it. Engle would raise bellowing hell if you misspelled a word or
used a wrong initial even in a one-paragraph obituary, but he
never failed to praise and reward with a $10 bonus what he felt

to be an outstanding job. Because of his goading I began to develop a style of my own, particularly in feature-writing and interviews, and frequent by-lines came along with occasional raises permitted by the National War Labor Board. "Everything is grist to the writer's mill," my father used to say, and I found that he was right. I also found that my family background and my education had prepared me to handle any kind of assignment I was given, and I was grateful.

In the summer of 1944 several things happened. Maggie Higgins was sent to England, and I died a little with envy, never having forgotten my college dreams of travel but aspiring in my own fantasies to nothing grander than the staff of the Paris *Herald* after the war. Also, early that summer, I started writing my San Francisco book. And I began going around with a reporter on the *Times* whom I'll call Abe. Abe was some twelve years older than I and something of a rough diamond, but he was amiable, a good reporter who taught me a great deal, and he loved me very much. I responded with affection, which at the time I confused with love, and pretended I enjoyed the horse races to which he was addicted. With these activities and my job, I managed to smother the loneliness I still felt for my father and for a man with whom I could truly communicate.

That fall the postwar formation of a United Nations was planned at Dumbarton Oaks, and during the winter of 1944–1945 the war gathered momentum for the final blazing climax, and by January 31, 1945, the Allied troops were pressing toward the German border. In February President Roosevelt, Stalin, and Churchill met at Yalta, and early in March five divisions crossed the Rhine over the famous bridge at Remagen. In the Pacific, Iwo Jima was invaded by our forces on February 19, and Okinawa on April 1. The Allies were so clearly moving toward victory on both fronts that a United Nations Organizational Conference was scheduled to meet in San Francisco on April 25. On Wednesday, April 11, I was called into the office of managing editor George Cornish, who politely asked me whether I would like to be a member of the reporting team which the *Tribune* was sending to San Francisco to cover the UN Conference. I managed to indicate that, yes, I would; indeed, I *would.*

The next day, one of our two days off, Abe and I were celebrating with a drink at the Empire State Building Longchamps when the Muzak stopped and a voice said: "Ladies and Gentlemen—President Roosevelt has just died at Warm Springs, Georgia." There were shocked gasps from everyone in the room, and many people put their heads in their hands and wept. So did I, for Roosevelt had been President almost since I could remember and for me, despite his arrogance toward youth and his failure to support the Spanish Loyalists, he had been a prime father figure. It seemed impossible that cocky little Vice-President Truman could carry on. But after a few moments we pulled ourselves together and, as is customary with reporters if big news breaks on a day off, went back to our offices to be put to work. Nature's law regarding women had gone into effect, I found, and I was given the overloaded-telephones assignment (a minor story which always accompanies big news developments). One week later I left for San Francisco.

Those two months at the San Francisco Conference were the two most intense, dazzling, heady months of my entire life; sometimes I think I never recovered from them, as in a sense I didn't, for they shaped my future. And from one encounter, lasting only seventeen days of those two months, I did not recover and never will.

I crossed the country on a special train, called "The Correspondent," which carried 300 newspaper people, many of whom brought along their own cases of liquor and others who considered themselves far too important to share the prevailing conviviality. I decided that I preferred the boys in the city room to most of the foreign and domestic egotists I encountered, and was glad that I was a "hack." But lanky Archibald Steele, the *Herald Tribune*'s Far East correspondent, who read quietly in his roomette most of the time, impressed me. I talked to him there several times, and he revived my old longing for Asia because he had recently returned from Tibet and told me marvelous tales of the search for the new Dalai Lama. Arch was one of the best and most serious foreign correspondents I ever knew, and when I myself went overseas I tried to model myself upon him.

One other man on the train, who was to become a dear friend, I met briefly and characteristically. The train stopped at Reno for fifteen minutes and I watched from the platform while most of the men pounded into the nearest casino to play the slot machines. The train whistle blew, the mob returned, and a man carrying two handfuls of silver coins approached me. He was six feet tall, but with his balding head, round blue eyes, and drooping mustache he looked a bit like the little man who used to appear on the cover of *Esquire*. "Put out your hands, child," he commanded in an English accent. I did so, he dropped the silver hoard from his hands into mine, and turned and walked away. I didn't know who he was then, but any of the hundreds who knew and therefore loved him will instantly recognize Charlie Campbell, director of the British Information Services in the United States.

In San Francisco a new world flowered. Instead of living in a shack on Telegraph Hill, I was installed in Room 1810 of the elegant Palace Hotel, with unlimited access to Room Service. Instead of drinking beer at the Iron Pot or the Black Cat, I drank champagne at parties in lavish hotels all over town, parties at which one might see anyone, ranging from Hedda Hopper in one of her fantastic hats to smiling Jan Masaryk of Czechoslovakia, or Prime Minister Herbert Vere Evatt of Australia, who liked to balance a full glass of Scotch on his gray head. Even our *Herald Tribune* "family" was awe-inspiring. Mr. and Mrs. Reid had taken a mansion out on Pacific Heights, where they regularly held formal dinners for Conference delegates and members of the paper's team. Walter Lippmann was a member of our working group, and so was Major George Fielding Eliot, the war analyst; Joseph Barnes, our foreign editor and a Russia specialist; Geoffrey Parsons of the editorial department; Marcus Duffield of the Sunday *Review of the Week*; Ned Russell, chief of our London Bureau; Bert Andrews and John C. Metcalfe of the Washington bureau; and the Asia expert, Arch Steele.

I was the only woman reporter, and the only member from the city staff, and I found most of these colleagues from the larger world bewildering. Bert Andrews, who headed our San Francisco coverage, would rush into our office with a shout: "Cuba's walking out!" So far as I could make out this assertion was based on nothing but rumor yet he would bat out the story, it would run page one, and Bert would bask in praise for a day. It didn't seem to matter that Cuba never did walk out, or many of the events happen which the big shots predicted.

Because I thought it was expected of me, I began writing the way they did: It was learned from a high source today that— Switzerland wasn't speaking to Russia or Jawaharlal Nehru's sister was going to assassinate Anthony Eden, or Bolivia was planning to oppose the veto. Engle would have bitten my head off if I had written a fact without attributing it by name to the source, but away from New York the rules were different. Looking back at my Conference clippings now, my stories seem stuffy and contrived, and I see how unnatural that way of writing was for me; in future years I sometimes had to do high-level political reporting, but I never enjoyed it or did it well.

Early in May someone took me to the San Francisco press club, and there I met Bob Considine, who quickly became a warm, platonic friend. The night of May 7, knowing that the peace announcement was imminent, we sat for hours in the press club discussing the approaching end of the war in Europe, and then wandered for a long time around Union Square, staring at ghostly rhododendrons in the fog. At 5:30 a.m. we went to the *Examiner* city room, and sitting on the rim of the sports copy desk listened to President Truman proclaim the end of the war, and a few minutes later, to Churchill broadcasting from England. "A historic moment, kid," Bob said. I felt so exhausted from the five long war years of sadness and the long night of waiting for it to end that all I could think of was that he was certainly right.

That night, after sleeping all day, I was taken to a party of British journalists who were celebrating Victory in Europe Day with particular vigor. I had never met any Englishmen before and I expected they would fit the stereotype—stuffy, formal, cold, humorless. To my amazement I found that these riotous journalists sang wonderful folk songs, danced with mad abandon, drank unbelievably, and made dry remarks like "An incredible bottom —what?"

I swooped through a number of wild waltzes with ebullient Charlie Campbell, the man who had given me the handful of coins in Reno, and when he asked me to lunch the next day at the press club, I accepted. When I arrived he greeted me very formally and led me to the bar. He was silent until the dry martinis arrived. Then he picked up his glass, took a sip and turned toward me.

"I say," he said politely, "would you be interested in sexual intercourse?"

I almost choked on my drink. But I managed to answer with

what I hoped was equal courtesy, "I'm afraid not. But I do thank you for the invitation."

"Quite all right," he said. Thereafter we became very good friends and he never again raised the subject.

Charlie and his deputy, Jack Winocour—another attractive madman—lived just down the hall from me in Suite 8002, and with the aid of their tolerant and pretty assistants, Margaret Fleming and Nora Thomas, operated a round-the-clock open house frequented by a select group of British correspondents and a very few Americans. I was invited in, and soon discovered that I was happier and more comfortable with these zany Britishers than I had ever been with my compatriots. For one thing, American men seem embarrassed by literacy, but these men took it quite for granted that if one has been to university, one is literate. Jack, for instance, would sometimes pull a copy of Catullus from a pocket, and read aloud in Latin. Once he read us the complete preface to the King James edition of the Bible, a performance we all enjoyed. Newspapermen are the most idealistic of cynics, and because they so terribly wanted the United Nations to succeed but suspected it wouldn't, there was an edge of hysteria to the Conference social life. In Suite 8002 we found relief from the tension in our deep concern for a baby turtle that Charlie and Jack kept in their bathtub. We argued for hours over whether he should go to preparatory school in England or public school in America, and hotly disputed the merits of Oxford versus Harvard for his higher education. At various odd moments during the Conference eminent correspondents could be seen prowling the hotel corridors in a search for dead flies to bring to the voracious reptile.

On Sunday evening, May 13, Charlie and Jack invited me to a dinner party. When I arrived at their suite, I was introduced to an Englishman of around forty, rather round and rosy, with hazel eyes and straight brown hair. He was (as I shall call him) Ian Thomas, a top official in the United Kingdom Government, and a member of its Conference delegation. We all had a drink, piled into Charlie's rented limousine, and drove to Vanessi's restaurant in the old Barbary Coast district at the foot of Telegraph Hill. I was seated at the table next to Mr. Thomas and we began talking. Two hours later we were still talking. The others, to whom we had said not a word during dinner, had left but we couldn't even remember their departure. Nor can I remember much of what we talked about except that he told me about his childhood in Shropshire and he quoted a Housman poem I had never heard: "Clunton and Clunbury, Clungunford and Clun / Are the quietest places under the sun." He told me about his early days on a newspaper and I told him about mine. He told me about London under the blitz, and I told him about Telegraph Hill before the war. He asked me to show him some of the places I had loved, so we climbed the Hill, I showed him the shack where I had lived, and led him through semisecret dark gardens and passageways up to Coit Tower, at the very summit of the Hill. It was late and no one else was there. We strolled around the tower, across the lawn in back, and sat down on the edge of a bluff overlooking the lighted ships in the docks at the foot of the Hill, the black waters of the Bay, the far lights of Berkeley and Oakland. It was very beautiful, and for the first time in several hours we were silent. Then at the same moment we turned to each other. "A lyric in time," he said later. Finally he took me home, and left.

The next day we met for lunch at the Black Cat, a favorite Hill hangout, which I also wanted to show him. "I have a feeling that you have a very steadying and deep relationship in your life," I told him, for he had said nothing about his family. "Yes," he said gravely. He had two children just approaching their teens. He had a wife to whom he had been married for nineteen years and to whom he was devoted. The implications of this were clear, but it was already too late for either of us to draw back—we had fallen in love. Not infatuation, not lust, not Conference madness, but love as I had never known before or ever have since; our minds and hearts seemed like two birds flying together, swooping and swirling in perfect harmony with no need for signals or explanations. With us, always, trickery or pretense was impossible, nor was there ever a need to think before we spoke; from the beginning we spoke the same language.

We spent as much of the next fifteen days together as we could manage, and all of the nights. We walked on the beach by the Cliff House and dipped our hands in the Pacific. We rode ferryboats in the moonlight. We folk-danced and drank beer at the bouncy William Tell Hotel. We talked and laughed and made love (how characteristic it was of him that he was amused and not hurt when I marveled innocently, "I didn't know love could be so peaceful"). We went for a weekend to Inverness, a little town on Tomales Bay, taking with us my book on San Francisco, which had just been published, and one of his; naked, bespectacled, and smiling we sat in bed reading each other's books. The next day we walked among the wild flowers on windy Point Reyes, looked at the distant sea, and quoted poetry we loved. For my thirtieth birthday he gave me a copy of T. S. Eliot's *Four Quartets* and an exclusive story about the probable future military arrangements of the United Nations, which amazed my colleagues and brought me fame for a day or so. He also taught me several new words: ancillary, adumbrate, *détente*. I could no more have helped loving him than I could help loving the sun and the moon and the stars.

We tried very hard to keep it "a lyric," part of a little world of our own and not the big outside world. But as the days went on this became impossible for both of us. For the first time in a relationship, I discovered, there was no need for compromising or justifying; with Ian I was simply happy and completely spontaneous. As the day approached when he would have to leave I felt that when it came there would be no *me* left, and I understood the true meaning of the phrase "tearing the heart out." We agreed that our emotions had gone far beyond that of a lyric, and talked of the future. But he could not leave his wife, whom he also loved, or his children, nor did I want to be responsible for the shattering of three other lives. I told him bravely, "Even if we do feel pain, it is all right. The only pain which is *bad* comes from the cruelty of other human beings. Our pain comes from good, from love, and therefore we will be able to endure and to assimilate it." Unable to endure it, we cried.

His last night my dear and sympathetic friend Dorothy Erskine let us have her beautiful apartment on Telegraph Hill, and we went there after a farewell visit to the place at the top of the Hill where we had first kissed. We ate the dinner she had left us, drank her wine, and sat by the glowing fire. Ian found a copy of Burns on her shelves and read, "O my luve is like a red, red rose. . . ." And Yeats, "Had I the heaven's embroidered cloths . . . I would spread the cloths under your feet. . . ." And, ". . . one man loved the pilgrim soul in you." We each gave the other a piece of carved Chinese amber, symbolizing the worlds we had shared. "A sign and a seal and a small world to hold in the hand," he said. Then the delegation car came for him, and he was gone. After a while I made my way back to the Palace and wrote in my journal, "I will try to do as he says, and use this love, this experience, as a positive force throughout my life."

I have tried to do so, as I know that he did also.

. . .

The next day Mrs. Reid invited me to one of her formal dinners, and I was dismayed because Ian was going to telephone me from New York before he caught his plane to England. I arranged for the call to be transferred, but it was necessary to explain its importance to Mrs. Reid, who didn't like to have her guests summoned from the table while Anthony Eden or Secretary of State Stettinius was briefing the others on the intricacies of the veto problem. With a gleam of curiosity in her shrewd blue eyes, she listened with sympathy to my stumbling explanations, but said nothing except that I might receive the call. Later, I suspect, she made a few inquiries and tucked the answers away in her orderly mind. Like so many other chances, the coincidence of the dinner party and the telephone call were to have a vast effect on my future.

During the next three weeks that the Conference dragged on I felt as if my stomach, my guts, and heart had been torn out by Ian's departure. Only two things helped: work, into which I threw myself ferociously, and the kindness of Charlie Campbell and Jack Winocour. Being English, they did not say anything directly but dozen of gestures of consideration showed me that they knew what had happened, that they understood it hadn't been just another Conference affair like the ones going on in so many hotel rooms. Yet they never gave me the feeling that they were pitying me, and I was grateful for this and tried to respond with a kind of stoic gaiety. Near the end of the Conference I made an effort, without being explicit, to thank them. They were embarrassed. "It is only because we love you," Jack murmured. Charlie patted me on the shoulder. "You're a good soldier," he said. I felt as if I had received the Order of Merit.

Every morning I found some funny little note from them slipped under my door. I still treasure one which was written on the crested paper of the United Kingdom Delegation to the San Francisco Conference:

Did it ever occur to you
that
The United Nations Conference on International Organization

Spelled backwards
And written backwards
Looks
Like This

Noitazinagro Lanoitanretni No Ecnerefnoc Snoitan Detinu Eht
??
No??
Well, it does.

Finally it was June 26, and we watched while President Truman and representatives of the other nations signed the charter which they assured us would keep our children from the horrors of another war. There had been many odd characters at the Conference, and one of the oddest was a small Frenchman who always carried a woolly toy lamb tucked through the handle of his briefcase. He sat just in front of me in the auditorium, and as we rose to our feet, applauding, he held the little animal high in the air and clapped its tiny paws together. The bedraggled lamb blocked my view of the solemn men on the stage, and has remained my sharpest memory of the historic day.

That night there was a farewell party at Dorothy Erskine's apartment, where Ian and I had spent our last evening together. As I sat on a big hassock staring into the fire, a shriveled man with a clever face came and sat beside me. He said he was Amin Yalman, editor of the newspaper *Vatan*, of Istanbul.

"Why are you sad?" he asked me.

"Because I was happy and now I am not happy."

"You are fortunate," he told me gravely. "You have stolen time from Felek. In Turkey we say that the malevolent god of destiny, called Felek, rules our lives and makes most of us unhappy most of the time. So if one has been happy, even for a short while, one has stolen time from Felek and is therefore fortunate."

. . .

Back in New York I told Abe I couldn't marry him, an emotionally rending experience, for he was understandably bitter. In the city room life went on, but I found that it had lost its old excitement since I had glimpsed larger worlds. But on August 6 we were shaken by the news that the human race had dropped an atomic bomb on Hiroshima, and mid-afternoon on August 14 the chief copy reader suddenly jumped up and slammed an exultant fist against the cowbell above his desk. The war was over. The bell's reverberations were almost instantly silenced by the bedlam in the city room, everyone shouting and laughing and some of us with tears of joy in our eyes. Then the city room began erupting with bellows and orders and assignments and reporters running up to the desk when their names were called, listening for a moment, grabbing some copy paper and a handful of pencils, and rushing off.

I had the mood-in-Times-Square story, and for the next nine hours alternated between the delirious celebration that was going on in the Square and the city room, where I updated the story every few hours and did a complete rewrite at midnight. By then I was exhausted and badly wanted a drink. But Bleeck's was locked to all except top *Tribune* executives and the nearby bars were full of drunks. Forlornly, I wandered back upstairs and in the ladies' room ran into white-haired Nellie Gardner, the religious editor. "Would you like a drink?" asked Nellie, fishing a pint of bourbon from her capacious black purse. So I toasted the end of the bitter war drinking bourbon out of a paper cup in the ladies' room of the *Herald Tribune*.

But it was a sad summer. My dear old dog, Christopher, had died while I was in San Francisco, and I missed him badly when I moved back to Sneden's with my mother. I was swept continually by waves of unbearable longing for Ian, and was uninterested when the handsome sculptor came back from the wars and again asked me to marry him. I was in no mood to marry anyone except Ian, and that was impossible even in daydreams; I could never figure any moral way to eliminate his wife without hurting Ian.

In November he came to Washington briefly and I went down to spend three days and nights with him. Soberly, we agreed that this must be the last time we were lovers, and although we knew that a deep and mutual love existed and probably always would, we must henceforth conform to the outward forms of friendship, not of love. I went back to New York determined that if I couldn't be his wife or mistress, I could at least find some comfort if I lived in the same country with him. Maggie Higgins had by this time gone on to Germany and growing fame, so I went to Mrs. Reid and pleaded to be assigned to the paper's London bureau. She looked at me with wise eyes and said, "We'll see." Several weeks went by. Then on January 30, 1946, foreign editor Joe Barnes called me to his desk and asked me to sit down.

"How would you like to go to Japan for six months?" he asked.

She couldn't have picked a country farther away from England.

❧ 10 ❧

Japan was probably the one country in the world I had never
wanted to visit. My family had always admired the Chinese, but I
knew nothing of Japanese history or culture and was, all in all,
about the most ignorant and unwilling correspondent the *Tribune*
could have chosen to send to Japan. However, I would have gone
to Hades itself if it meant becoming a foreign correspondent,
which seemed to me, as it still does, the most glamorous occupation in the world. So, gulping slightly, I told Joe I'd like very
much to go to Japan for six months.

As he described the assignment, I realized that it was the kind
that reporters dream of for their mature years. Ralph Chapman
would be going out at about the same time, and he would be responsible for daily coverage of the hard news. I was to rove
around the country and write stories about people, groups, and
places, stories which would indicate how the Occupation was
going, how people were living, thinking, and feeling, and whether
the Japanese were indeed being "democratized."

There were two people I hated to leave. One of them was
Engle, to whom I was devoted, who had taught me almost everything I knew about newspaper work, and with whom I had developed a warm if somewhat inarticulate friendship. "Going overseas
ruins good reporters," he grumbled once, biting viciously on his
long black cigar. "They start putting on airs and calling themselves *journalists*." There was a world of derision in his voice as
he said the detestable word. I promised him fervently that I
would continue to think of myself as a reporter, and never, never,
never as a journalist.

I also hated to leave my mother. She had never recovered from the grief of my father's death and she was increasingly dependent on me for decisions and companionship. Still, she was working and she had many loving and attentive friends. Above all, she wanted me to go. All her life she had been terrified of poverty, and perhaps for that reason had always urged me, as she did now, to remember that "JOB comes first."

So I plunged into the weeks of preparation. Applications for passport, Army travel orders and transportation. Fittings for the uniforms all correspondents in Occupation zones were required to wear. A trip to Washington to see our old-China-hand friend John Carter Vincent, talks with State Department Japan experts to whom he sent me, and with Herbert Norman, the distinguished Canadian scholar. The excursion was more bewildering than helpful, for nobody seemed able to explain what our Japan policy actually *was,* and the experts tended to laugh wryly at any mention of General MacArthur's name and to say darkly, "You'll find out." Meanwhile I read feverishly, trying to cram centuries of history into a few brief weeks: Sir George Sansom, Lafcadio Hearn, Herbert Norman, and Lady Murasaki; I began to glimpse the depths of my ignorance. The day before I left I had a final briefing from Joe Barnes. "Take a few weeks to get the feel of the place before you start filing," he said. "And Margaret, relax and have a good time. You'll be a better correspondent that way."

On March 26, 1946, I left by train for San Francisco, taking my mother with me to stay for a while at her sister Marion's after I left. I also took with me Ian's farewell letter, with a postscript which tore at my heart. "May I just once again say," he wrote, with a touch of that English formality I find so enchanting, "that I have loved you so much and go on doing so."

I had almost a month in San Francisco, talking to Japan experts, seeing old friends and my family, and trying not to glimpse Ian in every drift of fog. One night I had dinner with British friends and their infant daughter, Jennifer, whom I was allowed to hold. That night I wrote in my journal, "Seeing her two little new teeth, her smile, her pixie curls, I felt suddenly that all this business of being a foreign correspondent and going to Japan is utter nonsense—and that the only thing in the world I really want to do is to have a child like Jennifer."

But on April 25 I sailed for Japan aboard the *General Ernst,* a thirteen-thousand-ton Navy vessel guarded by Marines and transporting some three thousand enlisted men and officers, forty-four government secretaries, four USO actresses, and me. This initial encounter with military life was a considerable shock. I hated almost everything about it, but I managed to survive, thanks to Captain Richard W. Dole, who gave me a few cautious privileges including a cabin where I could study peacefully during the day.

As we approached the port of Inchon, Korea, on the morning of May 12, Captain Dole and his Executive Officer, Commander Forrest Allen (a former Washington newspaperman), let me stand all morning on the flying bridge, excitedly watching the soapstone-green Yellow Sea, the islands that looked like ones in Chinese scrolls, the tall, rectangular red sails of sampans. The next day was my first day in the Orient, and I was totally overwhelmed by looking, hearing, smelling, talking, questioning, and looking, looking, looking. The Captain had asked me whether I would like to drive to Seoul with him and Commander Balmer, the ship's chief surgeon, and while he picked up the jeep he was borrowing I tried to talk to a bright-eyed little Korean boy in the few phrases of Japanese I had learned; he patted my knee and the fender of the jeep and to both said, "Nice American," in English.

I loved Korea that day. The costumes, the convolutions of the hills, the eyes of the old men, everything. We opened cans of beer with penknives, we choked on dust, we marveled at the twisty streets of Seoul, we bought silly souvenirs, we were totally innocent of Korea and completely happy. In Inchon again we went to the Navy officers' club, joined Commander Allen, danced, drank, and sang; back on the ship for dinner in the Captain's cabin I held hands all evening under the table with handsome Commander Allen; the Captain, very shy and dignified, escorted me "home" to the stateroom I shared with the four USO actresses. It was, all in all, a most auspicious first day in Asia.

The first day in Japan was a different matter. Mac Johnson, a big, kindly man (whom small, kindly Ralph Chapman would soon replace), met me at the dock in Yokohama and drove me to Tokyo. I attributed my dreamy reaction to the shock of the devastation in the thirty miles between the two cities; not a single habitation remained standing, and only a few factory chimneys and stone outbuildings were silhouetted against the sky. Mac drove me to the "Press Nest," a Japanese house he shared with Darrell Berrigan and three other correspondents. I attributed my feverish reaction to all of them to excitement and novelty, but when Berry (who was one of the most sensitive and gentle of men) suggested rather early that I take a Japanese bath and go to bed I accepted gratefully.

The next morning I had a fever of 103 degrees. Mac drove me to the 42nd General Hospital, where Army doctors said they didn't know what I had but that I better stay. The next morning my over-all pinkness coelesced into red spots and there was no doubt of the diagnosis. So my first cable as a foreign correspondent wasn't an exclusive interview with MacArthur or the Emperor, as I had dreamed, but only the sad words, "Am in hospital with measles." The bright-eyed Korean boy, no doubt.

As the days passed and I grew well again, I also grew panicky. What did I know about the Occupation? Nothing. Even more frightening was the realization that I didn't have the slightest idea of how to be a foreign correspondent. I had always worked on assignment; Engleking had told me where to go and what kind of story was required. Now I must find stories for myself, interpreting the significant in terms of the specific, and to do that I must understand in some depth what was happening in Japan. But given all the complexities of both Japan and the Occupation, how should I begin to understand? I confessed some of these dark fears to my fellow patient Jack Service, an outstanding Sinologist, and his quiet reassurances helped me a great deal; I have always been grateful to the measles for introducing me to Jack, who became my friend, as did his wife, Caroline.

I was still frightened by my own faults of character: laziness, a weak capacity for self-discipline, procrastination, a tendency toward self-indulgence, a quick temper, and overemotionalism. The day I left the hospital and moved into the Keijo Building, where most of the government girls I had so unwisely ignored on the ship were quartered, I literally prayed for help.

. . .

To most Americans as well as to Japanese, General MacArthur was more remote and august than the Emperor; the only time a correspondent was likely to talk to him was at the formal interview he granted new arrivals, and, if he had approved of their coverage, once again on departure. Mac Johnson was going home and Ralph Chapman and I had just arrived, so an interview was scheduled—with some difficulty because the Supreme Commander had never before received a woman correspondent.

Everything I had ever heard or read about MacArthur had made me dislike him and want to disparage anything he had to say. We were not allowed to take notes during our twenty-minute off-the-record interview, but in the account which I wrote directly afterward I admitted that I had been impressed by his fluency. He talked steadily for all that time, and swooped smoothly from one topic to another: the dangers of the growing Russian complex; Russian regimentation which was worse than the Nazi or Japanese; bombs that were twenty million times more powerful than the one used at Hiroshima; there can't be another war because there can't be a victor and the Russians have missed the boat; correspondents should stop criticizing the Occupation and realize what a tremendous job was being done in Japan.

"What we are bringing to Japan," he said in conclusion, "is one simple, fundamental idea: the dignity of the individual human being. If we can't put that across, we can't put anything across. It's the idea of Christ, when he was tortured and debauched, and rose above it to affirm the dignity of the human spirit. This is the principal idea behind the Occupation, and the real story in Japan—that we have removed seventy million people from the enslavement of ten million, and given them a new dignity. This is the story I wish the correspondents would see, and write about."

. . .

I resolved to keep an open mind, and set out to experience whatever life and Japan had to offer. I walked miles through Tokyo and was appalled at the devastation, the blackened, skeletal office buildings, the three tattered waifs who lived in a large cardboard box behind the bombed-out railway station and apparently existed on air. I was also overwhelmed by the excitement and color of this strange new land, by cricket cages in the windows of the rebuilt Ginza shops, the fluttering of fans up and down the streets as the weather grew hot, the crackling cadences of the mysterious language, the women with babies strapped to their backs, the lovely young girls in bright kimonos and shimmering obis, the click-clacking on the pavements of thousands of the wooden clogs called getas. But within a month, I'm ashamed to remember, I went into an extreme case of what I now know is called "culture shock." The glamour wore off. I developed an alarming tendency to snarl, and a homicidal desire, when I was driving the *Tribune* jeep, to knock old gentlemen off bicycles. I found myself referring to "the nips" and even to "the little yellow bastards." I cursed plumbing that didn't work. I raged at Japanese pedestrians who insisted on walking in the middle of the street, apparently in a perpetual daze, and who stopped and bowed when they heard my horn. I sneered at carpenters because the teeth of their saws and the blades of their planes go in an opposite direction from ours, and I fumed at Japanese waitresses because they stood at my elbow while I ate and stared at me.

Before coming to Japan I had vowed that I was going to be sympathetic and understanding so I was horrified by these feelings, and not much comforted when other correspondents assured me that this happened to everyone sooner or later and that I would eventually recover (as I did). I had vowed, too, that I would stay far away from other Americans and "live with the people," but now I discovered that I didn't know any Japanese people to live with. Even our interpreter, young Ken Inouye, was no help in bridging the cultures, for he had been raised in Los Angeles and all of his attitudes were brashly American. Japanese theaters and restaurants were all off limits to Americans; I was forced to live in such an insular American environment that I even found it impossible to get a cup of tea.

Thus it was with mixed feelings that late in June I moved to the Tokyo Press Club, which had just rescinded its ban on women residents. This famous building on Shimbun (newspaper) Alley, which sheltered dozens of correspondents of many nationalities, was to be my home for the next eight months. It was a "modern" five-story building, which meant that in style it was very bad 1928 movie house, with ornate carvings, frowning fireplaces, repulsive stained-glass windows set into every possible nook, brown tile floors and walls, and oversize furniture in spiritless tones of gray and dark olive; in other words, it was typical of the dreadful taste which afflicts Asians whenever they try to build or decorate in what they conceive to be "Western style." But there was a shining and Broadwayish bar on the ground floor, a lounge with low divans and little red tables, and an elevator which sometimes worked.

American wives were not yet allowed to come to Japan, and

every morning the ladies' bathroom on the third floor was filled with pretty Japanese girls who had spent the night with various correspondents and who were enjoying the luxury of a shower. There were more girls every evening in the lounge and bar, as well as Eurasian, Chinese, Australian, and Russian correspondents—and just about every other nationality as well. The four Russian correspondents in Tokyo did not live at the club, but they often came by; they spoke no English, but I found that they had all had two years of high-school German, as had I. Thereafter we communicated on a primitive level and managed to discover that we all liked to sing. So I taught them "There Is a Tavern in the Town" and they taught me a rollicking tune called "Ukar Kupetts."

There was always something interesting going on in the lounge. As Japanese restaurants were out of bounds, the club was the only place where correspondents could entertain the sources and contacts who are so vital to the profession, and they were often to be seen whispering in corners to little Japanese men with brown fedoras crammed down over their ears; on any night one dining-room table might be host to General Eichelberger and his staff, another to Japan's leading Communist, while a third entertained General Deryvanko, head of the Russian Mission.

Coming back to the club late at night was hazardous, for the large consumption of whisky often turned normally platonic correspondents into leering wolves. One night I came in and found dear Lachie McDonald, a popular New Zealand correspondent for the London *Daily Mail*, lying on the floor in a sleeping bag and apparently dead to the world. It was necessary to step over him to get into the dining room for coffee, but just as I did so he wrapped his arms around my legs and grasped my right ankle with his strong antipodal teeth. When, after urgent pleas, he wouldn't let go, I picked up a heavy purple glass ashtray from a nearby table and tapped him briskly on the head. He yelped and let go, and a few minutes later writhed out of the sleeping bag. "The demm'd girl's cracked me head," he grumbled, and set off for the Army dispensary around the corner. I hadn't, and I thought the story so amusing that I wrote my mother about it. "Margaret, are you sure you're behaving like a lady?" she asked in worried reply. I was able to answer that only a few days before one correspondent had described me as "rather the Madonna type," and that the photographers had held a poll and decided that I was the most ladylike lady correspondent they had ever known. Lachie gave me a miniature carved ivory skull for Christmas.

Many of the men I began meeting after I moved into the club were former war correspondents who had covered the entire Pacific campaign. Most of them seemed to have been accredited to the Navy and they shared the Navy's disdain for General MacArthur; the few others seemed to dislike him on general principle—his ego, his arrogance, and his imperial style were, after all, in direct contradiction to the qualities a newspaperman most admires.

Everywhere correspondents go they write songs of parody, and now late at night I would sit with half a dozen of them in the bar, joining in the songs they taught me.

To the tune of "When Johnny Comes Marching Home":

SOLO: *When General MacArthur at last came back,*
CHORUS (softly): *I have returned,*
SOLO: *He followed the wake of a pig-boat track.*
CHORUS: *I have returned.*
SOLO: *Oh the battleship turrets emitted lead*
And the carrier planes were overhead,
So the General could go ashore, 'tis said,
CHORUS: *Singing I have returned.*
SOLO: *The General enlisted God's aid in prayer,*
CHORUS: *I have returned.*
SOLO: *But God He said He couldn't be there,*
CHORUS: *I have returned.*
SOLO: *But for help God went to the uttermost limits,*
For He sent Halsey, Kinkaid, and Nimitz,
So the General could go ashore to kibitz,
CHORUS (bellowing): *Singing I have returned!*

These were rough-and-ready nice guys who had been through a lot, whose answer to all problems was laughter, liquor, and poker. I liked them and enjoyed singing with them, but quickly learned they knew slightly less about Japan than I did. Their direct opposites, I discovered, were the men who had lived in Japan before the war, who had many Japanese friends, who could speak the language, and who knew all the customs, men who, with a few exceptions, were utterly scornful of newcomers like me. Gwen Dew, the only other woman at the Press Club at first, had also worked in Japan before the war and had been interned; we went our separate ways and it was only in later years that I came to know that brave woman.

The third group was the one into which I drifted and from whom I learned, a group composed of men who had not been war correspondents but who had been sent out fairly recently to study Japan and what was happening under the Occupation. I suppose I was drawn to them because, like me, most of them had grown up in the 1930s under the influence of debunkers like Charles Beard, Lincoln Steffens, and William Woodward, and unlike many other correspondents they cared very deeply about what was happening in Japan.

Mark Gayn, a stocky, passionately political man, who later wrote a good book about the Occupation called *Japan Diary,* taught me several techniques. One lesson I learned from him was the importance of getting out into the countryside in order to find out what was really going on; Mark traveled to more remote places than anyone else and therefore seemed to know more than anyone else. Joe Fromm, of *U.S. News and World Report,* a wiry little terrier of a reporter, set me an example of painstaking digging for facts, and of ferocious checking and rechecking. Gordon Walker, of *The Christian Science Monitor,* was a model of flaming idealism, and Carl Mydans, then of *Time* magazine, was a constant reminder of the need for objectivity, balance, and humor. But it was Bill Costello, of CBS, who was my real "guru." Bill, a balding man with a game leg and a gentle soul, very much missed his wife and two daughters and wanted feminine companionship which would make only professional demands; for my part I needed a buffer against the Press Club wolves, a father figure, and a teacher. For whatever reasons, we became deep and fond friends; it was probably assumed at the club that we were having an affair (which we weren't), for a rumor reached his wife, and when she eventually arrived I was cut dead for several months. Wives tend not to like single working women, and perhaps with good reason—but not in this case.

Bill taught me the important difference between working in a city room and working overseas. At home a general reporter does a quick study of one particular story when it develops, but over-seas you must try to make yourself as well informed as you can on many broad topics—education, politics, religion, militarism—and then when something happens in any of your areas, you can write about it with considerable knowledge; the more aspects of a country you study, the more diligent and unceasing your re-search, the better your stories. I, of course, was fortunate because my highly capable colleague Ralph Chapman was covering all the difficult areas like economics and political developments and I could waltz around anywhere I wanted to outside those topics.

I took Bill's lesson to heart, but I found it difficult to observe. The bar and the lounge were enormous temptations, particularly during the evening, for they were crowded with my laughing friends, drinking, singing, or playing "Cameroons" (a game I love which is akin to "Poker Dice."). There was a movie almost every night on the third floor where I lived, a Ping-pong table in the hall right outside my room, and a Japanese dance band every Friday and Saturday. Who could study at night?

But during the day I studied and looked, questioned, listened. And what I saw with my own eyes and heard with my own ears seemed to confirm what my friends were telling me: that a large bloc of American officers within the Occupation was cooperating with reactionary Japanese bureaucrats in order to turn Japan into a future bastion against communism and prevent the eventual election of any liberals or leftists. I met many of these officers and in the presence of Japanese guests listened to colonels criticize liberals within the Occupation as "dirty Jew Communists," or tell me they wished they had saturation-bombed Korea when they had the chance, "because the people are so filthy." How could such people possibly bring democracy to Japan?

Of course, they were not all like that. My old New York friend Bud Hauge was in Government Section (which dealt with politics and was responsible for Japan's new constitution) and I found him seriously worried about the reactionary old Japan hands who wanted to preserve the zaibatsu's economic stranglehold on the country and had joined forces with the military antireds in the fight against liberal and democratic ideals. So too was Com-mander Alfred Rodman Hussey, Jr., of Government Section, who later won the Legion of Merit for his work in setting up strong labor unions; Commander Hussey was a favorite of the correspondents, for he was intelligent, humane, and honest. And Dr. Alfred Oppler, also of Government Section, put down his pen one day when I had dropped by in search of news, and said wistfully, "I have just finished the proclamation which will emancipate Japanese women. Do you think they will be any happier than they have been?"

At meetings of the four-power Allied Council, representatives of the British Commonwealth, Russia, and China were supposed to offer suggestions to the Americans. These suggestions were always mild, but week after week I listened to the American representative and chairman, George Atcheson, Jr., reject them with such scorn and rudeness that as a fellow American I was ashamed. I became great friends with the Commonwealth representative, urbane and witty W. MacMahon Ball of Australia, and his economic adviser, Eric Ward, and listened with sympathy to their tales of frustration. Mac, who was regarded by the correspondents as one of the most brilliant men in Tokyo, adhered (in Mark Gayn's words) "to the unpopular belief that slapping the Russians down, with or without provocation, is a dangerous parlor game," and therefore was in open opposition to Atcheson. I wrote scathing stories about all of this, and was bitterly criticized by MacArthur's public-relations people and even by MacArthur, who told my friend Weldon James of *Collier's* that he couldn't understand why "a fine old conservative newspaper like the *Herald Tribune* would send out a correspondent like this red Ruthie Parkin." (Thereafter I was known around the club as "Red Ruthie.") But to my everlasting gratitude the paper supported me editorially right down the line.

A respite from these little tempests came in July, when I was asked by my paper to fly down to the Philippines to cover the Independence ceremonies. Manila had been partially destroyed, but the atmosphere compared to Tokyo was that of sunlight after deep shadow: cream and pink buildings, languorous air, orchids and hibiscus, tangos and sambas, gently indolent people who painted garlands of flowers on lavender jeeps. After the ceremonies were over, Bill Costello and I made three trips into Central Luzon, about a hundred miles north of Manila, to try to find out what was happening in the current Hukbalahap insurrection. We traveled with the Army in amphibious tanks and then, using devious contacts, shifted over to visit the revolutionary

Huks; we talked to dozens of people on both sides, but all we really found out was that the people on both sides were utterly convincing in their arguments and utterly charming. My most vivid memory of these trips is that at one point I asked myself incredulously: What the *hell* am I doing climbing around a lot of snorting black pigs to look for bullet holes on the underside of nipa hut in the middle of a Philippine jungle? I often had this sense of incredulity in Asia, perhaps with good reason.

Back in Japan I went on a long swing around the central and southern islands with Carl Mydans and Weldon James. I fell in love with the Japanese countryside, the green peacefulness, the patient farmers, the beautiful children, and in particular with Kyoto, the ancient capital of one thousand temples which had been saved from experimental atomic bombing only by the intervention of that great scholar Langdon Warner. But everywhere we found that the American military government teams, which were established in each prefecture to see that MacArthur's directives were carried out, were in charge of stupid men who found it easier to cooperate with the old-line Japanese officials than to chance the new. Only among the education officers did I find any realization that the United States of America was trying to carry out a social experiment such as no other nation in history had undertaken. And they were mostly young, powerless, and unhappy. So I returned to Tokyo and wrote a blistering series of four articles, which again created a tempest.

. . .

Many, many years later I came to know Commander Hussey very well indeed, and he told me much about Japan and the Occupation I had not known at the time. I had not realized, for instance, that the actual men who were charged with the conversion of Japan into a democracy were not career military men, but civilians who happened to be in uniform; Rod was a New England lawyer, who had specialized in constitutional law, and before coming to Japan on Naval orders he had been sent to Princeton for a year to learn about Japan from anthropologist Ruth Benedict, study Japanese, and compare various forms of constitutions in order to help draft one which would be viable for the Japanese. MacArthur, he told me, gave experts such as he few directives, and remained far from their work. Rod, who drafted the preamble to the new constitution, felt strongly that the Japanese people deeply wanted a democracy and that the militarist rule of Tojo and the others had been imposed upon them against their will; the fact that the new constitution has worked successfully for many years is proof of this, he later claimed, and proof, also, that by and large the Occupation *was* a success.

In the summer of 1971 I talked to Carl Mydans, who had recently returned from two years in Japan. The group of us who criticized the Occupation so bitterly during those early days, he thought, had been half right. We were correct in anticipating the political swing to the far right which came a few years later, in foreseeing that the zaibatsu would not be dissolved, and particularly in feeling that MacArthur was premature in his reiterated claims that Japan had already been democratized. On the other hand, he said, the constitution *is* working (although a natural process of Japanizing is going on) and Japan *is* a democracy.

So perhaps we critics didn't see the woods for the trees.

. . .

Aside from those correspondents I have mentioned, there were two others who taught me something. One, who was handsome and a Ping-pong champion, persuaded me to bed one night, and I went because I had decided that I should learn "to take sex like a man." Why not? I asked myself. But I found that I couldn't and that for me, without love, the act was meaningless and rather silly.

The other was probably the most charming man I've ever met. Like Ian and most of the others I've loved, he was one of those rare men who actually *like* women and think they are fun to be with even outside bed, who enjoy their minds and humor, and think of them as people. So we began an affair which lasted on and off for thirteen years; I learned from this affair that while I would never love anyone as I had loved Ian it was possible, as I had thought it would never be, to love again. And so I loved and was happy, until he feared that he too was falling seriously in love, which he was not free to do. He therefore retreated for a while, and I was bitter and agonized at the difficulties of being a sentient woman correspondent and thought, "Oh God, I didn't want my life to be like this," and felt that I shared all the loneliness of all the lonely people in the world. But then he came back and we learned how to be together without asking anything more than a few sweet hours.

The hot summer passed and the flaming autumn came. The streets were filled with festivals, with half-naked young men carrying golden shrines on long red lacquer poles, with parading geishas in elaborate black wigs and kimonos in hues of violet and peach, crimson and silver. Stately old men in flowing black robes waved golden fans and danced to the sound of the samisen. The plaintive trills of distant bamboo flutes seemed somehow poignant in the crisp autumnal air.

I had my own jeep by now, blue with red wheels and "New York Herald Tribune" proudly lettered in white across the front, and I made many trips out of Tokyo. To a sprawling mansion south of the city where one of the correspondents and his gracious Japanese mistress maintained a grand Japanese-style house and garden, and where I reveled in Japanese baths. With Bill Costello to the elegant Fujiya Armed Forces rest hotel at Miyanoshita, where all the rooms were named after flowers and you could see Fujiyama from the top of the mountain above the hotel. And most memorable trip of all, to Aburatsubo on Izu Peninsula south of Tokyo, where Haru Matsukato had a small Japanese summer house overlooking a turquoise bay. Lovely and aristocratic Haru, who later became the wife of Edwin O. Reischauer, American Ambassador to Japan, was interpreter for Gordon Walker, and we three spent a magic weekend at the little house, lying on the tatami in the moonlight and listening to the sea and Beethoven on the wind-up phonograph; at night we slept on mats under great white tents of mosquito netting and the next day naked old Watanabe, the fisherman, brought us lobsters still dripping from the sea.

Other women correspondents appeared and occasionally shared my room. One of these was congenial Lee Martin, of Overseas News Agency; we found we worked well together and spent a week in Kyoto, researching textiles and lacquers and, as a supreme climax, spending an evening with Kajiro Kawai, one of Japan's two greatest potters—a simple, friendly old man in a simple, friendly thousand-year-old farmhouse.

Lee went back to Shanghai, which was her base, and early in November Dixie Tighe arrived. She was at the time a well-known columnist specializing in the light touch; she had covered all battle fronts during the war, knew all the correspondents, and had a prodigious reputation for liquor and sex. She had blond curls and wore heavy make-up and although she was only forty-three, that seemed pretty old to my callous thirty-one. I was rather scared of her, and stayed at a distance, but I was having a drink with her one afternoon when the mail, containing her divorce decree, arrived. She stared at it bitterly for a long time. "My marriage was a marshmallow," she said slowly. "But still, it *was* a marriage." And then with forced gaiety, "C'mon, let's have another drink."

Within two weeks Dixie had fallen in love with one of the middle-aged correspondents, and he with her, mostly out of loneliness I think now. But it looked to all of us very much the real thing for both of them, and since his wife was already en route to Japan aboard a ship due to arrive on Christmas Day, we were all worried. It was a strange Christmas, as Christmases always are in non-Christian countries. On Christmas Eve, in a mood to escape the club conviviality, I went to a midnight mass with Art Mathers, a nice Australian reporter, and later, in my room, decorated my little bonsai tree with costume jewelry. Christmas Day I had dinner with the Costellos and that night I went to a party at the Press Nest.

Dixie's man had left the day before to meet his wife in Osaka, and by the time I arrived at the party, Dixie was already half drunk. She sat crying on the edge of a Ping-pong table, wearing a black satin dress with a silver collar which I suppose was meant to make her look sexy but only made her look like a floozy; her disordered hair hung in wisps over her ravaged face and the mascara ran down her cheeks. We all took turns talking to her and trying to console her. A great many people were deeply fond of Dixie.

"I never liked you much, Margaret," she said to me. "But I want to tell you this: life is hell. You fall for a guy and then he goes away and you do it over and over. I just can't do it any more! And there's nowhere for you to go, because you can't ever go home—they hate you at home because you've been overseas. Well, I'm finished. I can't take it any more. This is the end of the rope."

The next day Dixie suffered a massive cerebral hemorrhage, and we all began taking turns on the death watch. By the time her correspondent returned to Tokyo with his wife, Dixie was dead.

. . .

Dixie Tighe was one of the single most important influences on my life, as haunting today as she was twenty-six years ago. For one thing, she scared me profoundly, for I could see myself in her ten years hence, if I kept on the way I was going. For another, while like most newspaper people I have had periods of heavy drinking, I have been aware ever since of the frightful danger of alcohol, particularly to a woman (who is usually a messier drunk than a man is), and have tried to be careful. I have also tried, with perhaps less success, to be careful of men. "This job of being a woman in a man's world seems to be a tougher task than I thought it would be," I wrote my mother.

Professionally, I was going stale: I had been in Japan eight months and had done all the stories I could do, short of settling down for several years, learning the language, and becoming a serious student of the country. I was therefore not too unhappy when in January 1947 a letter asking me to move on arrived from Joe Barnes. "We'd like you to come home by way of India, and file from there for a month or two," he wrote. "But you've done well in Japan and there's no reason you should not remain in foreign service."

There were a lot of farewell parties and at one of them a strange Australian soldier claimed to be psychic and recited a spontaneous chant about each person in the room. About me he said: "She has everything to make her the toast of every nation—but she will not be a toast, because of the quietness and secrets in her heart."

Then it was February 27 and I was on the train to the British base at Iwakuni, near Hiroshima, where I could catch an RAF plane to Hong Kong and Calcutta. I always have trouble leaving places, and as I gazed out of the window the sound of the wheels seemed to say "I don't want to go, I don't want to go." I looked with love at the green rice fields, the small gray houses with their thatched roofs, the abrupt little hills tumbling their pine trees up into the blue sky, the red torii standing before ancient shrines. But while I had often said, only partly in jest, "Japan would be such a lovely country if it weren't for the Japanese," I thought with love of my few real Japanese friends. Once more I opened the copy of *Double Lives*, by William Plomer, which Ian had sent me from England, and read again the concluding words:

Civilization has many dialects but speaks one language, and its Japanese voice will always be present to my ear, like the pure and liquid notes of the bamboo flute . . . when I heard it for the first time, speaking of things far more important than war, trade, and empires—of unworldliness, lucidity and love.

❧11❧

From the first moment I hated the swarming of India, the noise, the degradation, the dirt, the suppurating poverty, the religious tensions, the mobs screaming political slogans, and above all the heat which moved inexorably over the months from 90 to 95, to 100 to 115 degrees F. I longed for the cool green beauty of Japan, desperately missed my Tokyo friends, and was convinced that I would never, never be able to make new friends in India, never be able to love again, either people or a country.

At the time I arrived, in early March 1947, India was still British. But on February 20 Prime Minister Clement Attlee of Great Britain had announced that India would be free by June 1948. To arrange for the complete transfer of power, his representative, Lord Louis Mountbatten, would arrive in New Delhi late in March to discuss the transfer with Mahatma Gandhi, Jawaharlal Nehru, and other Indian Congress Party leaders, as well as with Mohammed Ali Jinnah, the Moslem leader who implacably demanded the creation of a separate Moslem nation to be called "Pakistan." My second night in Calcutta I dined with an English couple to whom I had a letter of introduction. Tall, gray-haired Jim Foottit was the representative of a British oil company, had lived in India for twenty years, and was deeply sympathetic to the cause of Indian freedom. He was a civilized human being of great charm and sensitivity and so was his brilliant wife, Rose Marie, who wrote editorials for the leading English-language newspaper *The Statesman*. These were the first of the people I met in India who were to become lifelong, beloved friends.

"Hinduism," Jim said, speaking patiently to my ignorance, "is a religion of tolerance, of acceptance, of universality. Islam, on the other hand, is an exclusive religion which claims that Allah is the only God, and that all who do not believe in him are infidels. These two points of view are irreconcilable, and in almost one thousand years the two religions, the two people, have never really mixed. Hindus and Moslems seldom intermarry, for instance, although they may live side by side amicably. Even their languages are dissimilar. The British occupation only served to keep dormant for two hundred years the fight which had been brewing between the two people ever since the Moslems first came in force to India hundreds of years ago. Now the British are leaving, and the fight *must* inevitably be renewed. From the point of view of economic expediency it is absurd to split India into Hindustan and Pakistan. But people do not act from economic expediency, they act from emotional necessity."

The evening drifted off into a discussion of Hinduism and Marxism. "Seek ye first the kingdom of God and his Righteousness and all these things shall be added unto you," Jim quoted. "That could be from a Hindu prayer book or a Gandhi text instead of from the Bible," he said. "It's what Hinduism believes, and it's why India cannot go Marxist. That and the belief that means, not ends, are important. In India—perhaps everywhere, really—a man must search for the kingdom of God before he can seek to revise the economic system of his own kingdom."

"But how can a hungry man search for the kingdom of God?" I asked.

That was my first Indian paradox, and it took me several years to understand the answer.

. . .

From Calcutta I flew to New Delhi and installed myself at the westernized Hotel Imperial, where most of the other correspondents lived. Then began weeks of covering the arrival of Mountbatten and the subsequent freedom negotiations.

As usual, my colleagues were friendly and helpful. Bob Neville, of *Time*, George Jones of *The New York Times*, and soon thereafter Bob Trumbull, who replaced George; Percy Wood of the *Chicago Tribune*, Eric Britter of *The Times*, London, all lived at the hotel and we saw a great deal of each other. Percy, a big easygoing ex-police reporter with the prejudices of a mule and the sentimentality of Daisy Ashford, became a particular friend, and not only because he nicknamed me "Pretty Legs." Once, in shirt sleeves and with hair disheveled, he burst into a formal British dinner party I was attending with the shout "Hey, Pretty Legs! Somebody just tried to shoot Jinnah! C'm *on!*" Eric Britter, who was born and raised in India and who spoke Urdu fluently, was Percy's best friend and I, too, soon learned to respect Eric's vast knowledge and profit from it; after he took me dancing several times at the hotel's Tavern, I began to feel something else and to regret that he would soon go off for summer leave in England.

But the man who became really central to my life, and whose memory I shall always cherish, was Abdul Aziz Khan, my bearer.

Four days after I had settled into the Imperial, George Jones's wife, Toni, came into my room and found me close to tears, surrounded by a pile of dirty laundry.

"For two days I've asked the desk clerks how I get things washed around here," I wailed. "They keep saying 'Just now,' but nothing ever happens!"

"You should have a bearer to take your clothes to the *dhobi,*" Toni said.

"The room boy broke a bowl I brought from Hong Kong when he cleaned the room this morning—or pretended to clean it. Then a little man kept squatting on his haunches outside the door, muttering something. . . ."

"That was the sweeper," Toni said. "He wanted to mop your bathroom floor with that rag he swooshes around. You should have a bearer to clean your room properly, and supervise the sweeper."

"I have to take a note over to the American Embassy this afternoon," I complained, "but the thermometer's already over ninety. Would you mind very much if I asked Fazil to go?"

"Not at all," said Toni, smiling. "But Fazil has a brother who just happens to be looking for a job. He's been waiting outside your door."

Abdul was a wiry, middle-aged Moslem, with black hair streaked with gray, a neat black mustache, and merry black eyes. His pointed red shoes were gleaming with polish, his softly draped pantaloons were a shining white, and his brown zoot-suit jacket was spotless. He also wore a polka-dotted green and white ascot, and a pink and gold brocaded cap, shaped something like a beehive and encircled by a starched white cloth, wound so that it ruffled up in pleats on the left side and hung down the shoulder at the other. His references were equally impressive.

"Well," I said doubtfully, "perhaps just for a few days . . ."

Abdul beamed. He scooped up the dirty clothes from the floor, and disappeared with them.

"Finish tonight," he said when he returned. During the next two hours he mailed my letters, filed a cable, delivered the note to the embassy, dusted the room, rearranged the furniture, called in the floor boy and the sweeper, and in peremptory Hindustani made it quite plain to them (I gathered from his manner) that he was in charge now.

Instead of a few days, Abdul stayed a year. He took all the burden of living in an alien land from my shoulders; he tiptoed about the room solemnly when I was sick, saying that he "hurted" too; like a queen's jester he made respectful little jokes to amuse me when he saw that I was sad; he always knew, apparently by telepathy, the exact time I wanted a bath drawn or a drink mixed. He brought me morning tea in bed, sewed on buttons, and mended rips—and he never, never appeared at the wrong moment. For all this I paid him $25 a month, which my friends told me was much too much.

A few years before, Abdul said, he had had Hindu friends, but now he did not have them any more. All the Moslem bearers were puzzled about how the division between Hindus and Moslems had come about, he told me, but they spoke vaguely of Mohammed Ali Jinnah, the Moslem League, and Pakistan, and they all were afraid that "the troubles would get much worser."

"Is all very different religions in India, please madam," he explained. "But I think maybe life all same for poor Moslem, for poor Hindu. For poor people, always trouble. I poor man, too, but I no poor man in heart, by God!" Indeed, Abdul had as rich a heart as anyone I have ever known.

During lulls in the freedom negotiations I traveled "out of station" as the British used to say. To escape the Delhi furnace and the dizziness and prickly heat from which I suffered, I went to Simla in the foothills of the Himalayas, where I was invited to stay at the Viceregal Lodge with Mountbatten's press representative, Alan Campbell-Johnson and his wife, Fay—another English couple who became lifelong friends. Those were three days of paradise, with the air cool and fresh, silver monkeys leaping among the pine branches, English flowers growing in the gardens near the tennis court, and in the sprawling white mansion with its scarlet-clad servants an atmosphere of nineteenth-century viceregal splendor.

A week or so later I set off with Andy Roth, a free-lancer, for a trip through the Punjab and the Northwest Frontier Province— Moslem areas which would become part of Pakistan should India be divided. In Lahore we were introduced to the fervors of Moslem nationalism by the beautiful Begum Shah Nawaz and her sparkling daughter Taazi, both of whom were leaders in the drive for independence; listening to them and to the dozens of activists to whom they introduced us I was reminded again and again of what Jim Foottit had told me: "People act from emotional necessity." There was no doubt at all in my mind that whether they were right or wrong, they truly believed that only by separation from Hindu-dominated India could the Moslems achieve economic and cultural progress. After that had been achieved, Taazi and her friends insisted (all talking at once between mouthfuls of chicken curry and rice) India and Pakistan could be reunited in a nation which would give justice to all its peoples. In their enthusiasm and idealism they reminded me of all the other young people I had known in Greenwich Village and on Telegraph Hill, sitting on floors and planning the world we would build; I glanced at the Begum and saw that she, too, was smiling a little sadly.

In Peshawar, up near the Khyber Pass, I discovered the most romantic city I had ever known. For thousands of years conquerors and traders from Greece, Afghanistan, Russia, and China have poured through the passes leading into what was Northern India, and in their march they left their mark upon Peshawar in a mingling of races, costumes, languages, and arts. Here in the bazaars was a Tibetan selling turquoise prayer necklaces, a pointed cap flaring up above his ears; here a pale Afghan, with blue eyes and curly hair; here a Persian scholar reciting fairy tales; here a nomad, with his string of camels bearing raisins, almonds, and fruit. Each narrow street exhibited its wares on the platforms in front of each shop: one street displayed mound upon mound of green and purple grapes from Afghanistan and great piles of yellow Persian melons; around the corner was the street of coppersmiths, with dozens of burnished trays and huge pots glinting in the sun. There was a group of shops selling brilliantly colored birds in tiny bamboo cages, and a slipper market, with thousands of gold and silver and red slippers hung up along the walls. Beyond the busy central square, merchants offered great bags of spices, the scarlet of chili powder alternating with the canary of mustard and saffron. The air was pungent with the smell of spices and fruit, herbs and roasting chickens, horses and men, and an unidentifiable, drowsy perfume, which might have been opium or hashish, or merely the exhalation of enchantment.

The day we were planning to fly back to Delhi, Dera Ismail Khan, a town in the tribal territory some two hundred miles to the south, began rioting. There was no public transportation which could take me there, but the Indian Army (still largely commanded by British officers) gave me a staff car, a driver, and a young lieutenant who was in charge of a following truckload of sixteen Gurkha soldiers, who were sent along to protect me. The killing had stopped by the time we reached Dera, but half the town was still in flames and snipers still fired occasionally from sandbagged rooftops; the main street, which two days before had been a thriving bazaar of silks and spices, looked as if it had been hit by a blockbuster and an acrid stench made our nostrils flicker. That night a young sublieutenant of Skinner's Horse Regiment gave me his room and insisted that I sleep with his pistol under my pillow, and when I returned to Peshawar the officers of King George's Own Gurkha Rifles welcomed me back with a champagne party. Dera had been depressing, but I enjoyed the Kiplingesque glamour of these last days of the British Empire.

* * *

In Delhi it was politics and June heat again. Mountbatten presented his plan for independence, which included the creation of Pakistan; with deep reluctance the Hindu leaders accepted it, for anything else would have meant civil war. The independence date was moved forward to August 15, which left only two months in which to work all the complicated details necessary to the splitting of one country into two; it was clear to me that I would have to remain in India to cover the transition ceremonies. In the interim I visited many villages near Delhi, and made a month-long swing through Southern India, and blessedly joyous Ceylon. There was really only one story everywhere I went in India, and that was hunger. Leaders of the Indian National Congress, which had led the fight against the British, promised great reforms after independence, but from what I saw of greedy and corrupt Congress politicians in the south, I doubted whether much would change.

The independence ceremonies took place in Karachi and New Delhi with great pomp, and two days later the killings began. In the West Punjab, which had become part of Pakistan, Moslems began killing Hindus and Sikhs; simultaneously Hindus and Sikhs began killing Moslems in the East Punjab.

My memory of those weeks is a montage of dazed horror. I traveled in planes, Army jeeps, and on foot, shuttling back and forth across the border in an effort to keep my reporting objective and to cover this gigantic human tragedy in whatever way I could. I stood at an office window in a flaming town and watched a Sikh throw gasoline and a lighted match into the mouth of a wounded Moslem child. In a refugee camp I talked to a Hindu woman who had seen her baby's brains dashed out against a stone wall and her husband castrated and murdered; she herself had been abducted, raped repeatedly, and had finally escaped to the camp. In an Amritsar railway station I saw a train which had carried 5000 refugees toward safety but which now bore 4900 corpses; I watched while ten Communists lifted the wounded from the train and begged in vain for the Sikh guards to help them bring water to the dying. I visited hospitals on both sides of the boundary and saw infants with their eyes gouged out and old women whose hands had been hacked off. Along the dusty roads we drove by flocks of vultures tearing out the entrails from the bodies which had been thrown in the ditches; eventually the vultures became too sated to fly. Driving with a British photographer in the West Punjab we discovered some men armed with spears crouched behind low scrub growth on both sides of the road; they motioned us on with ferocious scowls and when we rounded a corner of the hillside we encountered a little train of refugees heading unknowingly into the ambush. "We've got to stop them!" I cried. "Do we have to?" he asked wistfully. "It would make some great pictures." But we stopped them, and after a while some Army jeeps came along and escorted them to safety.

Both nations accused the foreign press of distortion, lying, and favoritism toward the other, but I don't think anything we wrote could have adequately reflected that month of nightmare. As for favoritism, in my own case at least, there was none, for if there was a pro-Moslem bias to begin with, I quickly lost it. On both sides of the border there was nothing but a babble of hysterical unreason, the stench of death, and the same sated, faintly sexual smile on the faces of men who had done much killing. Even the intellectuals seemed to have gone completely mad and no one except the foreign correspondents and a few other outsiders saw the killings and migrations for what they were: a mass tragedy in which there was no right, no wrong, but only human suffering.

Early in September the riots spread to New Delhi, and from the hotel rooftop we correspondents watched houses burning in the bazaars. A curfew was imposed for everyone except the police, armed forces, and the press and the men all piled into a car to go find out what was happening. They refused to take me on the grounds that they might be killed while protecting me from the mobs, so I put on my old Army uniform from Japan and started walking toward the burning bazaars. I passed a couple of corpses on the hotel lawn and watched a hysterical policeman fire at a scurrying shopkeeper; when he turned his shaking rifle in my direction I zipped across the street to the residence of American embassy girls and rented a jeep from one of them. After that I covered the riots in solitary comfort.

It became too dangerous for Abdul or any of the other Moslem bearers to stay at the hotel, and with great sadness we drove them to the refugee camp which had been set up on the outskirts of town. There were no latrines, no tents, no blankets, and an inadequate water supply; every afternoon the road was jammed with cars carrying tense blond Englishwomen bringing food, hot tea, and blankets to their old servants, as I did to Abdul. One of the gray-haired bearers said to me, "All our life we take care of Sahibs and Mem Sahibs. Never we think that they take care of us!" There were tears in his eyes, and mine.

Rereading my old clippings of this whole period I am amazed at the factual tone I managed to retain. Yet the truth is that by mid-September I was close to breaking down. I couldn't sleep or else I had continual nightmares about the horrors I had seen. Impulsively, I bought a furry little puppy on the street for five cents, took him to my hotel room, fed him, cuddled him, played with him. When keeping him became impossible I gave him to the kindly *dhobi*, but the soft closeness and innocence had been comforting for those few days. One night on the hotel rooftop I cried almost hysterically on the shoulders of an understanding United Press correspondent; he said that all the men had been having nightmares too, but he thought I should ask the paper to bring me home. I drafted two letters to Joe Barnes telling him I couldn't take any more of it, but I never sent them.

The rains came and flooded the country; every day we counted the corpses floating down the swollen Jumna River. But the rains helped to stop the rioting, as did the arrival in Delhi of Mahatma Gandhi. It did not really stop, however, until troops were brought in from Madras in the deep south—little black men who seemed to be completely impartial in reinstating peace and order. Naturally, they were hated by both sides.

Abdul came back, and Eric Britter, the London *Times* correspondent, returned to India from his long summer leave in England. I was glad to see him, for he is a man of great charm and integrity and I had thought of him often during his absence. Also, I have always been attracted to men who are authorities in whatever field I happen to be interested in—so when Eric asked whether I would like to go along on a swing through Northern Pakistan I said yes. After all, it had been a month since I had been there and I was supposed to cover both sides.

In Lahore we went dancing.

In Rawalpindi we held hands.

In Peshawar we decided we were in love.

In Kashmir, where we guiltily planned to take an illicit vacation, we moved into a houseboat floating among the lotus blossoms. We were very happy.

After we had been there a week, tribesmen from Pakistan cut the only road out and invaded Kashmir. We had dutifully planned to leave our paradise that day and return to work on the plains; now, thanks to the tribesmen, we could continue the idyll. Within a few days, however, the tribesmen had advanced so quickly that we could hear machine-gun fire on the outskirts of Srinagar; it seemed probable that the town would be sacked and the inhabitants murdered, as had already happened in other towns. When the RAF arranged to evacuate British citizens we decided to go with them, and were already at the airport when the Indian Air Force planes filled with soldiers and machine guns arrived. So we stayed to cover the story, chortling with pleasure that aside from Alan Moorhead (who wasn't competition) and

Bill Sydney-Smith (who was, but who soon managed to get himself captured by the tribesmen) we were the only foreign correspondents in Kashmir and that none of the scores of others who were howling in Delhi could get in because of lack of space on the planes; kindly Indian pilots filed our stories for us when they got back to Delhi, and for about a week Eric and I had the kind of exclusive all correspondents dream of.

. . .

Gradually the Punjab killings subsided, although everyone feared that the undeclared war in Kashmir would soon spread to an all-out war; both countries turned to the desperate problems of resettling millions of refugees. December drifted by, then January 1948. On January 30 came the assassination of Mahatma Gandhi by a Hindu fanatic, an event I wrote about with shaking hands, knowing that it would be the greatest story I would ever cover. As it was.

My "six months in Japan" had stretched to almost two years in Asia. For a year my mother had been writing me letters full of her agonized loneliness and pleading with me to come home. My clothes were in shreds and my Indian-made shoes all squeaked. So when in mid-February Joe Barnes wrote for me to return for home leave and reassignment, I was relieved. Yet two things tormented me. One was the feeling of my own failure to find "the soul of India," not only among the brilliant, arrogant Brahmins, but with far simpler people in obscure villages; maddeningly, I felt, the fact that I had not found it was my fault, not theirs. I tried to comfort myself with the fact that intelligent men I had met in India, like Kingsley Martin of the *New Statesman and Nation,* Edgar Snow, and Vincent Sheean regarded me with apparent respect and friendly affection—but it was not much comfort.

The other concern was Eric, for he had asked me to marry him. I loved him, but I could not decide, for despite the harmony between us there were also difficulties. He was rigid and orderly, I tended to be slapdash and easygoing; he set great store by outward conformity to convention, I believed that "the letter killeth, but the spirit giveth life." He had been married once before, and was basically afraid of another failure; I hadn't, but I had begun to doubt that I possessed the qualities of a good wife. Above all, marrying Eric would mean accepting the probability of another ten years in India. When Eric suggested that I go home to America and decide from there, I agreed to do so. I had not forgotten Dixie Tighe.

. . .

I flew to Paris for a few days, and then took the boat train to England. I saw Ian for the first time since we had parted more than two years before; he showed me the places in London he loved, and our eyes talked. Then I met his wife and children, understood instantly why he so loved them, and bade my eyes be silent. I went off by myself on a long bus-hopping trip through Shropshire and the Cotswolds, and found some solace among fields of daffodils and in discovering the England I have loved ever since.

My last night aboard the *Queen Mary* I tried to sum up in my journal my two years in Asia. "I really don't know what I have learned," I concluded, "but I find myself much more of a *conscious* Quaker than before I saw Asia. And I have come to believe in the genius of Christianity; more than anything, I have felt the lack of human tenderness in the East. I have also become more aware than I ever was of the true goodness that is in America, the warmth, the concern, the kindliness that peoples of many other countries do not seem to think of as values."

. . .

One summer day, when I had been back a week on temporary assignment in the city room, the managing editor called me into his office.

"We'd like to send you to China," he said. "How do you like that idea?" (This was more than a year before the Communists took over.)

"I think it's a wonderful idea," I answered. "But I want to go back to India and get married."

He smiled and said, "Well, in that case, fine." I could go to India instead of China.

Today, when I yearn to go to China, I often think of those moments in George Cornish's office. What if I *had* gone to China? Would I have met someone else to marry? Would my fate have been very different? But then I would have missed so much joy, and would never have known the person whose life gives infinite blessing and grace to my own. But of course I would not have known what I had missed, just as I do not know now the what-might-have-been in China.

I spent the summer working in the city room, buying a trousseau, and enjoying the dear pleasures of Sneden's and the comfortable companionship of my mother, who was so happy that I was finally going to be married that she didn't even complain much about my going back to India. Mother had been married in a blue-serge walking suit, and she was relieved by the fact that I thought I was too old for white satin and lace and chose instead an ivory silk suit with gold buttons.

Late in September I sailed for India on a British freighter, a three-week trip which was nothing at all like the one on the *West Notus,* as the officers wouldn't speak to the passengers and the only other passengers were three elderly missionaries returning to Indian outposts. ("If you come to visit us in South India you'll have to pack a pistol," said white-haired old Pappa Puffer. "Mamma Puffer always carries one in her belt whenever she moves around the bungalow—to shoot the snakes, of course." Somehow I never did go visit the Puffers.)

. . .

On October 30, 1948, I was married to Eric in the old Church of England edifice near the Kashmir Gate, which was known as "Skinner's Church." The entire membership of the Foreign Correspondents Association of New Delhi was there, as well as some of our Indian friends. We went to Kashmir for our honeymoon, and then returned to live in the Cecil Hotel in Old Delhi.

The Cecil, which was owned and managed by a Swiss family and catered to foreign diplomats, was one of the loveliest hotels in the world. We had a living room with a fireplace, a dressing room for me, a bathroom with a refrigerator, and a bedroom large enough to accommodate a huge double desk and our files. Outside were courtyards, fountains, arcaded walls dripping with pink or purple bougainvillaea, gardens which glowed from October through March with roses and pansies, marigolds and asters, a swimming pool, tennis courts. At the front of the hotel was a long veranda, where we drank coffee and brandy after dinner. We ate in the hotel dining room, and servants, of course, took care of our apartment and our clothes, so I had no housekeeping to do. My dear Abdul had gone back to Pakistan to live, and our bearer was Bhag Singh, who had been with Eric for several years. Bhag Singh was a tall young Hindu from the foothills of the Himalayas, with very little command of English; I liked him, but had far less communication with him than I had had with Abdul, since my knowledge of Urdu was rudimentary and Eric was so fluent that I lazily let him do all the translating.

An active social life was basic to Eric's job, although not to mine, and we entertained or went out to cocktails and dinner parties almost every night. I generally disliked these events, and I resented the convention which forced me to sit on the sidelines with taciturn Indian ladies while the men all stood in the center of the room discussing serious matters. Even more I hated the British dinner parties, where there was nothing but chitchat until after the savory, when the ladies were banished to the dining room for coffee and more chitchat and the men settled down to port and good conversation. I learned to grab the living-room chair nearest to the dining-room door, in which case I could sometimes eavesdrop on the men.

Far better, from my point of view, were frequent trips away from Delhi. Eric and I went to Hyderabad to cover the aftermath of the Indian government's takeover of the Nizam's princely kingdom. Then I drove to Benares with Bob Lubar, the *Time* correspondent, and his wife, Pat, formerly of *Newsweek*—both of whom became close friends. In April 1949, Eric and I made a long swing through Pakistan, drove through the Khyber Pass, and spent a few days at Kabul in Afghanistan. A week later we were riding horseback in Kashmir's Hunza on a four-day trek along the edge of outrageous cliffs, to visit the remote little kingdom which only a few other white foreigners had ever seen.

In the summer of 1949 Eric was due for home leave. I wasn't, but I took a leave of absence and we set off on a grand tour, knowing that as we intended to have children it might be the last chance for a long time. We went first to Japan, because I wanted Eric to see some of the places and people I loved and I also had a secret hope that if Eric could transfer from exacerbating India to calmer Japan his quick temper might improve. After Japan there were a few magic days in Hawaii, and then California. It seemed strange to be walking the San Francisco hills again, with their insistently vivid memories of Ian, but I firmly tried to suppress them and build new ones. Colonel Wood had died in 1944 but Sara was still at Los Gatos, so I was able to take Eric to one of the places and persons closest to my heart; we had a few days of sunlight on the hillside and communion under the stars in the fragrant courtyard.

Then it was Sneden's and my excited mother, and for the first time a man in my girlhood bedroom under the little dormers. After several weeks at home we flew to London and spent a month in a housekeeping flat near Sloane Square. I met a lot of Eric's English relatives and enjoyed them. We dined with Ian, and to my relief the two men seemed to like each other. In Paris we did a lot of sight-seeing and quarreling over trivialities. Rome was better, possibly because we spent most of our time with amiable George Jones, who had been transferred there from India, and his sprightly wife, Toni. In Florence it rained all the time and we quarreled again; perhaps we were both tired. In any case, after two more stops in Istanbul and Damascus, we were both happy to return to India in the early fall and to settle down in the Cecil with Bhag Singh and our joyous dachshund, Jimmy.

Despite the quarrels, those first two years of our marriage were happy ones. True, I had come to understand the loneliness which probably exists in most marriages, and had long since recognized that it was impossible to share with my husband the kind of spontaneous communication I had had with Ian; it seemed necessary to plan carefully what I intended to say in order not to irritate Eric. Still, there was love between us, and a perfectly satisfactory sex life. Because of his vast knowledge my understanding of India had deepened and become far more sympathetic than it had been; he himself wrote high-level political "think pieces," but at his urging I began writing emotional and colorful background features, which evidently pleased the *Tribune* because they were always prominently placed on the editorial page. I, too, was now considered an "expert," and we were sought out by visitors to India and even by scholars who were far more informed than we were.

As I, in turn, learned more and more from these specialists, I came to believe that the true role of serious journalism was to function as a bridge between the detailed knowledge possessed by the representatives of the academic disciplines and the intelligent but uninformed public. I remember in particular how much I learned from Gittel Steed, the American anthropologist who had lived for almost a year in an Indian village, giving Rorschach and other tests to the villagers; there was just as much neurosis and psychosis in the supposedly contented villages, she said, as in any urban community. Dr. Gardner Murphy, an expert on racial and religious tensions, taught me to look upon communalism with a more objective eye, and darling Dr. W. Norman Brown, the University of Pennsylvania Sanskrit scholar, gave me a deeper feeling for the underlying meaning of Hinduism than I had ever had before. With David E. Lilienthal I watched the great Bakhra Dam being built by hand labor rather than machines, and I was interested to discover that he found this rather a good idea. There were many others from whom I learned—American, English, and Indian—and what I wrote was strengthened and informed by everything they taught me.

. . .

In March 1950 I discovered that I was pregnant. We had wanted a child for many months, so there was great rejoicing. I felt the race-urge strong within me, for I had always believed that no woman's life was complete until she had had a child, helped it, loved it, raised it; I felt that if my child could bring my father's qualities of gentleness, tolerance, and humanity to the *beingness* of another human, then my father's life would continue, my mother's, Eric's, and mine, part of the endless flow of life. What was a career, I thought, compared to that kind of creation?

I was supremely happy and superbly healthy. Until September I kept on working and we traveled as usual: to Pakistan to interview the ebullient Prime Minister, Liaquat Ali Khan; to Srinagar in Kashmir, where one can always write a story about how lovely it is in May; to a remote area of Northern Bihar, near the Nepalese border, where Eric's pretty sister, Marjorie, and her husband, James Broucke, still lived on one of the last British-owned sugar plantations; to Burma, to study politics and people, ruby mines and the current state of the Burma road. (Under "visible distinguishing marks" on the Burmese entrance form I wrote, "Pregnant." I still remember the young Burmese policeman who, when he read this, showed a lovely mixture of shock, amusement, and suspicion that he was being ribbed.)

But happy as we were, it is not only today's parents who worry about the future of the children they are bringing into the world. For us the cold war had begun and there was much talk of war and of atomic annihilation; on June 25 came the somber news of

North Korea's invasion of South Korea. I trembled for my unborn child, but finally decided that if he only lived long enough to smell pine needles and to dig his toes into wet sand, his life would have been worth the living.

On August 12 came the terrible news that our dearest friend, Unni Nayer, a newspaperman who was serving as a public-relations officer with the Indian Army units in Korea, had been killed in a mine explosion in Korea, along with Ian Morrison, a fine and sensitive London *Times* correspondent, who was also our friend, and Christopher Buckley of the London *Telegraph*. I thought of Ian's blue, blue eyes, in which I had once almost felt I was drowning, and of how he had told me of the Chinese woman he loved and wanted to marry. I thought of Unni's serious voice: "Meg, if you would just sit for a long time in the greenness of the Malabar jungle you would understand India." And of Unni's teasing voice: "Oh Meg, I like you because you wear such low-cut dresses!" Most Indians are hard to love, but the ones I love I love very dearly—and Unni most of all.

On September 1, with the baby due at the end of October, I went on six months' maternity leave. Then I concentrated on matters like the importing of layettes from the States and all the other details which I had learned from Pat Lubar, whose son John had been born a few months earlier in Bombay. Once these chores were accomplished I was free to sit in the sun, cherishing the warmth of the child within me and feeling the earth turn and my own place in its turning. My mother wrote me scolding letters, saying that she feared I was growing too maternal and I mustn't forget the importance of Job, Job, Job and Work, Work, Work, but I knew that she was wrong and that these dreaming hours, this time of coming to understand in a deep, nonintellectual, and totally biological way my own part in the flow of time and life, generation and death, nature and the eternal spirit, was of fundamental importance to me and to the child. I felt at one with the birds above me, the sweating old white cows in the street, the shy women in the sweepers' quarters, the grass and the trees; with all that was born, lived and died; in some obscure way death was vanquished in this new recognition that I, too, was part of the oneness of the eternal *whole*.

November 5, 1950, on a late Sunday afternoon, Lemuel Parton Blakeney Britter was born in Hindu Rao Hospital, a former Nawab's palace atop the ridge in Old Delhi. As I came out of the anesthetic I heard a baby crying and I asked foggily, "What is that sweet voice I hear?"

"It's your son," cried the Matron. "It's your *son!*"

Then I knew that miracles really did happen. Nobody else ever made a baby before that one, or ever has since.

❧12❧

I had Spock and Gesell and other baby books from America to guide me, our adoring ayah, Parvati, to take care of the baby when I grew tired, and the ecstasy of nursing Lem for the first few months. There were many times I nursed him in the dawn hours, with the hotel silent and only a far-off rooster crowing, when I felt we two were the only reality that existed, or ever would.

But then came March 1, 1951, and I went back to work. The first time I left him I went to Bombay for a week to cover the Indian Congress for Cultural Freedom; I stayed with the Lubars and spent a lot of time talking to delightful people like Stephen Spender and W. H. Auden, but I found that all I really cared about was getting back to Lem. Before I had a baby I had assumed that as I was a professional newspaperwoman, nurses would have to raise the child, which would be something of a pity, but necessary. In Bombay on this first absence I began to feel differently. My maternal hunger for the baby was primitive and rather agonizing; I felt frightened, for I didn't want to be a possessive mother. Intellectually, I believed that it was good for me to continue to work and to go away on trips, but my heart told me that there was something wrong about this concept and I wondered whether nature was not wrenched by a separation at a time when mothers and their babies are usually so closely united.

Just the same, Lem was a happy baby. At five weeks I saw his first smile, and to me it matched the sunrise. After that there were many smiles, gurgles, and giggles, and he developed a deep belly laugh that made people jump the first time they heard it. I began

to feel that he had come into the world with his own Scorpio
character, strong, decisive, joyous, and that while we could chan-
nel it we would be powerless to change it even if we wanted to.
"He will be very bright and shining," said his Indian horoscope.

When he was seven months old we flew with him to London,
where my eager mother met us and first beheld her grandson. We
left Lem for a week at an efficiently run children's nursery, while
we toured Southwest England, but back in London I found that
despite the good care of the rosy-cheeked young nurses, Lem was
not only pale but somehow lackluster and apathetic. A wonderful
summer in Sneden's and my steady companionship quickly re-
stored him to his normal bounce, but back in India in the fall the
problems resulting from my necessary absences began again.

One night in October 1951 most of the correspondents were
having drinks at Bob and Jean Trumbull's when a voice broke
into the radio music to announce that Prime Minister Liaquat Ali
Khan of Pakistan had been assassinated; in accordance with the
swift Moslem tradition of hot climates, his funeral and interment
would be held the next day at noon in Karachi.

Eric's paper had a Karachi correspondent, but most of the rest
of us were responsible for the coverage of Pakistan as well as of
India. We absolutely had to be in Karachi the next morning, and
thanks to miracles accomplished by an American Express man at
the party, by 5 a.m. we were all at the airport and in possession
of the proper official stamps and papers. I had had twenty minutes' sleep that night, because the baby had wakened, cried, and
had taken a long time to lull to rest.

By 9 a.m. we had checked into a Karachi hotel. The temperature was around 90 degrees, the streets were boiling with hysterical masses; the place of interment was about three miles off and
there was no means of getting there except to fight on foot
through the crowds. I became separated from the others and for
two hours battled my way between packed and shouting bodies,
praying that I was going in the right direction, but I finally
reached the funeral mosque, the only correspondent to make it
except for a *Life* magazine photographer. After that it took me almost an hour, while prayers sounded over an amplifier, to claw
my way among the wailing bodies which packed the big courtyard around the open grave; Liaquat's body was just being low-
ered into it, and his sixteen-year-old son was standing beside the

grave, calmly taking pictures of the event with a new movie camera.

After a hot walk back to the hotel, there were officials to see for information on the assassin, a religious fanatic who had been torn to pieces by the mob, and assessments of the probable political consequences. Then the story had to be written, passed by the censor, and filed in a telegraph office filled with pushing correspondents, each one shouting that *his* story must have priority. None of us had eaten for almost twenty-four hours and except for the twenty minutes and a short doze on the airplane I hadn't slept for more than twenty-seven hours, so perhaps our nerves were shot.

Back in Delhi two days later I found Eric, who had adapted most wonderfully to fatherhood, placidly mashing a banana for Lem. While I was gone, he told me proudly, he had broken the baby from the bottle to the cup. There would be no more nonsense about sterilizing bottles and all that mess! It was very simple, he said—he had just refused to give Lem a bottle no matter how much he howled, and had positively insisted on the use of the cup. I was worried, for that was not the method prescribed by Spock, and I thought that Lem looked a little frightened. I didn't say much about it, but thereafter I began to find more stories around Delhi and to make excuses for not going out of town. Articles for *Look, The Reporter,* and the *Ladies' Home Journal* also gave me a good excuse for staying close to home. But Eric soon caught on to this trickery and began to scold. "I thought I married a devil-may-care, hell-for-leather career girl," he fumed. "I didn't know you were going to become just a *woman!*" The last word, as he said it, sounded indecent.

This seemed a strange reversal of attitude to me, since the basis of most of his criticisms of me were my failures in the domestic line. I had tried not to make the fatal error of neglecting Eric in favor of Lem, but my failures in other ways were many and evidently heinous. I spent the days rushing in panic from one duty to another yet always there was bitter reproof because I had forgotten to answer the Japanese invitation or tell the hotel one of our chairs wanted repairing. "You never try to please me," he said often, but it seemed to me that life had become a constant succession of grim efforts to try harder to please him, and a constant succession of failures. One New Year's Eve I changed evening dress six times and he was still not satisfied that I was fit to appear in public; I went back to my dressing room, changed into a skirt and sweater, slipped away through the sweeper's door, and spent most of the night walking in a Moslem graveyard, with hyenas howling around me, trying to think about the story on which I was currently working and not to think about my marriage.

During the previous summer Eric and I had agreed that life might go more smoothly for us if we were transferred to another country. Eric knew India so well that it was no longer a challenge to him and he barely needed to lift a phone to gather material for one of his "think pieces." Then, too, India was fine for a baby, but it was a bad place in which to raise a child of Western parentage. As I had hoped he would, Eric had liked Japan during our brief visit there two years before and so, when the *Times'* Japan post fell vacant in the fall he applied for it. Early in January 1952 we received the news that his request had been granted.

That day I felt both sorry and glad. Driving home from New Delhi I noted many of the things which made me love India: a swami in his orange robes feeding a flock of fluttering birds, peasant women in gaudy silver jewelry and red head-scarves, homecoming cows kicking up sun-crimsoned clouds of dust at the time the Indians call "the cow-dust hour," the quarters of the untouchables boiling and pulsing with a kind of primitive, eternal life which Japan, with her silence and orderliness, had never known. And yet I loved the green beauty of Japan, and truly prayed that a happier and more serene life awaited us there.

The *Herald Tribune* agreed to transfer me to Japan with Eric, although Mac Johnson was already there for them, and the months of packing and farewell parties began. We sailed from Calcutta on April 5, on a British ship which stopped briefly at Singapore and Hong Kong, and arrived in Yokohama near the end of the month. Lem, who had long since learned to walk, explored the decks ceaselessly every day, wearing a little blue harness with a strap that had to be held by one of his weary parents. "God knows how two old crocks like us are ever going to raise a boy who is obviously destined to be an acrobat," I wrote my mother. And: "What a curiously emotional little person Lem is! Rocking with passionate sorrow one moment, glowing with joy the next. 'Like his mother,' comments Eric gloomily."

. . .

In Tokyo, where we arrived on April 25, we found that thanks to a good friend we already had the services of a nurse for Lem: a middle-aged lady named Sumi-san, all gold-glinting smiles and bobs and curtsies. But no one had been able to find us a house, so we settled temporarily into Frank Lloyd Wright's famous Imperial Hotel, a dim place with rough concrete walls and rocky excrescences, which I hated because they tore at Lem's skin when he tumbled against them, and because they made me feel as if I were living inside the abdomen of a diseased toad. I shed no tears when it was finally torn down.

A few days after our arrival I was sitting in the dear old Press Club, picking the brains of Keyes Beech, the knowledgeable and gallant correspondent of the *Chicago Daily News* who had worked for months with Maggie Higgins in Korea and helped to protect her from her own foolhardiness under fire, when another correspondent dashed in from the alley and shouted, "Hey! They're rioting outside the Imperial Palace!" "Come on!" yelled Keyes, and followed by a pack of other correspondents we dashed out of the club and sprinted two or three blocks to the Palace grounds, which we found to be a bedlam of tear-gas bombs fired by the police, showers of rocks thrown by some 7000 rioters, who, led by 100 indoctrinated North Korean Communists, had disrupted a peaceful May Day parade by a sudden attack on the police lines.

For two hours Keyes and I ran like mad whenever the rioters broke through the police lines, and several times he pushed me to the ground just in time to escape a hurtling rock. Near the end, we crouched behind a pine tree and watched a gang of young Communists overturn a big black Chrysler, stave in the gas tank with a crowbar, and set the car on fire. Even from twenty feet away we could feel the heat of the flames. As I watched, I heard Keyes make a slight noise of incredulity and I saw that he was looking at me with an expression of wondering disbelief. It had just come to him that I, too, worked for Maggie Higgins' paper. "My God!" he exclaimed. "Another girl from the *Herald Tribune*! How many more of you are there?" I could see that kindly Keyes envisaged an endless future of protecting *Herald Tribune* girls, and even with the bullets and rocks flying above our heads, I began to laugh.

Keyes was one of the more amiable of the new correspondents who had replaced my old friends in Japan. The new men were in their twenties and basically war correspondents, on their way to and from Korea; with the exception of a few, like Keyes and Robert Elegant, they had little interest in the sociology and politics of Japan. And less in me, about whom they knew nothing except that I worked for "Maggie Higgins' paper." I discovered what this meant when Mac Johnson asked me in June to go over to Koje Island in Korea, where North Korean prisoners were incarcerated and rioting.

I was quartered with the Red Cross girls, but the men all lived and worked in an enormous press tent next door and traveled to the prison compounds, three miles away, in a three-quarter-ton Army truck. I arrived with two male correspondents, who were immediately welcomed by their fellow correspondents and offered the courtesy of a "fill-in" on current news developments while I hung around, ignored, in the background. After a while a lieutenant in charge of public relations rushed in and said, "They're tossing tear gas over in compound Sixty-two. Anybody for the truck?" When I made a motion to join the men, a little twerp from *Time* said pompously, "Mary, women don't belong in a place like this—or at least not up around the compounds. I guess it's all right if you want to stay here in headquarters, but you just endanger all our lives if you go out in the truck with us." That night I crouched in the dark outside the tent and collected information by listening to the wire-agency men bellowing their stories over the weak phone connection to Tokyo.

The next morning I got up at 6 a.m. and walked three miles to the compounds. By luck I found that an informer had escaped from a compound the night before, and was just returning with camp officials to point out 102 top Communist leaders—a big and unusual story. Two hours later, when the press truck drove up loaded with correspondents, I was in possession of the full story. I could have had a good exclusive if I kept it to myself, but I gave them a complete fill-in. After that they decided I was all right, and I rode in the truck without endangering anyone's life. That's the way it often was, alas.

. . .

In India we had become great friends with Peyton and Margaret Kerr, who now were based in Tokyo. Andy—as we always called him—was a guitar-playing economist in the U.S. foreign service, and Margaret, a pianist, was one of the best hostesses and most generous people I had ever known. When it became evident that in house-hungry Tokyo it would be months before we could find a place to live, they invited us to spend the summer in the Japanese wing of their huge, Western-style house in the suburbs. In June we happily moved into the three rooms with their tatami-mat floors, sliding paper doors, and a view of a perfect Japanese garden.

The Kerrs had five children, ranging down from thirteen to a little boy who was Lem's age; Lem was happy with these playmates, with the swing and the sandbox, and even, most of the time, with Sumi-san. Eric, too, was happy, at least in his work, for he had made the transition very competently. But I was unhappy, for a number of reasons. First of all, because the lovely, graceful Japan I had known seemed to have been supplanted by bars, pinball-machine joints, Muzak from street-corner traffic boxes, dance halls with strip-teasers (in a country which before the Americans came had never thought nudity salacious), neon signs, and cafeterias. I concluded that there was something shoddy about the Japanese which made them want to adopt the more vulgar aspects of American civilization while ignoring the profounder implications of our democracy; not until several years later did I learn from one of Toynbee's books that this inevitably happens when one culture encounters another. I was worried, too, about my own professional life. I had my own car and could use the *Herald Tribune* interpreter and office, but I was distracted from work by the job of finding a house for us to live in, which had somehow become my exclusive responsibility; instead of writing, I seemed to spend most of my days looking at one dreary and expensive dump after another.

At home we had Sumi-san to care for Lem and to cook for us, and a part-time university student to do the housework, but they needed much more supervision than our Indian servants had required, and on one dreaded day each week Sumi-san was off and I had to do the cooking. I had never learned to cook anything except scrambled eggs and a simple meatloaf and I didn't have and couldn't find a cookbook. I don't remember why I didn't turn to Margaret Kerr for help, but I suspect I was too embarrassed to confess my domestic inadequacies; often, on those awful nights,

Eric returned furiously to the Press Club for a decent dinner and I cried myself to sleep. Mid-summer, Lem began waking at 4 a.m. every morning, and bellowed until he was picked up and played with; in order not to disturb the whole Kerr compound I had to take him to the far end of the garden and push him in a swing for three hours until Sumi-san arrived. I think if I had had adequate sleep that summer, the rest of my life might have been very different.

Most of all, I missed the old, tolerant atmosphere of the Press Club as I had known it during my first stay in Japan. Almost all of my friends were gone, or had moved out to houses with their wives, and the new, younger men were a different breed. One pimpled weasel, whose arrogance was only matched by his inadequacies as a correspondent and I suspect as a man, started a movement to bar all women except Japanese prostitutes from the club; it was called AWWAS, which stood for All White Women Are Slobs, and quite a lot of the younger men signed the petition. Eric didn't, but he thought it funny. I didn't think it was funny at all, nor did I like the fact that most of the parties now, Japanese and American, were stag and that night after night I sat alone with Lem on the Kerrs' veranda, cradling my boy's warm and sleeping body, staring at the moon, and trying to figure out what had gone wrong with my marriage.

We had asked my mother to come to live with us when we found a house, and I dreamed of the time when she would arrive and I would feel again an atmosphere of love, understanding, and kindliness, which I had not felt for a very long time. It was my parents who had taught me the values of intelligence and responsibility; it was my Western education—as it had been my mother's—which had led me to believe that a woman not only could be but should be an intellectual as well as a physical companion to a man. She would understand why, in the steamy sexual atmosphere of Tokyo, I now felt that everything I believed and *was*, had been rejected by my colleagues in favor of mindless little Japanese whores who knelt at the feet of their patrons and licked their toes. Eric, I knew, did not share these attitudes, but he taunted me with them and his amusement was salt in my wounds.

If only there had been someone to talk to! But one talks to friends about lovers, I felt, not husbands. In those days I was credulous and sometimes believed the women's magazines, so I pored over the "Making Marriage Work" pages of the *Ladies' Home Journal,* and found no help. I looked for marriage counselors or psychiatrists in Tokyo (as I had in India) and found none. As a last, no doubt foolish, desperate effort to build a deeper security of love into my life, I pleaded to be allowed a second child. I was refused.

It is not fair for one person to describe the breakup of a marriage, for there is always the other side—and I know that my failures were many. So I will only say that on September 1, 1952, I concluded that I must go home to people to whom I belonged, whose virtues were my virtues, and whose love was my love. The choice was for Lem as well as for me: a constantly quarreling family and a father, or no father and peace? I chose peace.

The next day I borrowed the air fare from sympathetic Mac Johnson, and Lem and I flew away from Japan toward America, toward home.

❧13❧

I was Lem's only security, his only continuity in this swift transition from one environment to another, and for weeks he howled every time I left his sight even for a moment. It was impossible to go back to work, but the *Tribune* was understanding and gave me a six weeks' vacation. The Sneden's house was too small for an active two-year-old, and it was full of precious antiques; every day resounded to the crash of another silver luster vase, the splintering of a prized Victorian slipper chair, and the sounds of my mother's anguish. In my innocence, I had thought I could hire a loving and capable old Aunt Jemima to care for the house and child for around $30 a month. I learned painfully and quickly that the only help available were dirty old slatterns, ignorant and uninterested, who demanded $40 a week. We had a succession of them, each one more dreadful than the last. The contrast with the pampered life I had led for seven years overseas was traumatic.

I also quickly discovered the facts of life for the single woman in the suburbs: almost total exclusion from the social life of the community. I have found over the years that only persistent (and expensive) entertaining and volunteer work in community organizations can even partially overcome the suburban prejudice against lone women. Most surprising of all was what I felt to be massive social disapproval of my separation from Eric. I had thought, reading about America in my years in Asia, that divorce had become so widespread that it was no longer as severely condemned as it had been previously—and Eric and I were not yet even contemplating divorce. But I had failed to take into account the pressure of what is now called "the feminine mystique," and the popularization of Freudian psychology: over and over I read in newspapers and magazines the assertion that if a child didn't grow up with a father in the house he would turn out neurotic or homosexual. "*You* can't expect to raise a normal child," a pediatrician told me scornfully. The few friends I saw seemed to reflect this attitude, so that I was torn between the guilt they imposed upon me and my own sure inner knowledge that I had done the right thing for Lem as well as for myself.

But all of these problems were nothing compared to the ones presented by my mother. Her first reaction to what she called "the bombshell" was one of support and understanding, for she had seen the difficulties at first hand. But this was soon followed by deep fear of the future and a conviction (which she did not voice to me, but which I find now on each page of her diary) that I would be unable to support my family or raise my son. Her already melancholy temperament therefore deepened, and, except when she was playing with her adored grandson, the atmosphere of gloom and apprehension she communicated dragged me down into further depths of depression.

The nearby Lockhart Nursery School was one of two elements which helped to save my sanity, for it gave wonderful care to children by the hour, the day, overnight, or even for years. After I went back to work in the city room in October, the school took care of Lem whenever we were between nurses or Mother was sick or I had to be out of town on assignment. He loved it and was very happy there. The second and most profound element of helpfulness was Dr. Janet Rioch. I was so worried about raising Lem by myself that I decided I needed professional advice, and fortunately I found Dr. Rioch, a psychiatrist and an adherent of the William Alanson White School of psychiatry. She was a handsome, middle-aged woman with short gray hair, a direct manner, and was one of the easiest persons to talk with I ever met. She saw Lem and put him through various tests. "He is an extraordinary, wonderful child," she said, "with great inner strength." Then her attention turned to me, and I found myself seeing her twice a week for several months and feeling that she was the only person in the world to whom I could talk honestly.

She eliminated my guilt about leaving Eric. A stronger person, with more assurance and self-confidence, might have survived my marriage, she said, but I would have been destroyed had I remained. "Thank God you still had the emotional strength to get out!" she exclaimed. "All a child needs is *one* good parent," she assured me. Nor should I worry because I had to be away at work all day and only had one hour to play with Lem when I came home at night: "It's the quality of the time a parent spends with a child which matters. Not the quantity." She helped me with my feeling of guilt because I coudn't seem to make my mother happy: "You can't take on her melancholy. That's her problem." And she encouraged me in my determination to move away from my mother's house and establish a home of my own.

In 1936 my father had built a Cape Cod two-story cottage at the far end of the meadow from the old house; white-washed cinder block with a slate roof, a small patio, and a grape arbor. It had been rented to various tenants for years and although it had been put in my name the rental had always gone to my mother; I now proposed that when the present tenants' lease was up the following May Lem and I and a housekeeper move into the house, and I would continue to pay the same rent. We would still be close, I pointed out to my mother. We would see each other every day, and Lem could run safely across the meadow between the two houses.

The explosion was volcanic, and marked the beginning of a battle which lasted more than fifteen years. She would *not* live alone. Why couldn't she live with me? She was sure that I wouldn't pay her the rent as faithfully as her tenants had paid it and she would be starving and penniless in her old age. I was selfish, cold, and unloving. "At seventy-five," I commented in my current journal, "my mother's emotions are like her kidneys— uncontrollable."

Reading her diary now I am appalled at the depth of the hostility to me I find there and the bitterness of her criticism of me in everything except my professional role. But there is much love also, and it was this ambivalence which so confused and disturbed me, and which kept me constantly off balance. It had confused me, too, in my adolescence, and in a way our battles involving my identity as a woman were very similar to the ones we had then; now that I was on my own she wanted me to play the role of a breadwinner like my father, while she would be mother to Lem and housekeeper for both of us.

But why so much hostility? I recently asked Berta Hader, who knew and loved my mother for more than fifty years.

"She was a jealous woman and very moody," Berta said slowly. "I think she had strong moods when she was jealous of you because your father loved you so dearly. And perhaps she was jealous because you were a more successful writer than she had ever been. And, of course, there was competition over the love of little Lem. But don't forget that she also loved you deeply."

I knew that even then, and I knew her loneliness and her need for possession. But I was determined to reject as much of the masculine role as I could: "Lem must grow up a male," I wrote in my journal, "with no twisted senses because of the masculine role which life has imposed upon his mother, and which she hates." And then, in an honest afterthought: "No—life didn't impose it. I chose it." But I wanted to cook and shop and arrange flowers and to play with Lem in my free time instead of working on the books and magazine articles my mother was always urging upon me. And I wanted, if I chose, to take a lover without having to remember that her abnormally keen ears were always alert for just such a dread possibility.

Dr. Rioch had told me that it was all right, even healthy, to cry in front of Lem, and sometimes, worn down by the inconclusive fights with my mother and all the other swarming problems, the tears would fall. "Don't cry, Mommy," Lem said earnestly when he was two and a half. "You *good* boy." He was my great comfort, and my happiest times were when I held him in my arms and lulled him to sleep with the old lullabies. Often I stood by his crib in the dark of midnight, praying that the angels would protect him from all evils, all dangers, even the danger of my own adoration.

On October 20 I went back to work in the city room of the *Herald Tribune.* It seemed strange to be back after so many years away, and I felt like a cub reporter and mourned for Engleking, who had been shifted to the editorial page. But the daily round of local stories was boring now, and I was glad when Irita Van Doren, editor of the daily and *Sunday Book Review,* gave me Han Suyin's *A Many-Splendored Thing* to review. I found the book profoundly moving, partly because I had briefly known the wonderful correspondent she calls Mark, and partly because her re-creation of their love affair reminded me so vividly of mine with the man I have called Ian. I let some of my personal reaction come through in the review: "Those who have encountered love and lost it will understand the necessity which drove Dr. Han's pen, and say 'I know'; those who have missed love will say 'I believe. . . .'"

The review made an impact on the editors and I was asked to take over the daily book-review column for three days a week, alternating with John Hutchens, when Lewis Gannett went on a six-month leave of absence. At the same time my salary was raised from $120 a week to $150 (good for those days), and I was told that I could go overseas again whenever I wanted to. The book-reviewing job began in mid-January of 1953, and I loved it. I went to the office daily but I kept my own hours; I had a thrice-weekly guaranteed by-line; and I loved Irita, her assistant, Belle Rosenbaum, and John, my considerate colleague.

One of the books I reviewed was Simone de Beauvoir's *The Second Sex*, a germinal work in what has now become the Women's Liberation Movement. Rereading my review, I find that I pretty well summed up what I still feel:

It seems to this reviewer that the central problem of woman is the same as that of man: to find serenity and strength within herself, to achieve imaginative understanding of others through which love for the whole of the human race can become possible. To the extent to which women are balked by men in this search for fulfillment, they must fight men. But if they find serenity, strength and the ability to love in their present role as women, then the battle becomes pointless. As the Hindus suggest, there are many paths to God. Mme. de Beauvoir, an important pioneer, suggests one. There are others.

When May 1 arrived and the tenants left, I took joyous possession of "Margaret's House," and in the next three weeks painted all the rooms, sanded the floors, and bought furniture from warehouses and an old piano from a friend moving to Haiti. It was all battered stuff that Lem could bounce on without reproof. May 25 came, and Lem and I moved in. That first night I made Lem's dinner, played the piano with him in my lap, put him to bed with lullabies, and sank onto my couch in front of the fire with a sense of peace I had not felt for many years. Then in the dear silence I began to hear sniffles outside the front door. I went to the door, opened it, and found my mother standing there, sobbing, and clutching a wilted bunch of pansies. "I came to bring you a welcome-home present," she gasped, managing to indicate with a slight gesture of her left hand that she was on the edge of a heart attack.

I was torn between fury and pity. I knew that her anguish was real. I knew that she was old and arthritic, although otherwise healthy, and that she had spent many wearying hours caring for my son. I knew that my desire to live apart from her was, as she charged, selfish. Mea Culpa! But I also knew that Janet Rioch had said to me, "There are times when you have to be a bitch." So I was. "How kind of you," I said in a formal voice. "Do come in and have a cognac. After that I will drive you home." Which is what happened.

. . .

I was fortunate in having a few old friends who didn't seem to mind my unorthodox life style. One of these was Edgar Snow, whom I had come to know and like in India, and who had now settled in Sneden's with his second wife, Lois Wheeler, a beautiful young actress, and their two small children. Ed and Lois were two of the warmest, most loving people I have ever known, and alone with them or at their frequent parties for old-China-hand friends I could feel comfortable and happy, as I never could with people who had not lived overseas. My old "brother" Peter Grey, who had been in Japan during the war, lived nearby and I began seeing a great deal of him, his wife Ty, and their son Chris, who was Lem's age. Ty was a product of the Maine backwoods, blue-eyed, black-haired, and as strong and vital as a Penobscot pine. It was fun to go to their house, for Ty was always painting a picture, building a tree-house, or working with Peter on the charming little swimming pool they designed and built, even when she was pregnant with the little girl who became Katy. Peter, effervescent and compassionate as ever, roughhoused with Lem as well as with his own son, and I was profoundly grateful. When, a few years later, Ty and Peter were divorced I mourned, as one always does when there is separation instead of the unity which the soul craves.

A few men came around, including a couple of old lovers to whom, for some reason I couldn't fathom, I said no. Then Greg, my first, came back and for several months I said yes, mostly because Dr. Rioch had told me that "body contact" would be good for me. But I wanted so much more, and in any case I felt hideously guilty because I knew and liked his wife. So I shut the door. After that there was no one else for a very long time.

In August Lewis Gannett returned from his leave of absence and I went back to the dull city room. But the boredom did not matter, for my central happiness lay in Lem. I had found a wonderful German girl named Susi to care for him, and by the time I arrived home at eight every night she would have fed and bathed him; all my weariness disappeared as I walked into the house and found him bouncing up and down in his little plaid bathrobe, crying, "Up me, Mommy! Up me!" So I would up him on my shoulders and for an hour we would play "horsie," practice sommersaults, read books, or learn new songs on the piano or the guitar. Then it was bedtime.

One night when he was two and a half I began teaching him the little Quaker prayer I had been taught as a child: "Jesus tender shepherd hear me, bless thy little lamb tonight. . . ."

"Whobody lamb?" he asked.

"Why, you are, darling."

"No I *not*," he said indignantly. "I *boy*!" There was never any doubt about that, thank God.

By the time he was three he was showing, to my great delight, clear signs of a sense of humor. "Good morning, Mommy," he said one day, climbing onto my bed. "Did you have sweet dreams?"

"Yes, darling," I told him benevolently. "I dreamed about you. And did you have sweet dreams?"

"No," he answered, twinkling. "I had bad dreams. I dreamed about *you*."

But there were sad times, too. After Lem went to bed I usually took a walk, and it was then that the waves of loneliness swept over me so strongly that wandering by summer meadows silvered with moonlight and mist or under black trees heavy with new snow, I could hardly bear the sound of laughter and voices behind the lighted, shaded windows of the houses I passed. I would think of Eric's mournful letters, and of the loneliness which he, too, was feeling, and go over and over again the old questions, the old pain, the old guilt. . . . If only once he had written "I'm sorry. I love you. Please come back," I think I might have, despite Dr. Rioch's advice. But he only implied the wish, and that wasn't good enough.

The new year of 1954 began, snow fell and melted, and I did

another happy month of book-reviewing. One night in February I was invited to dinner by my friend Lauri Shaffi, the Pakistan Consul General in New York, and Pakistan Ambassador Syed Ahmjad Ali. The city of Cortland, New York, had become affiliated with the city of Peshawar, Pakistan, they told me, and for the last year had entertained a series of visiting Pakistanis. Now Dr. Robert H. Kerr, the surgeon-mayor of Cortland, was going to visit Peshawar with his wife and a few other prominent citizens. The Pakistani government feared that the Cortland junket would not receive much publicity, so they thought it would be pleasant if I accompanied the group, as a State guest at their expense.

My heart leaped up, but I felt I had to tell them that if I went I could not guarantee that my stories would be uniformly cordial. The two men assured me I would be under no obligation and could write as I pleased, and so I said I would go if the paper agreed. The paper did agree, and furthermore decided to pay my way on to India, East Pakistan (now Bangladesh), Hong Kong, Japan, Hawaii, and home. The trip would last two months and I was worried about Lem, but not deeply. He was in nursery school every day now, Susi was a jewel, and Mother would stay with them while I was away. On March 20 I left for London, mostly to see Ian and his wife (even a few hours were still precious), and a few days later I arrived in Pakistan.

Even after two years everything seemed the same: the camels with their strings of blue bead necklaces, the mingled smell of dung and jasmine, the refugees in their miserable barracks, the idealistic dreams of my old friends in government service. And Peshawar, when I reached it, was more wonderful than ever.

Although I had met the Kerrs in Cortland and liked them, I had seen so many American tempers crumple in the face of Asian inefficiency and heard so many inept remarks made publicly and in all innocence that I had worried about their reactions on this official visit. But Bob and Ruth Kerr never put a foot wrong, and unlike so many other Americans they made me proud of being their countrywoman. The Pakistanis, for their part, outdid themselves with parties and parades, trips to the Khyber Pass to dine upon fat-tailed sheep and pilau, trips to see new dam projects and new schools. I had no trouble at all with my conscience when I wrote enthusiastic stories about the visit, and I acquired two more lifetime friends in the Kerrs.

New Delhi, when I reached it, seemed not to have changed at all, except that my lovely Cecil Hotel had been converted into a Jesuit retreat. The problems of overpopulation and mass poverty were the same, the heat was the same, the talk was the same. I had a conversation with India's Foreign Minister and he expressed bewilderment at the extent of America's hysterical anti-communism, which was then at its McCarthy-driven peak. "We ourselves see only two ways in which India could be taken over," he said. "Either from within or from without. Therefore, we keep strong forces on our borders and carefully control our local Communist parties. It is that simple." I had an hour with Prime Minister Nehru, who was, as usual, friendly and vague. I asked him whether he thought world communism was "expansionist," for I had begun to think that this belief could be a key to any country's attitude toward Russia and China. The question irritated him, and he snapped, "All new nations are expansionist! You Americans are expansionist with your dollars. China will probably make efforts to move across her present borders. We Indians would be expansionist in Southeast Asia if we had more money and airplanes." But we parted on good terms, with Nehru solicitously prescribing mango juice for the dizziness which always afflicted me in Delhi's hot season.

After India I rewarded myself with a few days in beautiful Hong Kong, and then came a day and a night with Eric in Japan. I left with a profound sense of relief, convinced as I had never quite been before that the marriage could never work. Yet all the way to Hawaii I felt as if the bottom of my world had dropped out, and my stomach roiled with the bitter recognition that now there was no possibility at all of reconciliation. The one remark about me which has hurt more than all others was made by Percy Wood and relayed to me by Eric during that brief time in Japan: "Meg treated you like a stud horse." God knows, a happy marriage is what I always wanted most in life.

I stayed in Hawaii for ten days, doing background research on an article the *Ladies' Home Journal* wanted to do on Hawaiian youth. Before I went there several correspondents around the world had told me to look up Sarah Parke, who worked for one of the local newspapers; none of them had thought to mention that she was of Korean ancestry, and when I met her I was slightly startled. But not for long, for Sarah was one of those breezy internationalists with whom it was possible to make instant friends, and because of her I had several unusual Hawaiian experiences. She took me to a Hawaiian wedding and barbecue in the back country, and to the local jail on Mother's Day, where we listened to a chorus of prisoners sing "M Is for the Million Things She Taught Me." We had a picnic with some Hawaiian beachboy friends on Waikiki, and I was taken on an exciting ride through the surf in one of their long canoes, all of us paddling madly to ride the crest of our in-rolling wave. I loved Hawaii, tourists and all, and I loved Sarah; correspondents all around the world wept when a few years later she was killed in a helicopter crash while covering a tidal-wave story, and so did I.

. . .

Back home, life became routine and lonely again, and I felt depressed because I was unused as a woman and unused as a writer. Janet Rioch said that it was "sob-sistery" to want to be interested in my work and it was the only thing she ever told me with which I profoundly disagreed. But she also told me forcefully that an unhappy mother cannot raise a happy child, and I managed to create many times of happiness for us both. We went on picnics in the woods with the Greys, we skipped stones from the beach down by the river, we sang simple rounds, we finger-painted, we read *The Wizard of Oz* and many other books aloud, and often we pretended (with great drama and hilarity) to be conductors of Beethoven's Fifth Symphony. We had no television, for I had been so horrified by its pernicious mindlessness when I saw it at the homes of friends that I paraphrased the old Jesuit saying and vowed; "Give me my child until he is seven, and then the advertisers can have him." (When Lem was seventeen he said he thought this was the single most beneficial decision I had made during his childhood.)

That decision was an easy one, but there were many others which were harder; one of the most difficult aspects of life for the single parent is the loneliness of decision-making and the longing to talk to someone of your own generation who cares as much about your child as you do. But no one ever does.

❧ 14 ❧

On July 5, 1954, I had read with mild interest of the brutal murder of Marilyn Sheppard, the pretty young wife of Dr. Sam Sheppard, a Cleveland osteopath, and a month later I noted that he had been arrested and indicted for her murder. I forgot all about the case until mid-October, when the papers were full of the impending trial. It began in Cleveland on October 18, and on that day I was assigned to cover it; the next day I was filing from the Cleveland courthouse. Why they chose to send a part-time book-reviewer and a minor Asia specialist to cover a sensational murder trial I do not know, but I know that the effects of the assignment brought about another of those profound changes in the direction of my life.

Those two months in Cleveland were among the most exciting I ever lived through. I became obsessed by the case, which I still believe to be one of the enduring mysteries in the history of crime, and for weeks swung wildly between a conviction in Sam's guilt and belief in his story that a "bushy-haired intruder" had murdered Marilyn. I was fascinated by the personalities involved: Sam, handsome, composed, inwardly hollow; his two brothers, one so brilliant, one so gentle, and their thoroughbred wives; the white-haired defense attorney, an old-style orator; the smooth young prosecuting attorney with his Florentine face, who added up point after telling point against Sam in a kind of deadly arithmetic; the honest, decent men and women of the jury, who deliberated for five days before they brought in a verdict of Guilty in the Second Degree.

Twelve years later, in 1966, the United States Supreme Court gave Sam a new trial on the grounds that this first one was "a mockery of justice" and had been conducted in "a carnival atmosphere," in which "newsmen took over practically the whole courtroom." I was incredulous at these assertions, as were most of the out-of-town reporters who had covered the trial; nine of us signed a letter to the Court asserting our belief that what we had witnessed was a fair trial, conducted admirably by the late Judge Edward T. Blythin in an atmosphere of complete decorum. It is, of course, impossible to catch up with lies, and our letter received little publicity and obviously had no effect on the Court. As recently as 1971 Charles Manson's lawyer said bitterly that "Manson had as little chance of a fair trial in Los Angeles as Sam Sheppard had in Cleveland." I sighed when I read this, and finally realized that the deliberately maneuvered confusion between the carnival atmosphere of the inquest and the fair and honest trial we saw is probably indelible in the American mind.

I must have been asked a hundred times since the trial what I myself thought. And what I thought and still think is that Sam was probably guilty. Most of the other correspondents thought so too, and they would have left out the word "probably." I think that Sam's mind, which all his life must have been under some tremendous pressures from his demanding family, snapped suddenly, possibly when Marilyn refused to sleep with him; that he went completely berserk and in thirty-seven savage blows took revenge for long-concealed resentments and frustrations; that still in a frenzy he made a clumsy effort to simulate a burglary; that he then became unconscious and when he awoke remembered nothing of what had happened. I am convinced that Sam believed in his own innocence and so did his brothers.

If I had been on the jury, however, I would not have voted for conviction, simply because of Judge Blythin's definition of reasonable doubt. How could anyone have "an abiding conviction to a moral certainty of the truth of the charge"? Yet even so, the case was in such delicate balance that I could not blame the jury for bringing in the verdict it did. Still, it left me depressed, for I could not feel that the punishment would in any way fit the crime; Sam would probably emerge from jail fat and homosexual, I thought, with the basic cause of his rage untouched. The courts are a hundred years behind Freud I had been told, and I agreed.

Otherwise, I was far from depressed. For two months I had had a glorious time, turning out 1000 to 2000 words of copy in a couple of hours late every day and then rushing back to the hotel to dress up for dinner and an evening of festivities with the other reporters. Most of them were seasoned crime and trial reporters, and they shared a kind of tough gaiety which seems to be common to those who must write every day about a man who is truly in the shadow of the electric chair. "If the testimony about the murder weapon outline on the pillow doesn't fry Sam, he's incombustible," a Chicago reporter quipped. It was all like that.

One of the men was a well-known crime reporter from a Midwest paper, a big man with glowing black eyes, a strong handsome-ugly face, vast experience in the rougher aspects of American life with which I was unacquainted, and no intellectual or aesthetic pretensions at all. He was the last type in the world to which I had ever been attracted, but he was so dynamic and our chemistries together so incandescent that he had no trouble at all in taking me to bed at the beginning of the trial and continuing to do so for many months afterward. We managed to convince ourselves that we were in love, talked of marriage, and only after many months realized it wouldn't work. Even so I have never regretted the affair. "Look what a beautiful body you have," he said, forcing me to face a mirror naked. "Be proud," he said. Because of him my confidence in myself as a woman, which had been destroyed by the failure of my marriage, returned at last. He did that for me and much more, God rest his battered soul.

Perhaps because of this satisfactory affair, I swung into a two-month spate of writing which I have never equaled. I knew nothing about covering murder trials, but I wrote what I saw and heard and thought, just as I might have from India—and it worked. Day after day my stories ran front page; other papers began withdrawing their own correspondents and subscribing to the *Herald Tribune* syndicated service; *Time* magazine's press section commended my "literate and low-keyed copy" as the best on the trial; letters and telegrams from judges, detectives, lawyers, and newspaper editors poured in, and one of them said: "England can just hush up now about Rebecca West." I glowed, tried to look modest, kept on pounding out the stories, drank coffee all day, drank bourbon all evening, smoked incessantly, went to bed with my tough guy every night—and not surprisingly near the end suffered an attack of tachycardia (fast heartbeat) which nearly scared me to death. So I cut down on coffee and kept on going.

On December 21, the day the trial ended, I went home in triumph. I had gone out to Cleveland a depressed has-been, and I felt I was returning on top of the world. The grateful paper gave me a three-week leave and Lem and I went to Florida's remote Marco Island (before it was so hideously developed) for a time together of sun and ocean and sand-between-the-toes. On New Year's Eve, while Lem slept, I walked beneath the glittering stars, listened to the cry of a loon from across the dark waters of the Everglades, and knew that I was happy.

. . .

But I have never been able to parlay my successes into further successes. I received a couple of awards and several publishers wanted me to do a book on the Sheppard case, and that is what I should have done, I suppose. But I feared the loss of a steady income, which a leave of absence from the paper would have entailed, and turned them down. Gradually, the glamour evaporated as I returned to the old humdrum of the city room, and no more sensational murder trials came along to rescue me from the routine obituaries.

One day in January 1955 I received a phone call from Bruce Gould, co-editor with his wife, Beatrice, of the *Ladies' Home Journal*. He asked me to come see him, and when I did he offered me a job on the magazine at $15,000 a year, which was roughly twice what I was earning at the *Tribune*. He said he wanted me to help broaden the readers' knowledge of foreign affairs by doing some stories abroad; that if I didn't like the *Journal* I could always transfer to one of Curtis Publications' other magazines— *Holiday* or the *Saturday Evening Post*—and that I would be in line to take over Dorothy Thompson's column on international affairs when she retired in a year or so.

I thought it over for three months. I talked to my friend Peter Briggs, an editor on the *Journal* staff, and he said it was a delightful place to work. I talked to Engleking, and he refused to advise me. I talked to Janet Rioch, and she wouldn't either. Finally, and miserably, I said yes.

There were many factors in this unhappy decision. One, and the least important, was the morale at the *Tribune*, which had been slipping badly for several years. Another was the money, for I had been having a hard time making ends meet—I was frightened of the future, and Eric was not yet contributing the $100 a month he finally agreed to give for Lem's support. A third reason was that the job would mean a move to the Philadelphia area and therefore would take us a comfortable distance away from my mother's increasing possessiveness; I could settle near Swarthmore, where I had friends. Also, Lem was approaching school age, and when I was in college I had often visited a wonderful little private school, called The School in Rose Valley, which had been started by my English professor, Elizabeth Wright, and a group of other concerned parents. I couldn't think of anywhere else I'd rather have Lem go.

But it was a hard decision and it nearly broke my heart. "You seem to have put the roots of your ego into the *Herald Tribune*," Dr. Rioch told me, and I guess she was right. When I told the paper, the editors too, were unhappy. They offered to send me to another foreign post, but I had seen too many overseas American brats to want to take the chance that Lem might become one. Brownie Reid (now Congressman Ogden R. Reid, Jr.), who had taken over as publisher, offered to meet the *Journal's* salary and told me (and I think this was shameful) that I could even have Irita Van Doren's job as book-review editor. But it was all too late and I had made up my mind.

As a farewell present they sent me off for a week in San Francisco, to cover the tenth anniversary of the founding of the United Nations—an event I found almost unbearably nostalgic. They gave me a party at Bleeck's, and Brownie's elder brother Whitey made a speech which almost made me cry, and Judy Crist presented a gold bracelet from the editorial staff, with a little gold typewriter charm, which did make me cry. And that was the end of the twelve years—except that my love for the paper continues to live in my heart, as it does in the hearts of all of us who worked for it in "the great days."

. . .

Early in June I spent several days in the Swarthmore area, looking at houses, and on June 7 I bought a two-story Colonial which, while conventional, seemed to me charming and livable. It was placed on an acre of grass and trees, set back from Possum Hollow Road in Wallingford—a mile west of Swarthmore and a mile east of The School in Rose Valley. I was tremendously proud of my choice, and in July took Lem and Mother to see it. Mother was polite, but back home that evening I heard her describing it on the phone to Berta Hader. "It's top, upper-class bourgeois, with *no* little ambuscades of beauty," she said. She always did have a way with words.

I found new tenants for the house I was leaving, and on August 5 we moved. On September 6, 1955, I became an associate editor of the *Ladies' Home Journal.*

❧15❧

"You're going to hate it," warned an old newspaperwoman who had gone to *The Woman's Home Companion* the year before. She was right for seven very long years.

I had been used to working with men, but almost all of my coeditors and co-writers were women. I liked most of them separately, but gaggles of them at the girly lunches made me writhe. Particularly on Thursdays. The editorial and art departments of the magazine were in Philadelphia, in the big Curtis Building on Independence Square, but fashion, beauty, and homemaking were in New York, and so were the Goulds during most of the week. We working editors and writers in Philadelphia dressed casually in skirts and sweaters, tended toward chipped nail polish and lipstick put on in rather a hurry, and we never wore hats. But on Thursday we tried to spruce up, for that was the day New York descended upon us.

At 10:20 a.m. the elevator doors would open, and out they came: Mr. and Mrs. Gould, poised and elegant; the dainty managing editor, who seemed to have a different hair color each week; and flocks of fashionable babes in furs and feathers and *hats*. They would all flutter down the halls and disappear into offices, and then we grubby ones—furtively applying fresh nail polish— would await the royal command from the Goulds' Philadelphia secretary: "Mrs. Gould wonders whether you would be free to join her at lunch today?"

I remember my first Thursday luncheon, one of what seemed like a thousand nightmare others. Six of us joined Mrs. Gould at a round table in the dining room of the nearby Downtown Club.

We were allowed one martini each, and we all dutifully ordered salad because, of course, everyone was always supposed to be dieting. After the martini had arrived, Mrs. Gould, smiling through all her words as she always did, opened the conversation. "Now girls, we all know some long words, don't we?" she asked. We all nodded. "But aside from that little difference," she continued, "there's nothing in the world to distinguish us from any woman under any hair dryer in America, is there? Or to keep us from feeling that we are closer to any of them than we ever could be to any *man?*" There was a short silence, and then she turned to me, the newcomer. "Don't you agree, Margaret?" she asked.

"Well, no, I don't, Mrs. Gould," I answered, unaware of the rule that one never disagreed with royalty. "I think it's more a matter of similar background and education and shared interests. I have known many men as friends who are far closer to me than a hypothetical woman under a hair dryer."

She looked at me coldly. "If you feel that way," she said in silky tones, "I don't see how you can possibly be a good editor of a women's magazine." I took a rather deep gulp of my martini—and thereafter enjoyed referring privately to the "steamy menstrual sisterhood" in which we were all supposed to live.

The next thing I learned from Mrs. Gould, after I had completed my first "How America Lives" assignment,' was that she believed *Journal* readers never notice by-lines unless they are those of very famous people, and that therefore no *Journal* writer must ever express an opinion in print. I was dazed by this news. During seven years in Asia I was expected to develop interpretations and opinions and pass them on to the readers, as I had been at the Sheppard trial and in my book-reviewing. I had assumed that the Goulds had hired me for the same kind of personal reporting, and it took me a while to realize the essential difference between working for the *Herald Tribune* and working for the *Ladies' Home Journal*: on the paper, the reporter's job was to find the facts of a situation and to write the truth as he saw it; on the *Journal*, the "truth" was determined in advance by the Goulds and the writer's job was to find the facts to fit.

Several years later, for instance, I was asked to do a story about Marilyn Monroe. I spent a February afternoon with her in her New York apartment and found her fragile and frightened (this was two years before her suicide) but also effervescent and courageous. I wrote a sympathetic story, called "Conversation on the Edge of Spring," and all the other editors who read it were enthusiastic. But Bruce Gould returned it with the simple comment: "If you had been a man I would have wondered what went on in that apartment." The story was killed, and I realized that what they had wanted was a hatchet job.

Gradually, I came to see that almost everything in the magazine was designed not to help the women who read it, but to sell products. The food department produced gorgeous pictures of elaborate meals, which took hours to make and used a great many of the ingredients advertised in the magazine. The beauty department featured many "before and after" pictures designed to show how a plain Cinderella could be made into a Princess by the use of any of a dozen different cosmetics, hair shampoos, and eye-liners. (I always thought she looked better *before*.) The fashion and home-decoration departments were so glamorous that surely any woman must have wept at her own shabbiness and the comfortable dowdiness of her living room, and rushed out to spend money on the clothes and furniture advertised in the magazine. It was all very professional, very beautiful, and as unrelated to real human problems and solutions as that wonderful dollhouse Queen Elizabeth II had as a little girl.

From the Goulds came a constant pressure for IDEAS. From Beatrice: "I do hope your suggestions will be COMPELLING!" From Bruce: "We are always in need of good Big Ideas, such as 'The Ten Richest Women,' 'The World's Famous Jewels,' and 'The Ten Best-Dressed Women.'" That memo really amused me. Those were Big Ideas?

In all those years on the *Journal* I only had one idea which resulted in a story, and that came from a chance seat next to a young minister's wife on the train to New York. Heaven knows, I kept on sending in suggestions, and many I think might today get into the magazine, but for the Goulds' taste they were too sociological, and sociology (like psychiatry) was a dirty word. I would have understood if only they had said, "Look, we believe in integration but we can't run a story about it because we would alienate our Southern readers, and we can't run a story about population control because we'd lose our Catholic readers." But instead, suggestions were constantly rejected because, in Beatrice's words, "It doesn't fetch me." One year, I spent days drafting a long, well-documented memo suggesting that we do a story about the corruption of American values as typified by the way Thruways were destroying the environment without concern for people. It was returned with Bruce Gould's red-crayoned scrawl: "I like Thruways—I can get to Martha's Vineyard in seven and a half hours instead of two days."

Eventually, I came to understand that there was only a limited amount of acceptable topics which could provide stories: love, marriage, sex, money, children, and the glamour of royalty, jewels, or movie actresses on which the dream fantasies of six million American housewives feed—although once in a while I was thrown off base when they ran an article on drug addiction or expressed an interest in hardened criminals ("Don't write about their childhood," Beatrice said in a memo. "The first seven years are not important"). I tried hard to think of new ideas in the areas of love and glamour, and came up with a suggestion on "How to Have a Discreet Affair," to be by-lined by somebody like Marlene Dietrich. Bruce Gould's reaction was: "Prostitutes have to be pictures on a wall, I guess, or characters in historical novels to be interesting." I am told that he was aware, or at least suspected, that half the members of his female staff were absorbed in discreet affairs, or had been; did he, I wonder, think of them all as prostitutes?

Now, in the hindsight of ten years' blessed absence from the magazine, I begin to see it all a little differently, and with less passionate dislike. The Goulds had come out of the Midwest and with their sure knowledge of that great, quiet and essential part of America, had built the *Ladies' Home Journal* into the country's leading woman's magazine. Who could blame them for thinking that what had worked in the past would work in the future? And often it did.

I think particularly of a story which had been written badly by a contributing editor and which I was asked to rewrite. It concerned monster babies and I thought it would be horrifying to young pregnant women. I said so to Mrs. Gould, and she was surprised. "But when you were pregnant, didn't you worry every day about the possibility of your baby being born a monster?" she asked me. I said, the thought had never crossed my mind. "Well, I did," she said. So I rewrote the story, but I thought it so awful I refused to let my by-line appear with that of the contributing editor. After it was published it brought in hundreds of enthusiastic letters and won a $500 award for the contributing editor.

I was incompatible with the milieu, that was all. After a few years, when I had developed aerophagia (abnormal air-swallowing due to tension and unhappiness) I went to see a Philadelphia psychoanalyst. "Don't you realize that when you took this job you walked right into your central problem?" he asked. He told me there wasn't anyone in Philadelphia who treated unhappy career women and that I'd have to move to Atlanta for help, so I dropped the whole idea and trudged back to work.

It seems to me now that I clung unrealistically to my snobbish rigidities, and failed to give the Goulds credit for producing a magazine which was truly loved by millions of American women. They must have realized soon after I went to work that they had hired me under the misconception that I was a hard-boiled, unscrupulous, front-page-type reporter who would bring box-office ideas to the magazine; our obvious incompatibility must have irritated them—once Bruce told another editor (who hastened to tell me) that "Margaret works harder at hiding the good in her than most people do in hiding the bad." Although over the years I wrote many successful stories for them, I really can't understand why they didn't fire me.

I was not alone in my misery, and I am reasonably sure that most of the other women in that Philadelphia office were as unhappy as I was. I remember the squeals of ecstasy in the corridors whenever one of the girls came in wearing an engagement ring, little cries of excitement which conveyed true happiness for her but which also held an undertone of wistfulness, not only because she had "found a man," as they hadn't, but the wistfulness of a prison inmate who watches one of his own escape beyond the walls. And I remember when, after I had been there five years, one of the few men writers on the staff sauntered into my office and asked me, "Have you ever written anything for the magazine of which you're proud?" "No," I answered. "Neither have I," he said gloomily, and drifted away. One fine woman had fainting fits, for which doctors could find no cause; another suffered from an equally mysterious diarrhea and recurrent nightmares. Their symptoms disappeared after they had left the magazine, as did my own aerophagia.

There were the women who never talked about their cancers or their alcoholic husbands, but who smothered it all in bouncy cuteness: "My dear, look what I found at Wanamaker's! The most *divine* toy rabbit—you just stroke its little head and lift its little arms and really, it blows *bubbles!*" We were forced to give the measurements of our legs and our opinions of sex for the benefit of various magazine projects yet our private lives were secret and carefully covered with gloss. Often I paraphrased to myself Matthew Arnold's line: "Most women live lives of quiet desperation."

The real problem, I think now, was that the Goulds were producing a magazine for average, normal, middle-brow, middle-class American women, with the necessary editorial aid of abnormal, often intellectual, and sometimes far above middle-class women. If we had been the norm, would we have been working on the magazine in the first place? Of course not. And so the only way to reconcile the difference was to pretend that there was none, to take part in an elaborate little game in which all must deny what we were and affirm what we were not. Is it any wonder that each day we were bored with the gray mediocrity which we were forced to pretend was excellence? With hypocrisy?

One day I found a copy of a speech given to potential advertisers by our current advertising director, and then I really understood. He had said:

One of the primary responsibilities of a magazine editor is to gather together an audience which is profitable for the advertiser to sell with his advertising message. It matters not, within the limits of good taste, how this is accomplished, as much as that it *is* accomplished. Of course, the advertiser doesn't want the editorial so spectacular that his ad is overshadowed, nor does he want it to be so humdrum that the reader does not page all the way through the book. Rather, he wants something in between, so the reader will not only see the ad the first time, but will be exposed to it again and again when she returns to read more articles or stories.

We did print some good fiction, now and then, even some that may have overshadowed the accompanying ads. But I have always remembered that when in the same issue we ran a superior story by Rebecca West and in a homemaking department an offer of a Bible quilt pattern, there were 3200 requests for the pattern and *one* letter commenting on the Rebecca West story.

For one thing I was grateful to the *Journal:* it was there that I met Helen Everitt, who became my close friend and confidante. Helen was about fifteen years older than I, but she was one of those women who never age. She used the tennis court and the swimming pool on her three-hundred wild acres in Hopewell, New Jersey, and sometimes, when her seventeenth-century stone house was snowed in, she would ski to the railway station. Helen's mind was as trim and lithe as her body, her eyes were full of laughter and wisdom, and she had the most perfect taste for people and for writing that I have ever known. The vulgarities of the *Journal* were anathema to her, too, but she was more philosophical about them than I was, and thus helped me to achieve an approximation of her own cheerful stoicism. Helen had been for years an editor at a Boston publishing house, and after the premature death of her husband had worked as a literary agent in New York. But she had four teen-age children to send through college and, like me, she had been driven to take the *Journal* job for the money it provided. When I first met her, the two older girls were married, one boy was just finishing at Yale, and the younger boy was beginning his senior year at preparatory school. "Only five more years to go," Helen would sigh over one of our three-martini lunches. And as time went on, "Only four more years . . ." Or, "Only three years now . . ." And I would sigh even more heavily and say, "Only fifteen for me." Or, "Only fourteen now!" And then we'd both laugh and order our third drink.

Often we were joined at lunch by Alberte Wright, a white-haired editor of great sensitivity and dignity and a widow with grown children who wanted to work even though she was a member of "Philadelphia society" and didn't need to. Alberte was, and is, a woman of intelligence, talent, and delicacy, but because she was an assistant rather than an associate editor, she was required to punch a time clock every day—just like the typists—and treated more or less like a lackey by employers who seemed to resent the fact that they could never break down her imperturbable good manners.

Why didn't I quit? One reason was that from time to time I had some fairly glamorous assignments. One of the first of these, just before the actress Grace Kelly announced her engagement to Prince Rainier, took me to Hollywood to interview all of her leading men and find out what they thought of her. Through arrangements made by Peter Briggs, who wasn't intimidated by movie stars, I talked to Cary Grant, Alec Guinness, James Stewart, William Holden, and Gary Cooper, and found them all, somewhat to my surprise, immensely likable and intelligent men.

Mr. Gould's assertion that he wanted me to help broaden our readers' knowledge of foreign affairs seemed to have been forgotten, but I did have two overseas assignments. The first, in 1957, was to Morocco to do a story about Lalla Aisha, daughter of the late Sultan and sister of the present King Hassan. I had never been to North Africa, and I was amazed to find so many similarities between Morocco, which had just been liberated from French rule, and Pakistan in its early days. There were many things I loved there, as I had in Asia: the relaxed.tension, the eagerness for a better life, the beautiful faces of old men, the quietness of a veiled woman at sunset, who sat with a baby in arms on the pirate ramparts above the Bou Regreg River. Above all, I loved the sense of the flow of tradition, which is something I think we hunger for in America. But also there was mass illiteracy, corruption, inefficiency, contempt for women, and the usual inability to think of an individual foreigner as anything except a generalized symbol of colonial oppression.

It was a relief to fly to England, for a few green and quiet days in the country I love so dearly. I saw Ian and his wife, and felt again the overwhelming joy of his presence. I went down to Lewes on the South Downs to spend a weekend with Kingsley Martin, editor of *The New Statesman and Nation*, and his lifetime companion, Dorothy Woodman; at dawn we walked barefoot in pajamas and nightgowns on the downs above the sea, and watched the sunrise. They were both such warm and vital people, with minds crackling with world-encompassing thought; it has been hard to accept the knowledge that they are both dead now.

My Calcutta friends Jim and Rose Marie Foottit had come back to England and settled in Patrixbourne, a tiny village four miles southeast of Canterbury, in Kent. I visited them there at "The Old Vicarage" for the first time, and fell in love with the great, sprawling house, and beds of lavender, the huge beech tree at the end of the lawn, the little Norman church next door, the winding village street with its brick and half-timbered cottages, the front gardens glowing with perfumed roses. After that visit, Patrixbourne became my English "home" and Jim and Rose

Marie, two of the most delightful and civilized human beings I have ever known, my English "family."

The other overseas assignment came in 1959, in connection with World Refugee Year, and took me to Switzerland, Austria, and Germany (which I loathed) in search of a refugee family which had been denied entry to the United States because of some trivial shortcoming. The Goulds set up the standards for the family I must find: Protestant, photogenic, with at least two girls and a boy or two boys and a girl. They must have lived in a refugee camp for several years but none of them must show any emotional scars. In other words, a typical, pretty, *Ladies' Home Journal*-type family with which our readers could identify. It turned out, not unexpectedly, that no such family could be found; almost all the refugees were from Eastern Europe and, therefore, overwhelmingly Roman Catholic. And what family can live for years in refugee camps and not suffer emotional scarring? After a six-week search we finally had to settle on a German Lutheran wife and her Polish Catholic husband and their two little girls, living in a camp near Münster, in North Germany. Later, the story I wrote about them resulted in their admission to the United States, where they have lived more or less happily ever since.

There were other perquisites of the job. I could take Lem with me when I flew to Puerto Rico to observe Nelson Rockefeller in action at a governors' conference, and to Hollywood when I went there to do a story about "Why Hollywood Marriages Fail." We had two winter weeks in Florida on several occasions, and in 1958 a wonderful three weeks, riding horseback at the Bar Sixty-three Ranch in Livingston, Montana—the happiest vacation of them all, I think. I had a full-time housekeeper (or rather, a series of them), I could pay Mother's medical bills without worrying, and have hothouse flowers in winter.

But these luxuries alone were insufficient to keep me at a job for which I basically had only contempt, or living in a suburban community which, while pleasant enough, seemed more and more like Siberia. The really decisive factor was Lem.

❧16❧

After Lem started kindergarten at The School in Rose Valley, I felt that for the first time since I had returned to America I had found a group of people who were also battling the corrupting influences of our society: television, violent comics, prejudice, precocious sexuality, conformity, unreason. With this help, I thought, it might yet be possible to raise a human being who was creative, inner-directed, and emotionally healthy. Rose Valley, which ran from nursery school through the sixth grade, taught the regular academic subjects but it also emphasized carpentry, clay work, dancing, theatricals, original writing, and nature walks.

Lem was happy, and grew in mind and spirit. "What is the best thing in the world?" I asked him when he was six. "Loving!" he replied. "And what's the most important thing in the world?" "I am," he said flatly. He'll be all right, I thought. In spite of everything he's going to be all right.

Eric had been transferred from Japan to New York to cover the United Nations, and we established a rather formal relationship. For many years he came every Christmas Eve and stayed through Christmas morning present-opening; during the year he came for a weekend every few months and in between Lem would visit him at his Manhattan apartment. One time, when Lem was six and a half and in an obstreperous and demanding period which I found difficult to handle, I picked him up at his father's apartment and was told that he had behaved admirably all weekend. After an exhausting trip home, during which he behaved outrageously, I finally wrestled him into bed.

"Oh, Lem," I wailed, "why is it you're so good with your father and so bad with me?"

"Daddy's strict!" he howled. "And I *like* him strict!" I took the hint and cracked down on manners and routine, and to my amazement discovered that we had achieved a degree of peace in the house.

Peace, that is, except for the times that my mother came uninvited to stay, which happened with increasing frequency. She brought the old dragging melancholy, and several housekeepers left because she nagged them all day and countermanded directions I had given. I overheard her telling a new one: "Don't pay any attention to Miss Margaret—she doesn't know anything." Once, when I had suggested mildly that she might consider my convenience in her arrivals and departures, she left a scrawled paper on my pillow: "The eagles have their aeries, tigers have their dens, birds have their nests, rabbits have their holes, dogs have their kennels. But alley cats—oh, alley cats, who cares!" At the time she had a Manhattan apartment and two houses in Sneden's. I had re-established friendships with some of the Swarthmore faculty and with old classmates who had returned to teach, and sometimes went out to cocktail or dinner parties. The departure was always miserable, for she would follow me to the car each time, cling to the door handle, and cry, "Why didn't they ask me too?"

Another complication of life was my mother's older sister Alice, who lived on the Main Line, only twelve miles away. Alice, with whom I had mercifully had very little to do until I moved to Wallingford, was to become of immense importance in our lives for the next seven years and, for me, even now.

In the eyes of my family when I was growing up, my mother's older sister Alice was a scourge, a horror, an eccentric, a reactionary, a social climber, a person to be patiently endured when she was present, and the subject of considerable hilarity when she had blessedly departed. But my parents tried to sublimate their rage with analysis of her childhood, made miserable by the brutal tyrannies of her Victorian father, who never forgave his first-born for being a girl instead of a boy.

During my college years I had been forced to see something of my Aunt Alice and her henpecked little husband, Walter Newkirk, and a few years later I stayed with her for a few days after

Walter had been killed in an automobile accident. But it was only after I moved to Wallingford that I began to see her regularly. Part of this was conscience and pity for a childless widow in her eighties, but the other part was Alice's shrewdness in coming to my rescue when my car collapsed and I couldn't afford a new one: she bought me a little English Ford and in return I somehow agreed to drive her around when she needed to be driven, and to have her to lunch on frequent Sundays.

Oh, those Sundays! Twice a month for seven years . . . twice a month for seven years, with a blessed respite in the summers when she went away or in the winters when the roads were too icy. Drive ten miles to Saint David's Church, to collect her after the service. Drive home, remembering to speak clearly into her hearing device, remembering not to shout. Assist her into house. Pour a daiquiri into her as quickly as possible. Assemble lunch. Remember telephone book and pillow on her chair because of her bad leg.

"Why do you have club rolls when you know I like soft rolls?"

"Why do you have soft rolls when you know I like club rolls?"

"Well, I suppose you *like* this welfare state—"

"Why are you wearing lipstick? I thought you were too intellectual for such foolishness."

"No, I don't want to watch your new television! Do you think I'm a fool? I'll go home now."

Drive home and deposit her in the spooky house she and Walter bought in 1913, the year it was built. Thanks to a once-a-week cleaning woman the house was orderly, but the atmosphere was one of funereal gloom. Partly this was due to the early Mrs. McKinley style of decoration: the heavy mahogany furniture, stained-glass windows through which no light ever seemed to fall, the huge sepia tint of the Coliseum which hung over the imitation fireplace. I don't think Aunt Alice had seen these things for years, or perhaps ever. In her old age she was so bent over that the flaking ceilings and the peeling wallpaper didn't matter—she knew they needed replacement but saw no reason to spend money on something she never looked at. She spent it, instead, on subscriptions to *The Wall Street Journal, Barrons Weekly,* and the *National Review,* copies of which were piled around the edge of the living-room floor and in towers on tables and desks.

Hidden behind the bathtub in the bathroom on the second

floor of the house, Aunt Alice kept a bottle of Mount Vernon rye, which lasted her for months since she took only half a jigger before bed. "You must have a weak bladder," she'd comment whenever I brought her home. "That doesn't come from *our* side of the family."

Seven years, every other Sunday, except in the blessed summertime when Aunt Alice went to Maine.

It is a wonder to me that Lem survived all the elderly females who tried to dominate him, but he was fiercely independent and went his own way. I worried continually about the absence of a male image in his life, and often, when we watched a neighbor wave good-by as he went off fishing with a young nephew I marveled that he never asked Lem to go along, nor did any of the other men in our neighborhood show any interest in this (in effect) fatherless boy. So, over the years, I taught Lem baseball, tennis, swimming, basketball, bowling, archery, typing, and chess. Fortunately, he had been born with superb muscular coordination and the fact that he was expert in many sports won admiration at school. It was sports which saved him, really, for at eight his feeling of alienation began to cut deep and he began to retreat from his own generation—except for the hours on the beloved playing fields of school and Little League.

Yet at the beginning of second grade his teacher told me that he was "socially adjusted, loving, completely masculine, extroverted, happy, well liked and highly verbal." This last was no news, for only recently he had given me an example of his capable use of language as well as of his particular brand of humor. "Don't twist people's knuckles when you shake hands," I had told him as he brushed his teeth at bedtime. "That's the kind of thing that might make them hate you—and it's not good to be hated." Lem, who was then seven, had looked up from his tooth-brushing with a cool, slightly amused expression. "You're telling me this from personal experience, I presume?" he asked.

That same year I learned from the school psychologist that Lem's class of twelve children was considered phenomenal because not one of them had an IQ of less than 130. So then I worried about whether it was good for him to be educated among such an atypical elite, and reflected that while my own IQ was high, I had nevertheless made a mess of my life. (When he was eleven, Lem pawed through my files of school reports, discovered that his IQ was 156, and began to boast about it. I told him that having a good brain in the head was like having a grand piano in the house—it won't make music if you don't learn how to play it. That calmed him down considerably.)

His mind was ceaselessly active, and sometimes exhausting. One morning when he was nine I made a list of the questions he asked me during the first ten minutes I was awake on one particular morning: "What is life for?" "Do animals know when they're growing old?" "I never noticed that earthworms have claws or teeth, so how do they get through the earth?" "What is the difference between fiction and nonfiction?" "Who was Alexander the Great?" "Why do parrots live so long?"

I had obtained a Pennsylvania divorce from Eric in 1957, and a few months later he told me that he was planning to remarry. I was shaken by this news, remembering all the dreams and the love that were now so irretrievably gone, but Lem was explosive. "If Daddy marries again I will still like him, but I won't *love* him," he swore. I tried to convince him that nothing in their relationship had changed and that his father would always love him, but arguments were useless. Finally, at my suggestion, Eric took him for a day of planetarium-viewing and to see *Around the World in Eighty Days,* and to have supper and spend the night with his new stepmother at their apartment on Sutton Place. She is a quiet, intelligent woman and Lem liked her; the next morning when I picked him up he was full of scrambled eggs and renewed love for his father.

. . .

I think of those years in Wallingford as unhappy ones, but there were many happy times and I should not forget them. Birthdays and Christmases, snowball fights, games, singing, laughter, dogs and cats and goldfish. But for me, as the years went on, there was also deep loneliness for the mate I was beginning to assume I would never have. Like most reporters who are trained to observe rather than to participate, I am allergic to group activities and volunteer work, but now I forced myself to do some of the things the lone woman in the suburbs is supposed to do: joined the library book-selection committee and became a Democratic committeewoman. But I only grew bored and lonelier, while three years and more drifted by.

As always, I found a certain amount of sublimation in work.

Not for the *Journal,* but moonlighting on book reviews for the *Herald Tribune* Sunday book section, for *The New York Times,* and for the *Saturday Review.* In 1957 Knopf gave me a contract for a book about India and I worked on it for almost a year at night, early in the morning, and sometimes during the long, empty days at the office. *The Leaf and the Flame* was published in March 1959, was widely reviewed and acclaimed, became a "standard" on every library's list of books on India—and failed to sell out even the first edition. Life resumed its old gray hue.

Then, on one of my out-of-town assignments, I met an old friend whose family had known mine since the beginning of time. We went to dinner together, we danced to "September Song," we went up to the hotel roof for a nightcap. We leaned on a railing at midnight and looked far down at the illuminated swimming pool, where a girl in a red bathing suit was floating. It had all been platonic and great fun. But suddenly he turned and kissed me, and the world exploded, for him as well as for me.

It was a complete disaster, because of course he was married and of course he had teen-age children. We both went rather insane and for several months managed to writhe our lives around to arrange frequent meetings between our separated hometowns, and agonize and weep and love and weep again. For me all of life became unreal—Lem, Mother, Aunt Alice, the house, my job —and nothing in the world mattered except to be with him. Only in a love relationship, I realized, is one completely free to be as joyous, as tender, and as wild as one is capable of being; only in a love relationship, I further realized, is one free to surrender and to give, to pamper and adore, to worship and to pleasure, in a surge of love which brings new freedom, new realization of self.

After a few weeks of emotional tumult I decided I needed help, so I went up to New York to see Dr. Janet Rioch. To my surprise I discovered that I, as well as he, was suffering from a disease she called *Crise de Midi,* which often afflicts people on the edge of middle age who have been intensely lonely and who have repressed their need for love for too long a time. She gave me a prescription for the tranquilizer Miltown, and warned me that alcoholism often starts in this period of a woman's life. "This is one of the major crises of your life," she told me as we said good-by. "Don't minimize it. Keep some air holes open." I tried to do so, and was much helped by an assignment to spend a day with

Adlai Stevenson at his farm in Libertyville, Illinois. We walked through snowy fields talking of King Arthur, we drank, we ate, we laughed, and we talked, talked, talked. I floated back to the hotel that night all shimmery from the sense of the greatness I had touched.

The next morning I received a letter from my lover, saying that while he would love me forever he thought that the injury which might be done to his vulnerable wife was too grave to justify continuing the affair. I went to the Chicago Art Institute and stared at Monet water lilies so long I will never be able to look at another. Then I retreated into silence and curled up around my misery like some horrid, instinctive animal nourishing a grievous wound.

Obviously, I decided when I was finally able to think again, I was never going to be happy. But I thought that perhaps I could at least try to make Lem happy, and Mother and Aunt Alice, and my Aunt Sara when she came East for a visit. But it wasn't easy. The three old ladies spent a great deal of time reminiscing about the iniquities of their father, and the rest of the time talking about Lem's deplorable upbringing, usually in his presence and mine. To Lem his Great-Aunt Sara was just another bossy old lady with white hair, but she was used to being courted by previous generations of adoring children, to whom she had given greatly of her time and generosity, and she kept accusing Lem mournfully of not loving her. It was perhaps no wonder that he did not take kindly to her, or to still another Great-Aunt, Marion, when she came East a year later to care for my mother during my absence on an assignment. When I got home from that trip, I found the two old ladies cooking up a scheme to send him off to reform school, and that Lem had developed a nervous tic in one eye.

· · ·

I once did a story for the *Journal* about old age. One of the things I learned from the experts is that the personality does not change as it ages, it only becomes more acutely whatever it was in previous years. So now I always think of 1960 as the year my mother became "more so." She had always been full of nameless terrors; now they consumed her with bitterness and she creaked angrily about the house all night, refusing to go to bed and keeping the rest of us awake. She had always been determined to be mistress of my household; now she became positively imperious in her orders to our housekeeper, Gladys Morgan. Gladys, who was with us for three tempestuous years, is a Panamanian of mixed Indian and Spanish blood; although she had an explosive temperament, she was remarkably patient with my mother and devoted to Lem.

That May, America's U-2 spy plane was shot down over Russia, and for a few days we believed—as did most of the country— that atomic war was imminent. The night of the deepest crisis I stood by the bed of my sleeping son, knowing that no protection, no salvation, was possible, but wanting only to throw myself across his body, to protect, to save.

"I hope you have a gun in the house," my mother said when I went downstairs. I asked her why.

"To shoot Lem if war comes," she said.

To get Lem away from the tensions in the household I sent him for two months that summer and the following one, to a boys' camp in the Poconos. Shortly afterward, I flew to Los Angeles, where I served as an Alternate Delegate (with no vote) on the Pennsylvania Delegation to the Democratic National Convention. I broke my heart over Stevenson's defeat for the Presidential nomination, learned a lot about machine politics, and concluded they were no place for anyone with a hide less thick than that of an armadillo. But a drive up the beautiful California coast was healing, and so were a few days in Carmel, Berkeley, and San Francisco, with its dear memories of Ian. Then I went back to Wallingford, where my mother had taken up more or less permanent residence, and sank again into the old emotional mix of rage, fury, guilt, conflict, hope, and hopelessness and hope again.

In desperation, I began to try some really serious self-analysis. One day in October the months of work exploded into understanding and for the first time I realized that my mother and I had been perpetuating the old, adolescent relationship from which I had never broken free. "I am *me*," I marveled in my journal. "I am grown up. I am not a whining, petulant, perpetually rebelling adolescent. It is *my* home, and the presence of my mother is only incidental." I felt suffused with joy at these discoveries.

I found that power was in my hands, not hers, and that I therefore could afford to be kind to her, and tolerant of what now seemed her pitiful efforts to dominate. And I found that as I accepted the break from the guilts she had imposed upon me and accepted myself as I was, I was free to love her not with a cutting edge to my love, but freely. I began to feel an inner calm, a confidence and gaiety I had not known for years; I could even look at my job objectively, merely as a way of earning a living. I realized I had value as a human being and felt as if I were in love with myself. And I learned, too, that I was human, fallible, and that I was mortal.

I do not know whether my fresh approach to life, which was reflected in a new peacefulness in our home, was responsible for what happened next, or only coincidental. But it seemed to me that no sooner had I learned how to understand and handle my mother, than she changed into someone else. During November she had two little strokes, one of which took her to the hospital for a few days, but by Christmas she was well enough for the usual festivities. Eric arrived, we had the lighted candles on the Christmas tree, carols, the reading of Luke and *The Night Before Christmas*. Lem went to bed and I stuffed his stocking. Mother said gloomily, as she always did, that this was no doubt her last Christmas, and went to bed. Eric and I talked trivialities until midnight.

At 4:30 in the morning Lem burst into my room. "Mother! Wake up! Nani's sick and calling for *her* mother!" I stumbled into her bedroom and found Mother writhing on her bed, moaning, her eyes glassy and wild, like those of a terrified bird. "This isn't the real me! This isn't the real me!" she groaned, over and over. Lem grabbed the Bible from her bedside table and began reading the 91st Psalm aloud; it was her favorite and had always calmed her during past seizures. But this time the psalm was of no help, and her groans increased. It was agony to call her doctor at 5 on Christmas morning, with the roads all ice and snow, but I did. Twenty minutes later he arrived, and Lem and I went down to the living room. Lem ignored the waiting stocking and the presents under the tree, and picked up a book from the coffee table. "Would you like me to read to you from *Amahl and the Night Visitors?*" he asked. I said yes.

He began at his favorite part, the section near the end where Amahl is leaving his mother to go off with the three kings to see the Christ child. "Feed my bird!" "Yes, I promise." "Watch the cat!" "Yes, I promise." "I shall miss you very much. . . ." Beyond the misted windows the skies began to lighten with the Christmas dawn. Then the doctor came down and said Mother had suffered an attack of labyrinthitis (a balance displacement) but would be all right when she awoke from the sedative he had given her.

In the weeks after that she was like a trembling child, needing constant care and utterly dependent upon me. I was confused and in a way infuriated; it seemed to me that no sooner had I learned to be independent of her attempts at domination than I had been brought utterly to heel by the necessity of learning a new role, that of the pretend-mama to a frightened woman in her second childhood. It was hard to recapture the euphoria of October, but as she grew better some of it came back and I was able to achieve a renewed sense of my own balance.

Lem, who had always had a tumultuous and ambivalent relationship with my mother, indicated in a poem he wrote at this time, called "Grandmother," that he, too, was growing toward detachment:

Old, tired, wrinkled, kind,
But hissing at cats who come upstairs.
Considerate and patient.
Yet she hides bananas and bits of graham crackers in her room,
And reads late at night.

1961 was a turning-point year, but it started out more or less as drearily as the years before. At the office the war for advertising was on with *McCalls* and we seemed to be losing it. Every month there were fewer pages in the magazine, which meant less chance for serious articles and less space for whatever we wrote. When my Marilyn Monroe story was rejected in April, I decided firmly that I must find a job somewhere else. Dorothy Thompson had died in January and for a while I wondered whether Bruce Gould would remember his assertion when he hired me that I would be in line to take over her column when she retired. But nothing was said, and by this time my self-confidence as a writer had been so thoroughly crushed that I never mentioned the matter to either of them.

I remembered Mr. Gould's promise that I could easily transfer to the *Saturday Evening Post* or *Holiday,* and I put out feelers with some of the editors and writers I knew on both magazines.

The *Post* people liked the material I sent them, but they were also in financial trouble and in a process of reorganization during which no one could be hired. *Holiday* informed me that they had never taken anyone from the *Journal* staff, and never would. I thought of the *Herald Tribune*, but the management and ownership had changed and the staff morale was said to be appalling. Besides, Lem had only one more year to go at Rose Valley and I didn't want to leave Wallingford until he completed it. There seemed nothing to do but to slog on, and take what pleasure I could in my rose garden and the coming of spring. It was with no premonition of impending change that I invited old friends from Washington for my birthday weekend in late May.

❧17❧

Commander Alfred Rodman Hussey, Jr. (USN–ret.) was an old friend I had first met in Japan, where I had also known the brilliant young woman who became his second wife. Rod and I affectionately called each other "cousin," for we both stemmed from the same family of early settlers in Nantucket. Rod, the son of a Unitarian minister, had been raised in Baltimore and Plymouth, and in the summers at Barnstable on Cape Cod. He had been graduated from Harvard and received a law degree at the University of Virginia. During World War II, he served in the Navy and spent a year in academic studies preparatory to his eventual work on the Japanese constitution; he was one of the true liberals on MacArthur's staff and near the end of his time in Japan received the Legion of Merit for his work there.

At the time our friendship was renewed, Rod was with the Central Intelligence Agency and a member of a minority liberal wing that was concerned with the cultural and psychological understanding of other peoples in the world and not with political operations like the Bay of Pigs—which drove Rod to fury. He was very much the Harvard-New England-Brooks-Brothers gentleman, with an Edwardian courtesy and sense of humor, and a conscience as solid as Plymouth Rock. At fifty-eight, he looked like the long-time captain of a whaling ship: foursquare, with white hair, a weathered rosy face, and eyes a seagoing blue.

During the past few years I had stayed several times with the Husseys in Washington, and while I had always enjoyed the visits I had been saddened to hear, late at night when they thought I was asleep, the sounds of bitter quarreling. Still, I enjoyed her dynamic intelligence, and once Rod and I began to talk about the behavioral sciences we found it hard to stop; it seemed reasonable enough (and quite innocent) to invite them for the weekend.

Saturday evening, Mother let the tub run over and part of the dining-room ceiling fell in. Lem went to bed in raging tears when his grandmother told him he wasn't a member of our family because he was more interested in sports than books. The Husseys and I sat up late, talking, and I kept wishing that his wife wouldn't keep interrupting him. Then she and I went upstairs to bed while Rod remained in the living room, reading. A while later I remembered I hadn't locked the living-room door to the screened porch, and wearily went downstairs to do so.

As I walked into the room Rod stood up and held out his arms. Without a second of hesitation I went right into them, put my head on his strong chest, and cried. That night my principal emotion was that after years of carrying problems alone for so many years, it was absolute bliss just to cry and be comforted. But the next night I went downstairs again feeling a somewhat different emotion, and that was the first time we kissed.

The following weekend he suddenly appeared at the house. We sat in the sassafras grove at the end of the lawn, and faced the fact that, in William Godwin's lovely phrase, our "friendship had melted into love." But I told him that I was damned if I was going to have just another affair with a hopelessly married man. He told me then that he and his wife had recently agreed upon a separation preparatory to divorce, and that they were already discussing the division of property. He reached over and put his hand on mine.

"I shouldn't ask this yet, but I'm going to," he said. "My dear, will you marry me?"

"Yes," I answered. "I will be most happy and honored to marry you."

. . .

It seemed very strange to be faced suddenly with the possibility of happiness. I worried at first that I might be suffering another *Crise de Midi*, but I soon realized that I was not and that this love was on very solid ground. Nor did I need to feel guilty, for to Rod his marriage had ended long before, and there were no children to worry about.

A little to my surprise, my mother approved of Rod, and tears of happiness for me came to her eyes when I told her of our plans. But I worried about Lem, at first. I had always made a point of telling him that I liked men very much and wished that I could marry again, but he had been alone with me for so long that I feared his jealousy.

"Mother, I want to know what's happening," he said to me one Sunday in June, when I was saying goodnight to him while Rod waited for me in the garden.

"What do you mean?" I stalled.

"When you looked at Commander Hussey in the candlelight at dinner your eyes were full of love—and so were his for you."

So I told him that we loved each other and that we hoped to be married. And then, impulsively and probably wrongly, I asked him, "Do you mind?"

He laughed. "Of *course* not!" he exclaimed. Then he patted me gently on the shoulder. "Go on downstairs to him now," he ordered.

At the beginning we had thought there would be no trouble with the divorce and that perhaps we could even be married by October. But it was not to be that easy. Rod's wife had already accepted the idea of separation, but once Rod started to press she began to balk; one day she would agree and threaten suicide the next. "You cannot build happiness on a foundation of someone else's pain," Rod said, and, of course, I agreed with him. So the summer drifted on and by autumn I was sick with tension and anxiety, subject to strange fevers and fainting spells, and back on Miltown.

Meantime, my mother's mental and physical condition had steadily worsened, and by early winter it was creating havoc in our lives. When Lem and I were home, she followed us from room to room, out into the garden, back indoors. She chased away boys who came to play with Lem. She wrote bitter letters to our relatives telling them that I had stolen all her money. Most disruptive of all was her restlessness, which led her to disappear without warning and often without money. Sometimes state troopers would bring her home. Sometimes she would make it to her New York apartment, where she usually had a small stroke, and I would have to drive up to fetch her.

One day I came home from work and found Lem sobbing on the living-room couch, with long scratch marks on his throat. His grandmother huddled in the big chair by the fireplace, ruffled like a chickadee with defiance and fright.

"Nani tried to strangle me!" Lem howled. "She tried to *strangle* me!"

Gladys told me what had happened. Our yellow cat, Chini, had recently produced a litter of kittens, each of which Lem deeply cherished. He was in the living room crooning over their box and watching them feed when his grandmother came in. "I'm going to drown them," she said firmly.

When Lem's temper flared he threw things. Never anything that could break or could hurt anyone, but something like graham crackers or playing cards. In this case it was newspapers, which he ripped into shreds and scattered furiously all over the room. His grandmother, thinking she was under attack, grabbed him by the throat and, presumably tried to strangle him.

Her doctor said that she was showing increasing evidence of arteriosclerotic psychosis, and that he thought she ought to be in a nursing home. A psychiatrist said her behavior indicated developing paranoia, and he strongly recommended a nursing home. So did Rod, whose compassion for Mother was great, but whose tender concern for Lem and me was greater.

But one does not lightly put a mother in a nursing home, and particularly one like mine. She was still so open to new experiences—only recently she had discovered Beethoven's "Archduke Trio," and one evening she had pleaded for more when I read her Dylan Thomas's "Fern Hill." She cherished seeds in her arthritis-twisted hands, pondering on their mystic potentiality; she had followed the recent Russian and American first flights in space with fascination; and she had wept at the death of Dag Hammarskjöld on September 18. I began visiting possible nursing homes, but I felt torn in two by the decision I had to make.

In Washington, Rod came to the conclusion that only by maintaining a Virginia residence separate from his wife for a year could a legal divorce be obtained. He found an apartment, and three times that winter he prepared to move into it, but each time his wife produced a new emergency for which he had to remain, and cope.

Life at my office was equally gloomy, and was made more so for me when Helen retired at the end of 1961. I was happy for her, of course, but without her crisp, unsentimental companionship I felt bereft. The office was filled with despair because of the continued decline in advertising linage, and every day there were new rumors of imminent collapse. All in all, it was good to be given an assignment at the end of January 1962, and one which interested me: to take three weeks going across the country talking to mothers of illegitimate children who were on welfare and whose children were receiving Aid to Dependent Children. There had recently been a great public outcry against these "immoral" women, who were supposed to be having babies just to get more welfare money, and Mrs. Gould thought it would be interesting to find out what they were really like. So did I.

I talked to twenty mothers of eighty-three illegitimate children and to dozens of welfare directors and social workers in New York, Illinois, Kansas, Colorado, and California. I learned that each of the women was very much an individual, that each had had a lifetime of trouble, that every one of them would far rather be married than be on welfare, that they loved their children and cared for them as best they could, and that more than anything else, they needed compassion. I came back with a heavy heart, because I knew that the story I felt compelled to write would be sympathetic and would also involve my own opinions—and therefore that I would not be allowed to write it.

Fate, for once, was kind. On March 5 the entire editorial staff was summoned to the office of Beatrice Gould to hear the news that an era which had lasted for twenty-seven years was ending; the Goulds had resigned. There were mixed emotions all over the office that day: shock, tears on the part of some of the younger girls who looked upon Bruce Gould as a father figure, and outright rejoicing.

Our new editor was Curtiss Anderson, who had been Philadelphia managing editor for the past year. Curt was tall, red-haired, and in his mid-thirties. He was intelligent, full of ideas for modernizing the magazine, and he possessed a lively social conscience. When I asked him how he wanted the illegitimate children story written he said, "Write it your own way." I did, and it ran in the September issue, over the protests of several of the old-time editors. The next year it won a $500 Sidney Hillman Foundation award for the best magazine article on social problems published in 1962.

Everything seemed to happen that March of 1962. Mother had

slipped so far during my absence—and Lem's facial tic was so pronounced—that it was imperative to put her in a nursing home. On March 9, with the approval of all her relatives, I took her to a nearby residence home where she would have care and companionship, but be relatively free of the physical constraints she could not bear. She telephoned every night, begging to be brought home, she wrote us streams of heart-wrenching letters, but our house was peaceful and Lem's tic disappeared.

On March 17, Rod finally moved into his apartment. And on March 30 Curt Anderson fired half the editorial staff and invited the rest of us to move with the office to New York. In mid-April Rod and I went house-hunting. Rod would retire in a year, at just about the time we could marry. He planned to work on a history of the writing of the Japanese constitution, which he could do anywhere, and I now wished to remain on the staff of the *Journal*; all this meant that we should live within commuting distance of New York. Rod thought both the Sneden's houses too small, for Lem was now a big, exuberant, boisterous, noisy eleven-year-old, and needed space; also Rod longed to return to New England. The house we fell in love with was on Greens Farms Road in Westport, Connecticut, on two acres of land, and surrounded by old apple trees, peaches, plums, raspberries, white lilacs, tall sycamore trees, and rambling roses. The main part of the house dated from 1718, most of the floor boards were a foot wide, and there was a huge Dutch oven fireplace (complete with swinging crane and kettle), and another fireplace in one of the four upstairs bedrooms.

Judy Wallace, one of the few nice real-estate agents I've ever met, took us back to her office after we had seen the house. The owner was asking $45,000 and Rod and I had agreed that our top price (pooling our money) would have to be $40,000. There seemed little chance that the owner would accept, but Judy said it was at least worth a try, dialed his number, and talked. When she hung up she was smiling. "He accepts," she said. The closing was set for July 16, and triumphantly Rod and I went out and celebrated with a three-martini lunch at a Chinese joint on Main Street. My God, but how happy we were!

. . .

It was a wild three months. Lem was graduated from his beloved School in Rose Valley at the end of sixth grade, and after that moped in the basement with his electric trains. I put the Wallingford house up for sale, but it remained unsold for several months. Gladys refused to move to Connecticut. I started commuting between Philadelphia and New York and suffered culture shock when I encountered all those fashionable ladies in the *Journal*'s Radio City office. Aunt Alice, who violently resented Rod ("that man you stole from his wife," she called him, and also "that fortune hunter"), had to be pacified. But at last Rod and I went to Westport for the closing and finally took possession of the home in which we hoped the fates might give us at least ten good years together. "The quality of the light . . ." he murmured as we wandered entranced through the empty rooms. "You shall have the carriage house for your study. . . ." "And you shall have the little bedroom with the fireplace. . . ." "Oh, my dear, my dear . . ." Two days later the moving men came and packed us up and Lem and I said a somewhat tearful farewell to the place where we had not been quite as unhappy as we had thought we were, and to the neighbors who had been so good to Mother and me. Then Rod and Lem and I, two cats, and three goldfish set off in two separate cars and headed north and into the future.

Remembering the rest of that summer, I think of sand and sun and gentle surf on Burying Hill Beach, and of Rod's great joy in being near the water and seeing red-winged blackbirds again. I think of our excitement when Lem and I went to meet his train from Washington. I think of the helpful new housekeeper I found, and of Lem going off happily to day camp. And I remember the five swans I saw every morning on Compo Inlet, as my commuting train took me to Manhattan. I think of my great happiness in Rod's mature companionship on frequent weekends and my knowledge that it would soon become permanent. But I remember, too, that there were explosions between Rod and Lem, for Rod, who was sixty, weary, and longing for peace, sometimes applied a kind of quarterdeck discipline which I felt to be over-harsh; often, hearing Lem weeping in his room at night, I would slip in and quietly offer comfort.

In September Lem entered public school for the first time. In contrast to Rose Valley where there had been only twelve in his class, there were ten divisions of the three hundred children in seventh grade. Lem was in the most advanced section, but he settled down to work conscientiously and actually seemed to enjoy it. Life went on. I found a pleasant nursing home in nearby Stamford and brought my mother there; she seemed more peaceful then, so that I felt slightly less guilty about her incarceration.

In the office, things were chaotic. There were new department heads, all of whom seemed to be flustered by their responsibilities. There were more firings, and now there were only three writers left on the staff instead of the previous dozen or more. There was a new publisher, a gross, bewildered man who took me to lunch with Betty Hannah Hoffman, another writer and a very good one. "What does a writer *do?*" he asked us in what seemed honest puzzlement. We tried to explain, but he looked as if we were making it all up. Two weeks later, in mid-November, Curt Anderson also took us to lunch. Over the martinis, the fillet of sole, and the watercress salads, he very gently explained that the publisher had decided the magazine no longer needed writers on the office staff. Henceforth, he said, we were to work at home, without a regular salary but with his personal guarantee of six stories a year, at $2500 each. Also, we would continue on the masthead with the title of "Contributing Editor." He made it all sound so reasonable that it took awhile for the news to penetrate, but as we stood outside waiting for Curt to retrieve his coat I said, "Hey, Betty, you know what? I think we're *fired!*" She agreed.

At home I tried not to panic each time I thought of the $112 a week for the nursing home and the $55 a week for the housekeeper, and tried to grasp again the essence of that talisman word of my life, "courage." On November 30 I walked out of the *Journal* offices for the last time and felt nothing but joy. The next morning I drove down to the station in my nightgown and coat, and chortled as I waved good-by to the commuters' train.

I had great plans for free-lancing, but until they resulted in some solid money, it was necessary to bring my mother home. It seemed a grim decision, but Mother was so euphoric about being back with what she called her "tribe" that for a long time she behaved very reasonably.

Curt Anderson kept his word about assignments. In January 1963 he told me he wanted me to do a story about a Peace Corps team, and thought it should be located somewhere in South America. I did some preliminary research in Washington, and on February 1 flew off to Lima, Peru. ("Good-by, Mother, I love you immensely," Lem said as I left, careful not to be too slurpy.)

From Lima I flew to Cuzco, which is 11,000 feet high in the spectacular Andes. From Cuzco, the area Peace Corps director drove me in a jeep over wild dirt roads, most of them skirting the brink of cloud-filled chasms, to the little Indian town of Calca. I lived there for two weeks with two young volunteers named Geraldine Keeley and Mary Ellen Patterson, sharing their lives so completely that I came to feel that I, too, was a member of the Corps. I slept on a mattress in one of the bare rooms of the adobe compound that was their home. I ate guinea pig cooked with licorice. I learned to speak some Quechua, and I washed my hair with Mary Ellen at the village fountain. I shared Gerry and Mary Ellen's anger at the upper-class Spanish-descended Peruvians' contempt toward the impoverished Inca-descended Indians, and, as they did, I came to love the Indians. I helped the girls carry loads of flour to the baker who made the bread for the school-lunch program the girls had started. I danced with solemn six-year-old Claudamiro to a modern record of ancient Inca music. And on weekends I sat with the girls and visiting members of other teams, drinking Peruvian beer and listening to the young people talk of their despair at the poverty of the Indians and their conviction that helping even a few people was something worth doing.

"We're happier than we have ever been in our lives," the girls said, and I realized that I was, too—or at least happier than I had been for many years. I was astonished at this discovery, and at the degree of my identification with the volunteers. Always before I had felt detached from any "movement," unable to participate because I must stand apart and observe. I could sympathize, but I have always found it hard to act, or to believe, even if I acted, that anything I did could in any way change the world's misery. But this had been an extraordinarily direct experience and my response was to wonder whether, when Lem went to college, I could join the Peace Corps.

On the way home I stopped for a few days in Cuzco, the old capital of the Inca civilization, found it full of fascination and excitement, and marveled with the other tourists at the Inca stone-cutters who had mortised great blocks of rock with such incredible precision. Then I went to Machu Picchu, wandered in the rain among the gray ruins of that stupendous mountaintop Inca city, looked at the boiling clouds in the valleys below and the still higher mountain peaks looming above, and knew that I had never seen and would never again see any place in the world more impressive, more awesome. All in all, I think that was the best single assignment I ever had.

. . .

On March 17, 1963, three weeks after I had returned home, Rod was free at last. And on March 30, in the presence of a few of Rod's relatives and of my close friends, we were married in the Victorian front parlor of our home by a Unitarian minister. In mid-April, we flew off to the Virgin Islands to stay at the lovely Caneel Bay Plantation on Saint John, something we could only afford to do because the hotel's publicity office generously gave us press rates. For two weeks Rod and I enjoyed it all, walked, swam, drank, ate, made love, and sat on the balcony overlooking the bay late into the evening, talking of Japan, of Tibet, of cultural differences between nations and peoples, and of all the other thousand things which interested us. And we marveled at the joy of true companionship, which had no further need of interruption.

One day, as we walked through one of the public verandas, I noticed a copy of the second section of *The New York Times* lying on a table. I was about to pass it by when I did a double take at a photograph of Curt Anderson. The paper was that of the day before and the story which accompanied the picture said that Curt had resigned because of a fight over editorial control with the publisher. The new editor was someone of whom I had never heard. I did not realize, at first, what this change would mean, for I assumed that my arrangement with Curt would be transferred to a similar one with the new man. What it did mean was that my name was eliminated from the masthead and that I never heard from the magazine again. An enthusiastic story I had written about Senator Birch Bayh of Indiana and his wife, Marvella, never appeared. The Peace Corps story, which Curt had thought "great," was pulled out of the July issue and in its place they ran a feature on Doris Day.

. . .

I would like so very much to write: "So we came home and lived happily ever afterward." But I cannot, for we didn't. Does anyone, ever? Euripides never wrote truer words than: "That mortal is a fool who, prospering, thinks his life has any strong foundation; since our fortune's course of action is the reeling way a madman takes, and no one person is happy all the time." (Richard Lattimore translation.)

The trouble that summer was that while there was harmony between any one of the others and me when we were alone together, there were usually cat-and-dog fights if either or both of the others appeared, and I was perpetually exhausted by the effort to adjudicate, scold, and maintain some shreds of peace.

Mother had now decided that Rod had stolen all her money and that he opened her mail and took checks from the envelopes. Consequently, she hissed and spat at him whenever she came upon him, exactly like a furious kitten. She had a downstairs back bedroom with a telephone and an intercom arrangement to our upstairs bedroom in case of need; she could not be taught how to use it and at night, lonely and bewildered, she would tap with her cane around the dark downstairs, calling "Margaret, Margaret, where are you?" When I woke and went down to her she would weep that her sins were scarlet and that God would never forgive her.

Lem, too, was a problem. Sometime near the end of the Wallingford years he had begun withdrawing from his own generation, and now the withdrawal seemed complete. True, he was a star pitcher with his Little League baseball team, and I will never forget my excitement and pride (or his) when he hit a grand-slam homer, bringing in four runs for his team and winning a game which they had believed lost. But he seemed to make no friends on the team or at school, and when I tried to talk to him about it, all he would say was: "The only things Westport kids talk about is how drunk their parents were the night before and how many sports cars they own." When school ended he was completely at loose ends, refusing to go to camp, reading comics and watching television, putting on weight, bored, waiting for us to take him bowling or swimming, and newly jealous of every moment I spent alone with Rod.

Rod was an even worse problem. He suffered from "retirement syndrome," I see now, and he was deeply discouraged by his failure to get a foundation grant for his Japan book. He had recently been through a destructive marriage and two years of cliff-hangers, his arthritis was hurting, and he was beginning to feel his sixty-one years; he needed peace and the long hours of quiet comfort which only I seemed able to give him. Instead, he was confronted by a burgeoning twelve-year-old male who constantly vied for my attention.

There was one happy day I remember, when we three drove up to Mystic to see the sailing ship Rod's grandfather had captained. On the way back, Lem exclaimed: "Isn't it *wonderful* to be a family!" If Rod had been able to do this sort of thing more often, to include Lem in our other expeditions, there would have been less friction. But he wasn't; his general reaction to the situation was to begin drinking at ten in the morning, to retreat all day to his studio in the converted carriage house behind the garage, and—when I tried to spread myself between the three of them—to accuse me of "utter and complete desertion."

Janet Rioch had moved to Baltimore, and so in my desperation I talked to a Westport psychiatrist. His advice was that I devote myself to my husband, "even if you have to neglect your son." I tried to do this, but I couldn't keep it up, for Lem had been too long entwined in the deepest part of my heart for any serious abandonment to be possible. Besides, the advice was wrong and I knew it, for I had come to realize that Rod's assertion, "I know how to raise boys, by God!" was based more on fantasy than reality, for the two sons of his first marriage were still very young when it was dissolved.

Our solution was to send Lem in September to a boarding school in Darien, which was close enough for him to come home on most weekends. It was coed and "progressive," so it reminded him of Rose Valley and he was not too unhappy. After his departure, Rod and I found peace and communion again. During the weekend following President Kennedy's assassination we were especially close, for we spent three days and nights watching television, holding hands, and weeping. When it was over we looked at each other and realized that we had both aged, as had Walter Cronkite.

We had hoped to begin new lives in Westport, working on books and reaching out to make new friends, but my mother made this difficult. Her senility was so far advanced that she needed to be dressed and undressed every day and could not be left safely alone in the house. There were bowel explosions on carpets and walls which no housekeeper could be expected to clean up, and daily attacks of terror which only my companionship could comfort. I had a contract for a book about two young Maryland blacks who had been unjustly convicted of rape, but after a week of researching it down there, I realized that the need for me at home was so desperate that I would have to give up doing the book, and also postpone the book on my mother's feminist generation, for which I also had a contract.

The doctor was adamant in his belief that she be placed again in a nursing home. By this time we were living on capital and unable to afford it, but I spent April 1964 visiting homes and early in May finally found a reasonably good one in nearby Fairfield. I did not tell her she was going, but the night before I was to take her there I felt deeply moved at the thought that this was the last night of our lives when we would sleep under the same roof. I gave her a bath, put her nightgown on, lifted her into bed, and smoothed the sheets and blanket. Then, feeling some obscure need for her blessing, I knelt beside her.

"You have been such a wonderful mother," I said.

"My darling," she answered, laughing gently, "I always think of *you* as Mother."

And so they ended, the years, the years that numbered almost half a century.

. . .

In February Mother's tenant had moved out of the old house in Sneden's. Late that month Rod and I went down to attend to it and snowbound for a day and night felt the peace which is always there enfold us. Together, then, we faced the fact that we could not afford to continue mortgage payments in Westport, particularly since in a fit of sentimental insanity we had bought the huge barn on the hill above the house. The year before, weary of the problems of absentee landlordship, needing money, and thinking I would never return to Sneden's, I had sold "Margaret's House." But the old house could be made livable again, we agreed happily.

In mid-May I drove the forty-five miles to Sneden's to spend the day alone at the house. It was a day of agonized strangeness, filled with the pitching sense of time past, present, and future all swirled together so that I became dazed as I tried to grope for reality. Mother's friend Irene Stillman had lived in the house like a gentle little ghost, using only three downstairs rooms and insisting that everything be left as Mother had left it. As my mother had taken no real interest in the place since my father died twenty-one years before, the whole house was preserved in the amber of time past, the time when my father was alive, the time when I was a child, a girl, a young woman.

I sat at my father's desk in his library, listening to the silence and trying to decide whether the house breathed or did not breathe. Against one wall, shelves were filled with hundreds of the books they had read, draped with cobwebs now. Yet vividly I saw my father in the room, pounding out his newspaper column, reaching up to check something in *The Golden Bough,*or turning eagerly from the typewriter to listen to me as I shared my discovery of Stephen Spender with him. He was almost palpable in that dusty room. Truly, love makes the passage of time meaningless.

So it was in the rest of the house. In the kitchen my mother stirred a great cauldron of spiced grapes, and once again I smelled the grapes, the cinnamon, the cloves. In the dining room, she played the piano, while behind her my father rocked from foot to foot as they sang, "The temple bells are ring-ing-ing . . . the young green corn is spring-ing-ing." In the living room, we three played rummy on a hot August night, my mother and I in white cotton nightgowns, my father in blue pajamas, and laughed together and drank ginger ale with a dollop of vanilla ice cream. The fireplace brass and the Victorian furniture shone with polish, and a soft night wind blew through the open windows, ruffled the fresh white curtains, and spread the fragrance of the flowers on the table, the phlox, the snow-white phlox. . . .

I sat down on a broken couch, one of its legs shored up with books, and wrenchingly returned to the present. The curtains were yellowed, tattered, and dirty. The wallpaper hung in strips. The ceiling was cracked. The fireplace no longer worked. The woodwork was the color of old tobacco stains. The gray velvet carpet, of which my mother had been so proud, was crisscrossed by threadbare paths.

The whole house was like that—full of ghosts and the bitter realization that the home we had loved so dearly for so many years was now a cluttered ruin. Somehow, on my occasional visits to Mrs. Stillman I had failed to notice what was happening; now I saw that every wall needed plastering, painting, or wallpaper, that the ceilings were falling down, mouse holes were plugged with steel wool, the closets and bureaus were stuffed with the detritus of the past. Outdoors was just as bad. Except for the lawn, the meadow, and the grape arbor, which had been regularly mowed and pruned, all else was jungle. The lesson was obvious: cut or be overwhelmed, crowded and sunless, die.

I went back to Westport full of determination to make the little house live again, and Rod and I agreed that we would spend the summer with Lem at Sneden's, putting the house into shape.

That was a beautiful May, that last May with Rod in Westport. With Mother gone and Lem still in boarding school we were alone together there, virtually for the first time, free of strain and tension, full of love and harmony. And for the first time I felt that we were achieving the good marriage which Sir Philip Sidney so beautifully describes: "A happy couple, he joying in her, she joying in herself, but in herself because she enjoyed him; both increased their riches by giving to each other, and making one life double because they made a double life one."

Even when Lem came home from school—still friendless, but loaded with honors—peace prevailed. Lem agreed with us that his overly progressive school was not right for him, and we began to look for another; eventually we chose Hackley, a somewhat more conventional school for boys in Tarrytown, New York, which was only a short drive across the Tappan Zee Bridge from Sneden's.

Then Rod fell ill. He went for tests, and took to his bed while we waited for results. They were inconclusive, and he went for more. The atmosphere became heavy with gloom, and Lem's vitality seemed an increasing challenge to Rod's waning health. Rod suggested that Lem and I go ahead with the Sneden's plan and insisted that our current housekeeper could perfectly well take care of his own needs. I didn't believe that Rod was seriously sick and I was desperate to keep my two men from driving each other crazy, so I agreed.

Lem and I spent most of that summer of 1964 at Sneden's, going back to Westport on weekends. We spackled and painted, pruned and hammered. We walked down the old road to the river and fished from the banks. We read *Oliver Twist* aloud in the evenings. He began cutting lawns and earned $18 a week. I worried at his lack of companionship, and he said firmly, "This is my life, and I accept it." But I had him take tennis lessons and after that he was at least with other boys on the court. September came, and he went off to Hackley, dutifully if not happily.

The doctors decided that Rod had a hiatal hernia, and sent him to Grace New Haven Hospital for a week's observation. It was discovered that he had a cyst on the lower intestine; the surgeon decided to operate on both conditions on the same occasion and the operation was scheduled for October 14.

The three weeks before the operation were an interminable nightmare, for Rod was convinced he was going to die. He drank heavily, and at night threw himself on his knees and prayed. "I don't want to leave you," he would sob. And when Lem came home for a weekend, Rod glared at us both at the dinner table, threw down his fork, and shouted, "I'll be dead in two weeks!" I felt that I had only stoicism to offer him, but I tried to be the mother-comforter he wanted because he was in psychic torment —and also, I truly loved him.

A week before the operation, Pat and Bob Lubar drove us to New Hamsphire, to spend a few days in an old farmhouse which had been loaned to them. One day Rod stayed alone in the house while we three went for a drive; after we came back, he told me he had found great peace "sitting by the small fire and looking at the sunlight on the yellow maples outside the windows." He did indeed seem at peace with himself at last, and I rejoiced for him. We held hands all the way home.

On the 13th I drove him the thirty miles to the hospital. "The only thing that worries me now," he said, "is that you and the boy are so alone." The house was very silent that night, and the only phone call was from Lem. "I thought I would like to console you," he told me.

The next day they operated, and in the afternoon the surgeon (who had told me to wait at home) called to say all was well. The following day was the day that Khrushchev was ousted as Premier of the Soviet Union, the day the Jenkins scandal erupted in Washington, the day the Labour Party won in England, and the day the Cardinals won the World Series 7–5. It was also the day that I found Rod reading *The New York Times* and listening to the World Series. The doctor told me his recovery was "phenomenal."

But during the next week Rod developed pneumonia, an infection of the left lung, abdominal distension, and septicemia of what the doctors called "the upper wound." On the 22nd, they operated again on the upper wound. Rod's elder son, Christopher, a Boston architect, drove down to be with me. The next day Rod's younger son—always called Pokey—arrived. So did Lem. And so did my cousin Kay's daughter, Sara Caldwell, a social worker who had recently moved to New York. After many days of driving sixty miles a day, spending six hours at the hospital, and returning to an empty house, it was good to have "family" there, even for only a day or so.

The next nine days were again a seesaw between better and worse, for it seemed impossible to lower Rod's temperature for very long. October 31 was a Saturday, and Lem was home for Halloween. We were offering cookies to swirls of small goblins and ghosts when the surgeon called to say that Rod's left lung had collapsed, and that he had developed "some pneumonia" and was worse. The next morning, when Lem and I arrived at the hospital, we were met at the elevator doors by Rod's doctors, who had been waiting for us. They took us into the small reception room and told us bluntly that there was now little chance of saving Rod's life. As well as the collapsed lung and pneumonia, blood clots had developed in his legs. But worst of all was what seemed to be an abscess at the site of the "lower wound," which was poisoning his entire system. They brought in another surgeon for a consultation, and he agreed with them that the only slight chance for survival would be an immediate operation on the abscess. Rod would surely die without it, they told us, and he might die with it, possibly on the operating table. We would have to decide, and very quickly. They left us alone and Lem and I looked at each other. "There's nothing else to do," he said. "No, nothing," I agreed.

I told the doctors our decision and they began preparations for an immediate operation. When we were allowed to, Lem and I went in to see Rod. He was weak but conscious, and he knew what was ahead. He looked at Lem, who stood at the left side of his bed, and whispered, "Take care of your mother." Lem said, "I will." Then Rod turned to look at me, and saw the tears in my eyes which always before I had managed to conceal. He asked for a linen handkerchief, and when I found one in a drawer and gave it to him he smiled and handed it back to me. I kissed him, and then he was wheeled away to surgery.

I telephoned Christopher, and Rod's sister Emily, whom we both loved. Then Lem and I went into a convulsion of grief for which I could find no comfort except the hospital chapel. And there we both did find a kind of peace in the thought that there should be only one true time for mourning, and that should not be while there was even a flicker of hope left. Neither of us had ever practiced any conventional religion, but we read aloud the Episcopal prayers for the sick, and prayed silently. After that we went out and had hamburgers with onions and were strong.

By the time we came back to the hospital, Emily was there. "He's back in his room," she said. "He's alive." Lem said later that of all the events of that day the one thing he remembered most vividly was the expression on my face when I heard Emily's words.

I was allowed to see Rod. He was unconscious and looked dreadful. Christopher arrived. The doctor told us the end might come at any moment, and also that he had performed a heart massage during the operation. We four huddled at the end of the hall, and waited. Suddenly a young resident who might have won an Olympics sprint event came dashing down the hall, followed by what seemed like a hundred nurses, doctors, interns, and odd-looking machines on wheels. They all disappeared into Rod's room. After an eternity, the surgeon came and told us that Rod had stopped breathing but that they had caught him just in time and that he was now attached to a machine which would do his breathing for him until his body could take over again. He said he thought we should go home and wait, so we did.

We were all very Anglo-Saxon and controlled that evening, and only jumped a bit convulsively whenever the phone rang. Lem even drew me into a game of poker dice, and thus distracted me for an hour; only later did I realize that it was an intentional distraction on his part. At dawn I awoke, watched the sunrise, heard Rod's wind-bell ringing in the apple grove, and knew that he had lived through the night. A few hours later Christopher, Lem, and I walked into his room and found him conscious, breathing quietly on the machine, his blue eyes shining.

"Well, darling, you've won your fight," I said. He had had a tracheotomy, and he could not speak until the nurse showed me how to hold my finger over the little metal circle on his throat. (Odd, how even the most squeamish of us becomes accustomed to the horrors of surgery when we love the patient.)

"Of course I've won," he said proudly.

"The doctors say you have the constitution of an ox," I told him.

"Of a whale," he insisted.

All week he improved, and I was convinced that a miracle had taken place. Lem went back to school, but came home on Saturday, November 7, to celebrate his fourteenth birthday with me. We drove up to New Haven to see Rod, and found him gently teasing the nurses, who all adored him. Then we drove home, and I cooked a special birthday dinner and gave Lem his presents. We were sitting by the fire, reading Sherlock Holmes aloud, when the phone rang.

"I'm sorry," said Rod's surgeon. "But his heart just couldn't take all that he had been through."

. . .

There was, of course, the usual bustle that follows a death. Authorization for autopsy and cremation. Friends. Neighbors. Relatives. Tranquilizers. Obituaries. Food brought in. Kindliness. Clothes disposed of. The simple Unitarian service in Barnstable, and tears shared with Christopher and with Rod's ninety-two-year-old mother. The drive home with Lem, Helen Everitt, and my cousin Sara. Then Lem and I were alone.

"It's as if you had a wonderful present, and suddenly that present was snatched away from you," Lem said. "After all those years, at last we had a *family*."

We sat together on the edge of a couch, trying to be brave. But then Lem put his head in his hands and sobbed. "How can we go on?" he cried. I put my arm around his shoulders and I, too, wept at last.

"I don't know," I said finally. "But we must find a way. We can. We *will*."

❧18❧

Grief does not pass; one only learns to endure it, as one would a physical affliction. It was not my own mourning which preoccupied me that bitter winter, but Lem's profound reaction to Rod's death. Throughout the whole ordeal he had been strong, supportive, and infinitely loving. A few days after we returned from Barnstable, I said I wished more people had sent flowers because I found them consoling; that afternoon he bicycled off to his savings bank, withdrew some of his lawn-cutting money, and arranged with a nearby florist to deliver to me a great arrangement of copper and gold chrysanthemums. Daily, in many ways, he showed his love and concern.

But he would not return to school. Seven times he said he would go, and seven times that November I drove him to Tarrytown, but each time at the foot of the steep hill which leads up to the school he would begin to cry and to insist that he could not go back just yet. Christopher, whom Lem much admired, came down from Boston and tried to help. Emily came. Peter Grey held long, urgent telephone conversations from Sneden's. Eric wrote letters of stern admonition. Nothing worked.

The eighth time, Lem promised to go if I drove him there alone, and we actually got halfway up the hill before he began to sob. His sobs grew wilder, and suddenly he grabbed the door handle and started to open the door. "I'm going to kill myself!" he shouted. I jammed on the brakes and stopped the car at the edge of a cliff, with Lem's door on the outer side. "No you're not," I said, trying to sound calm and authoritative and to keep my voice from trembling. "Close the door," I ordered. He did, but he kept on crying hysterically. "Why do grownups hate their children so much they have to send them away to school?" he sobbed.

After a while I drove the car very slowly up to the parking lot below the school. I knew that I couldn't handle the situation alone any more, so I left Lem huddled in the darkness of the car and went up to the school office to talk to the vice-principal and the guidance counselor. They were wise and they knew what to do. The guidance counselor went out and talked to Lem for an hour in the car, and when he came back he advised immediate psychiatric help, that same night. They made an appointment with Dr. Abraham Chaplan, the school psychiatrist, and we drove straight to Manhattan to see him. Luckily, Lem was intelligent enough to realize he did indeed need help, and he made no objection. I will never forget that first of so many anguished hours that I sat in the gray-walled, dimly lit waiting room with its hideous bronze bust of Sigmund Freud.

Lem's talks with Dr. Chaplan were effective enough so that he went back to school on a day basis for the three weeks before Christmas. We moved temporarily, with the two cats, to Sneden's, and I drove him back and forth every day. Lem applied himself to his studies and just before school closed for the holidays he passed all his subjects, despite the fact that he had missed three weeks in November. He promised to go back on a boarding basis after the new year.

Except for my Uncle Elliott (my mother's only brother, who lived in Virginia), we wouldn't have had any Christmas, I guess. I felt so beaten down by life at that point that the thought of putting up all the old decorations and playing the familiar carols was more than I could bear. I must have conveyed this in a letter to my uncle, for he sent me a quotation from Albert Schweitzer which profoundly affected me and my behavior during that long, grim winter. It went something like this: "Example is not just one important element in the raising of a child, it is the *only* important element." And so, to demonstrate to Lem that we must celebrate life even in the face of death, Christmas was accomplished in all the lovely old ways.

But just the same, during the holidays Lem went into some kind of deeper tailspin and adamantly refused to return to school, even on a day basis. Nor would he go back to the Westport school, which he had so hated. He might go to the "right" school, he said, but he could not say what the right school might be. Dr. Chaplan, whom Lem was seeing two or three times a week, maintained that he was a boy who could not be pressured and must be left to come to his own decisions. By this time, relatives and friends were screaming at me to throw him in jail or at least military school, and when I did not do so they one by one retreated into a silence of disapproval and Lem and I were left alone.

. . .

Another cause for anguish was my discovery, shortly after Rod's death, that we were only a few thousand dollars away from bankruptcy. When Rod and I were married, we agreed that he would handle all the finances; I felt that perhaps my financial independence had harmed my first marriage and thought that it would be a fine change to be dependent on my husband. I knew vaguely that he had some stocks and that he received a government annuity every month, but that was all I knew. Shortly after we returned from the memorial service, I began going through his papers in the studio where he worked. First, I discovered a whole drawerful of unpaid bills, which he had evidently been too upset to cope with in the months before his operation. Then I found he had sold all his stocks; that for a year we had been paying more than half our monthly expenses from capital, and that it was nearly all gone. I didn't even know if he carried life insurance, and going through his papers I did not find anything I could recognize as a policy. Mother's nursing home, Lem's psychiatry and orthodonture, and the mortgage payments, I discovered, were running well over $1000 a month, and all that was coming in was the $100 Eric contributed to Lem's support. I knew I would eventually receive a portion of Rod's annuity, for I had filled in sheaves of government forms and turned them over to our lawyers, but I had no idea how much it would be or when it would begin.

All that lonely January and February, when I wasn't worrying about Lem I was worrying about money. I began waking at four every morning, staring for hours into the bleak dawn, smoking too many cigarettes, and going round and round in the trap of my mind. If we could only sell the house! But it had been on the market for more than six months and it hadn't sold . . . the agents said it looked shabby and neglected . . . but it would cost

money to fix it up. If I could find a cheaper nursing home . . .
but I had looked at six others and they were unbearable and
some were even more expensive. If I could get a job . . . but how
could I leave Lem alone all day, when even now I was scared to
leave him for a few hours to go to lunch with an editor? It had
been more than two months since he threatened to kill himself
. . . but still, there were so many articles in the papers about
teen-age suicides! The Lippincott deadline for the book about
Mother's radical days had passed, but I hadn't been able to work
on it for months.

Housework was a third major concern. We said good-by to the
maid, of course, as soon as I discovered our situation, and in my
late forties I began learning the routines that most women learn
at twenty. I had never operated a washing machine or a vacuum
cleaner, never cleaned floors or washed windows. "OH SHIT!" I
would scream as another machine bit me, knocked me down,
chewed a thumb, and broke a rare Chinese vase. And then I
would look around guiltily, hoping Lem hadn't heard me, for in
my old-fashioned way I had taught him that this and certain
other four-letter words were in common use among men but were
never used by a gentleman in the presence of ladies. And untan-
gling myself painfully from the coils of the vacuum cleaner I
would whisper again very softly, "Oh shit!"

Yet cleaning had to be done daily, for the real-estate agents
said the house must always be spotless and shining, and potential
buyers were likely to arrive at any time of day or night. Lem,
somewhat to my surprise, was an enormous help in these tasks,
and he often worked with me till midnight, polishing floors and
cleaning windows. Yet week after week the buyers came, admired
the house as if it were a museum, and went away forever. And so,
in a trance of terror, I watched the dollars in the savings account
whirl away with the swiftness of the last oak leaves in a winter
storm.

Just at a time when it seemed to me that everyone I knew was
telling me that Lem was insane, my old college friend Margaret
Pohe came to stay for a few days. "Don't worry about Lem," she
said when she left. "He's a wonderful kid. He's going to be fine." I
went to bed hugging her words to my heart as if they had been a
goosedown pillow. A young Indian friend, Raghavan, said the
same thing after a visit of several days, and his words were cool-

ing ointment on my wounds. Dear Raghavan, an impecunious journalist with thin wrists and frayed cuffs and collars, was touring the country on a grant which allowed him a per diem of $6 a day—but "Dear Meg," he said as he was leaving, "I am hearing that you are having troubles about money. If one hundred dollars would help you I could give it." I declined the offer, but the fact that he made it brought tears to my eyes.

One cold gray afternoon in late February I sorted the mail in the kitchen, and found it the usual junk. One long white envelope bore the return address of an insurance company. I thought it an advertisement and almost threw it away, but in idle curiosity I opened it. Inside, made out to me, was a check for $18,000—Rod's life insurance. I stared at the check for an incredulous moment, then crumpled onto a kitchen chair, sobbing with relief almost as deeply as I had cried a few months earlier with grief.

The money couldn't solve everything, of course. It couldn't bring back Rod or get Lem to go to school again, or make my twice-weekly visits to Mother any less painful. But it gave me time to breathe, and once again I began to sleep through the night.

The patient Hackley authorities had been so impressed with Lem's potential that they had given him until the end of spring vacation—Monday, March 29—to return. Saturday came, and he had still not made up his mind. We drove the fifty-mile trip to New York to see Dr. Chaplan. Sunday came, once more we saw Dr. Chaplan, and we were still cliff-hanging. Dr. Chaplan insisted there should be no pressure. Lem implied that if I wept and went into hysterics he would go. I refused to do this. Monday morning he was no longer a student anywhere, with a psychiatric excuse from Dr. Chaplan for his truancy.

Up to this point I had been depressed, but perfectly strong and healthy and able to drive the hundreds of miles a month which had been required of me. But gradually I had begun to feel pain in my lower back and in that violently emotional first week of April I could not move without severe agony. The doctor said it was an inflamed sacroiliac, but I know now that it was psychosomatic as well as physical. A New York telephone call told me that our beloved family friend Lucile Swan was dying of cancer. A California phone call said that Jim Caldwell, the "cousin" I had loved so deeply all my life, was hospitalized with a second heart attack. Lem and I visited a number of impossible and appallingly expensive tutoring schools. On Sunday, a call came saying that Jim had died; I wept most of the day. On Monday, my Mother fell and broke her hip and was taken to the Norwalk Hospital, where we visited her. On Tuesday, I saw her twice on my way to and from Hackley, where I sadly cleared out Lem's room. On Wednesday, she was operated on; I saw her again and found she was recovering. On Thursday, my back was so bad that I was unable to get out of bed and Lem brought me breakfast, with flowers on the tray. Friday, I was completely unable to move.

That morning a book arrived from Berta and Elmer Hader, who in their seventies were still vigorous and healthy. It was called *Strong Medicine*, it was written by their own physician, Dr. Blake F. Donaldson, and it made me well again. Get out of that bed and *move*, ordered the stern old Scotsman. Even if it's agony and you can't get your hands below your knees, try to touch the floor without bending your knees—thirty times, night and morning. And take a fast walk before breakfast, working up from one minute (if that's all you can stand) to half an hour. On Saturday, feeling I had nothing much to lose, I began painfully following his advice. On Sunday, my back felt much better. On Monday and Tuesday, Lem and I walked for half an hour along the shore.

The morning walks became part of our routine, and they were as good for Lem as they were for me. We studied birds and trees, marsh grasses and wild flowers. We learned poems and chanted them as we marched along. I taught him Elizabethan rounds and we sang in time to the rhythm of our feet. Sometimes we drove to unfamiliar Connecticut towns and studied the architecture and the historical signs as we walked along the quiet streets. As Lem grew healthier in mind and body his love of sports returned, and he became an enthusiastic golfer. He took tennis lessons at a nearby court, and began to lose weight. He studied the stock market, read *The Wall Street Journal,* and made some cautious investments with his lawn-cutting money. He even made a friend of his own age—another fatherless boy who was having school trouble—and the two spent many hours working on the electric trains in the basement. Free of his interruptions, I managed to finish an article for *McCall's* on the trials of widowhood.

But there were more deaths in May. On May 2, Lucile Swan,

who had shed her serene and sheltering love over me for all of my life, died in New York. And on May 26, Aunt Alice, after a week of round-the-clock nursing, died of pneumonia at her home in Radnor. After the interment of the ashes in the beautiful old graveyard of Saint David's Episcopal Church, I, as her principal heir, stayed behind with Lem to clear the house of whatever I wanted to keep. The job took a week, for Aunt Alice could have given lessons to a pack rat. Every room was filled with old shoes, pillows, and cracked vases and there were suitcases, files, and cardboard boxes filled with papers—invitations to tea in 1926, tickets to the 1939 New York World's Fair, carbons of letters to newspaper editors asking why General MacArthur was not invited to Yalta, and Herbert Hoover campaign literature. This litter of a lifetime had to be sorted through because old family photographs would unexpectedly emerge, or letters from great-great-grandparents—all of which I felt an obligation to preserve, as I did, too, my own recent understanding of my aunt's uncomplaining courage. I prayed that I would inherit it.

The week after we returned to Westport our house was sold, at the price I had been asking, and life moved into high gear, for we had only two months to clear out. Wallace Heath, a family friend and a great architect, had already drawn up plans for the rebuilding of the Sneden's house and now that I knew I would have the money from Aunt Alice to do it, I told him to go ahead. Irving Thomsen, the contractor, moved in with his men and every few days when I drove down to Sneden's I found a new room gutted or a chimney torn down to the ground. One day I watched as most of the broken, unrepairable furniture my mother had loved was carried out of the house by the local junkman, and felt only a twinge of sadness as the old maple bed of my girlhood, which I had later shared (on separate occasions) with two husbands and a lover, disappeared forever.

The whole process of destruction of the past and rebuilding toward the future took on an enormous symbolism. Everything I touched as I cleared out closets, attics, and upstairs rooms in Sneden's was an evocation of the past. I found a "John Peel" music box and remembered how my father smiled when he first listened to its tinkling tune on one of his October birthdays. I wound it up and amid the dust and desolation listened to it play, wondering why there had been a particular fascination with music boxes in our family, and for golden Chinese wood carvings and pieces of old wrought iron—my parents didn't deliberately collect these things but somehow just seemed to accumulate them.

My parents' touch was upon these objects, as it was on the Spanish candlesticks, the Japanese prints, the old clock from Vermont, the Käthe Kollwitz lithograph, the monastery bell, the Renaissance angel, the serene soapstone statue of Kuan Yin, goddess of mercy, and in the grape arbor the statue of Pan with his bronze pipes. Everything I now touched with my living hands forced upon me a decision, for I did not want to be weighed down by what was gone forever, but to build toward the future, Lem's and mine.

What do other people do with their families, I wondered? With memories? With the lovely acquisitions of people who are now gone? Who picks up the pieces of the past, palpable and impalpable, and brings them into the living present? "You do," said an inner voice. But for a long time I could not find the way, for the house was a treasure box, full of mysteries and surprises, and more and more I became obsessed with the personalities of the two sentient human beings who had been my parents, and the dynamic generation which had been theirs. In the bottom of the linen closet I found a ukulele with a pineapple decal and no strings. My father played the guitar, my mother the piano, and I the recorder, but I could not remember anyone ever playing a ukulele. I had thought I knew everything that had ever gone on in the house, but suddenly I felt that the silly, 1920s pineapple ukulele was almost laughing at me. Can we ever grasp all the realities of our parents?

At least 1000 books had to be weeded out. But I could not resist browsing, and leafing through *British Poets of the Nineteenth Century*, I stood bemused in the dusty sunlight, reread my mother's favorite poem, Matthew Arnold's "The Buried Life," and heard once more the slight quaver of her voice as she murmured, "Light flows our war of mocking words . . ." I kept the book. One day I found her diaries, neatly packed in a cardboard box, hidden at the far end of the attic. She had told me when I was in India that she intended to burn them, and I had assumed that she had done so. But here they were, the familiar red volumes filled with her copperplate handwriting—from 1911 through all the years to 1961 (and there were three more in Westport). Now that she was no longer the same person who had written them, now that she had gone into some other dimension of the mind, I felt morally justified in reading the pages of the past that had been present.

As I skimmed the pages covering the time of my own adolescence, I found in them the old ambivalences, the overwhelming love, the lashes of ridicule and hostility. ("Margaret irritates me, with her large awkward frame, her large, awkward dreams. Oh how I love her!") I found that at that time and place, surrounded by dirt, desolation, and memories, and utterly confused about the meaning of life, I could not yet face the hurt she still inflicted, and sought instead for references to the house.

1928: "Lem is down at the end of the meadow, cutting back the jungle. In time there will be nothing to stand between us and the jungle save one little girl-stem. . . ." And two years later: "We stood for the first time on the steps to the new library, watching the setting sun over the fields and wondering who would build on this house, after us."

My parents' function, I began to see, was to build outward from the house, while mine seemed to be to strengthen from within and to examine and preserve what was good of their past and discard what was no longer healthy or appropriate. Could these separate functions, I wondered, be symbolic of our differing generations? Theirs had been radical, opinionated, noisy, outreaching, and moving always in new directions politically and socially, even if it meant discarding the past *in toto*. In contrast, my own generation—now in middle age—seemed quiet, inward-looking, Freudian-oriented, concerned with assessing the work of our parents, and conserving that which we found to be good. And now another new generation had appeared, the young people in their twenties, and like their grandparents they were radical, outgoing, scornful of the past, and eager to discover solutions which they believed to be new. Could this be an endless cycle? An eternal swinging of time's pendulum? Maybe so, I thought morosely as I sorted through boxes of old letters and newspaper clippings, but the far more interesting, outgoing generations sure leave a hell of a mess for us dull little girl-stems to clean up!

During the final frantic week of clearing out Westport, Pat and Bob Lubar came for two days of 91-degree heat to pack dishes and pictures and to clean out the garage and attic; I wondered what saintliness I had achieved in a former incarnation to merit such friends in this life. Lem and I summoned up far more physical and emotional strength than we thought we had, but without the Lubars' help I think we both would have collapsed into screaming hysterics. We didn't, but nevertheless I am not proud when I remember how I behaved much of the time during those harried months. I drank more than I should have. I had bouts of extreme self-pity and remember one awful night when I threw myself on my father's grave, sobbing passionately. I flew into wild rages with Lem, and once, when he had mischievously locked me out of the Sneden's house, I drove my bare fist through a pane of glass in the kitchen door and was badly cut. One day Lem said, "Mother, I don't think your fits of anger are good for me." That ended them, for he had chosen his final pronoun well.

August 16, 1965, came at last, and so did the movers. Because reconstructions on the Sneden's house were far from finished, everything had to go in storage; Lem slept that night on the Sneden's sleeping porch, which hadn't been slept in for twenty-five years, surrounded by packing cases and possibly spiders. But, "Oh, Mother, we've *moved!*" he marveled. And I, about to bed down in the spare room amid a litter of Chinese screens and old suitcases, echoed his amazement, "We've *moved!*" Two days later I cleaned the Westport house (preparatory to the closing at which I would turn over the key to the new owners), relived memories of happiness and despair, and for the last time stood in Rod's studio, where his presence had always been for me particularly vivid. "Rod, what have I forgotten?" I asked aloud. Inside my head a voice spoke in his dear New England tones which sounded so much like John Kennedy: "The future. Go ahead to the future!"

That warm, summer-smelling night at Sneden's, Lem and I filled a little plastic pool in the rose garden and sat with our bare feet in the cool green water, looking at the fireflies darting over the meadow. "We're *home,*" Lem said, his voice full of wonder.

. . .

In June Lem agreed to return to school in September if we could find one he liked. I had been brainwashed by everyone I knew; they assured me that only a boarding school could cut a teen-aged boy's silver cord, so we visited several boarding institutions for boys without finding any we liked. Finally, we reached

Oakwood, a Quaker school in Poughkeepsie, and there my brain was gently rewashed by the kindly admissions officer. "Did it ever occur to you," he asked, "that boarding schools are not *right* for some boys?" Lem and I went home and talked it over. He wanted to stay home for his high-school years and God knows I dearly wanted him at home. So we went to visit Rockland Country Day School, twelve miles north of us, which several Sneden's children attended. The school had been started some six years before by a number of literate parents who were dissatisfied with the education their children were receiving in public schools, and it emphasized both the academic and the creative. The country campus and the scattered buildings were pleasant, and the boys and girls we saw looked happy. Lem responded cautiously, took the admissions examination, and passed it (according to the headmaster) "brilliantly." He was enrolled for September and agreed to "try it out for a few days."

Now it was mid-August, our house was still in chaos and would be scarcely habitable for some weeks to come. When a friend told me of a small inn near a golf course on the edge of the ocean near Ingonish, on Nova Scotia's Cape Breton, I made reservations and three days later we were on our way. We flew to Sydney, rented a car, and drove through a sparkling morning on to the Cape. The road wound along the shoulders of mountains above the sea, and, occasionally, signs pointed to small towns, most of whose names seemed to end in the Scottish word "Dhu." One sign read "Skihr Dhu," and seeing it, Lem (who had picked up a lot of my old slang) exclaimed, "Wow! Twenty-three Skihr Dhu!" We both started laughing and the more we laughed the harder we laughed; I finally had to stop the car by the side of the road because my eyes were full of the tears of laughter and released tension. It was the first time we had really laughed in many months. As we finally drove on, Lem broke the relaxed silence. "I didn't think it would really happen," he said. I knew that he meant that we would go on an idyllic vacation, but also that he would ever be happy again. It was only through these shorthand clues that I sometimes caught a glimpse of the depths his unhappiness had reached.

Cape Breton is one of the most beautiful places I have ever seen, and the inn was as charming as my friend had promised. Lem golfed all morning, and surrounded by peace and beauty I was free to mourn for Rod with a silent intensity that had not been possible in the months following his death. We ate good food, we swam, we clambered on rocks, and wandered over pink sands. One night, lying on the beach beside a bonfire, we looked up at the clear, star-pulsing sky, and over the murmur of the waves Lem suddenly recited a poem called "In the Field Forever," by Robert Wallace, which I had clipped from *The New Yorker* and pinned to my bulletin board:

Sun's a roaring dandelion, hour by hour.
Sometimes the moon's a scythe, sometimes a silver flower.
But the stars! All night long the stars are clover,
Over, and over, and over!

The nice New Jersey family which shared the bonfire with us looked at Lem in amazement, as if a fourteen-year-old boy reciting poetry was something extraordinary and a little embarrassing. But I was filled with joy, and pride, too, for I had not known that he had memorized the poem or that he could summon the self-confidence to say it aloud in front of strangers.

When we returned to Sneden's early in September, we found that nothing had been done to the house during our absence. The kitchen fireplace was still a gaping hole and there was no flooring, no stove, no refrigerator, no sink. The living-room walls were stripped to plaster and laths, the ceiling was gone, and the fireplace a jumble of bricks. The old refrigerator had been temporarily placed in the dining room, where there was just barely space to set up a card table for our meals. I had one small electric burner to cook on and dishes had to be washed in the bathroom basin. But we managed to live this way for a month, and I was proud because we not only coped with the difficulties but even had linen, flowers, and candles on the rickety dinner table.

Monday the 13th was a day of apprehension, for Lem (looking very handsome in the hated but required tie and jacket) actually went off to school in the arranged car pool. He had not promised to remain and I waited all day to hear his reaction, but when he return he was noncommittal and I did not dare to press him. The next day he went again, came home, and after dinner settled down resolutely to homework. At exactly 9:05 p.m. he looked up from his books, grinned at me, and said with light solemnity, "Mother, I hate to admit this—but I think I *like* this school." I felt within me the soft release of the breath I seemed to have been holding tightly for so many months, and I wanted to jump up and scream with exultation. But I said, "I'm so glad, darling," and went on knitting. He had lost a year, of course, and had to begin again in ninth grade. I had thought this a tragedy and it took me a while to discover that it was a fortunate loss. Lem, who was born in November, was always one of the youngest in his class at whatever school he attended and his emotional development had been slower than that of his older classmates; now, in a slightly younger age group and possessing the superiority of the earliest birthday, he finally felt comfortable.

Those first few days I discovered that I had forgotten the simple joys of a home with a schoolgoing child in it: a boy quietly working out fractions while I cooked dinner, discussions of words and ideas and books, the phone ringing with messages about car pools, ironing white broadcloth shirts for the next morning, the alarm clock set at night because now there was a serious reason for rising in the morning. How unfamiliar it all seemed, and how lovely!

Gradually the house made progress, although I lived for weeks with the whine of electric saws, surrounded by coveys of plumbers, electricians, bricklayers, plasterers, and painters. Walls and ceilings were finished, floors painted, and wallpaper appropriate to an eighteenth-century cottage bloomed freshly in living room and hall. Soft yellow kitchen appliances arrived and were installed. Men burrowed underneath the house putting in ducts for the hot-air furnace and miraculously, by the day of the first frost every room was warm. The two chimneys rose like Jack's beanstalk, and the old mantels went back in place. I watched all this with wonder at my own daring, and with fear that the special quality the house possessed might be lost, but when at last it was done and I was left alone, I walked through the rooms, smiling. It was there, it was still there, the *ambiance*, the love. But was it just in my imagination? A hangover from my girlhood? But then, why did Lem feel it? And new friends who had never been here before and who knew nothing about my parents? How did the *ambiance* come about?

One day, burrowing through a great box of Mother's papers I found all the letters my father had written her over a period of thirty years, chronologically arranged. I settled down in the grape arbor to read them, expecting only to revisit the outward aspects of America as it was during the decades he was traveling and observing. I did find a great sweep of Americana, but I also found something else which to me was far more fascinating:

The little house was cool and lovely and filled with the aroma of you two beloved ones. I fondled your clothes on the hooks and felt overwhelmingly grateful for having you. Mary, my blessed Mary, I feel rich beyond measure—somehow the little house seemed to whisper to me. I have become a firm believer in the Charcot theory of aura, and I can feel your beloved presence in everything in the little house.

Our funny little house is sound as a bell and quite clean and orderly, and full of the blessed and luminous exhalations of your garments and your pots, and pans and your typewriter.

The only goodness is being happy and the only happiness is a worshipful acquiescence to the mysteries of life, sensation, substance, function, being. Even these words with which I try to reach you are just intrusive intermediaries as I feel that I am reaching for your hand. I feel that I have had a wanton disregard for life itself in futile indignations and useless theorizing. Life is so much more important, and that means you and Margaret and our grape arbor. . . .

After many hours of reading through the years I put the final letter down. I felt dazed, not only by the letters themselves but by the discovery that he, too, had felt the aura, just as Lem and I now felt it. Was this the answer then? That simple old word in which no one seemed to believe any more? A place where *love* abideth?

. . .

On October 1 the furniture arrived from storage—the books and the lares and penates which represented the melding of Rod's life and mine and Lem's. There was an enormous job of sorting and arranging ahead, but I felt triumphant because we were all together at last and I vowed that our life in the house would be creative and loving, doing credit to the past but moving on in new directions which I could not yet foresee. Two days later, dear Berta and Elmer Hader came over for the "christening" of the new living-room fireplace. They brought champagne, and we drank to the past, the present, and the future, while Lem, our symbol of the future, lighted the first fire.

That night, as Lem was going to bed, I called up to him that there was a beautiful half-moon scudding through the autumn clouds. He grabbed a bathrobe, plunged his bare feet in galoshes, and we ran outside into the cold October wind to watch. Suddenly we found ourselves not only singing but *bellowing* "Sweet Adeline" to the moon, and afterward we chortled for five minutes and danced in circles on the frosty lawn.

"I can't quite believe it," Lem said as we started back indoors, panting, "but I'm beginning to think that I'm happy."

"Me too," I said.

🎜19🎜

It is a strange place, Sneden's Landing, and I found it more ingrown, resentful of intrusion, and malicious than it used to be. Artists had been supplanted by television types, well-to-do physicians, and the merely wealthy; the people themselves seemed to me to be far more divided into cliques and coteries than they were in other years, a matter apparently dependent upon amount of money, age grouping, and propinquity. As time went on I discovered that they were also more alcoholic, and more adulterous than in earlier years, and that some parents shared drugs with their children. In the 1930s, people used to walk to the post office or on Sunday down the road to the river, stopping to talk to friends and neighbors along the way; now no one walked and everyone existed in the isolation of automobiles. Yet many second-generation children, like me, have returned to Sneden's.

People were not the lure, I believe, and no one, not even Marian Grey, was Circe. The appeal lies in the incredible fact that this tiny enclave, only a short drive from New York, was physically almost exactly the way it was in our childhoods; in an unstable world and in an unstable community of people we found stability of place. The woods, the meadows, the road to the river. The river and the willow tree. The eighteenth-century cottages and the gingerbread Victorian mansions. The smell of the locusts in flower around the tennis court, the goldenrod and the wild red sumac in autumn. That oak, this pine tree, so well remembered, so well loved.

But people matter, too, and once I had unpacked seventy-two cartons of books and papers, I vowed that I would reach out and find them. During my previous three-year residence, when Lem was an infant, I had been too preoccupied with my job to take part in the community chores which seemed to occupy other mothers, and gradually I had become aware of a slight frostiness on the part of the neighboring ladies. Now my hours were my own and I swore to myself that I would become a PTA-type mother, a den mother if necessary, and that I would even try to concoct popcorn balls for school fairs. In order to make friends (and by this time I well knew that in the suburbs a woman only makes friends with other women) I was determined to try to be *just* like the other mothers, even if it meant only writing at night, in secret. Unfortunately, none of this worked out quite as I had planned. On our first Halloween, when I detected a bunch of darkly hovering figures behind the stone wall, I became convinced that a rough gang from Nyack which had threatened to descend on Sneden's was about to attack the house and, with what I thought was enormous composure, I fired Lem's .22 eight times into the brightly lighted lawn. The "gang" disappeared hastily, and I went to bed feeling like a pioneer woman who had defended her home and child against an attack of Iroquois. The next morning, I learned that all the boys were from Sneden's, intent only on Halloween mischief, and that all of them had informed their parents that my bullets had creased their hair. After that my hopes of being accepted as the conventional mother became rather dim. Anyway, I don't suppose I could have played the role for very long—I guess one just has to be what one is.

· · ·

After so many years of emotional turmoil, I found it hard to believe that I was finally entering into a peaceful, creative period of life. I felt dazed at the change and immensely weary; instead of returning to work on my Lippincott book (now eleven months past deadline), I sat for hours at the kitchen table, watched the birds at the bird-feeder, and agreed with Lem when he said, "I think a bird-feeder must be one of God's greatest gifts to humanity." I consistently fell below my own expectations for myself, but I also realized that I had been somewhat more battered by life than I had thought I was. It was perhaps no wonder that three days before Christmas my contract was canceled—although I thought my editor's timing rather brutal.

Despite my anguished pleas, Lem and his father had refused to see each other for a year. Eric disapproved strongly of Lem's defection from school; he also thought that psychotherapy was nonsense, and that the answer to emotional problems was to be more "robust." Lem, in turn, was deeply hurt by Eric's lack of understanding, said he never wanted to see his father again, and at one point asked if he could change his last name to Parton. I said no. But this Christmas of 1965, after a series of cautious postal exchanges, Eric came as before loaded with expensive presents, and a stately reconciliation was effected. The following November, on Lem's sixteenth birthday, we went to Eric's Sutton Place apartment for a formal luncheon, during which Eric expressed no curiosity about his son's life. On the way home I allowed myself a rare outburst.

"I *can't* understand why your father never asked you a single question about your school, or sports, or any of your interests!" I exclaimed.

"Oh, that's easy," said Lem. "He isn't interested. But just the same, I think he's a very fine man."

In the new year of 1966 I tried to go back to work, but it was difficult because one of my greatest professional weaknesses is that I cannot write unless I know there is someone, somewhere, who *wants* me to write. I felt guilty about this until one day I heard Truman Capote in a radio interview say something which so accurately described what I felt that I copied it down and pinned it consolingly to my bulletin board: "There is nothing lonelier than writing in a vacuum—in not having a sounding board for your work." Beside it I pinned a quotation from Dorothy Parker: "The writer's way is rough and lonely, and who would choose it while there are vacancies in more gracious professions, such as, say, cleaning out ferryboats?"

I could have looked for a job, and I suppose I should have, as Rod's monthly annuity check and the dividends from Aunt Alice's inheritance were not really enough to support us without dipping into capital. But I didn't want Lem to come home from school to an empty house, and also, for fear of rebuff, I was afraid to try. My ego had collapsed like Silly Putty, and with the latest rejection at Christmastime, any self-confidence I ever possessed had melted down into the basement. So I stayed home and immersed myself in the journals and letters, sure that somewhere in them there was a book which would say something meaningful about life.

Early in January 1966 Marguerite Higgins died, and I felt strangely shaken. For twenty years—in the same profession but far more famous than I had ever been—she had been the shadow-dancer on the other side of the screen, the glimpsed figure beyond the looking glass, like mine but not mine at all. We had only danced some of the same steps in different worlds. A few weeks later I went to the Memorial Service at the Overseas Press Club with Lucy Freeman, and to my surprise found that my eyes were full of tears. Afterward Lucy and I joined Bob Considine and Hal Boyle in the bar, and Bob and I held hands for old-times' sake. It seemed very strange to be once more in the glamorous big-time world I used to inhabit, and I felt fractured when I went home to the bird-feeder, the cats, and Lem's problems with French verbs. But there were no real regrets, for it seemed to me that I had chosen a path leading away from that world, and from Marguerite's, and that I must follow it to the end.

In mid-March I moved my mother to a Rockland County nursing home, where I could visit her twice a week. She was now completely bound to wheelchair and bed, but in her poor, addled mind she was still a vigorous forty and the determination to come home and take care of Lem and me never abated. When I came she would weep, throw herself about, beg for poison, and claim she was being tortured; the hours with her were agonizing and my heart broke with pity each time I saw her, particularly at the contrast with the self-assured, dynamic woman who emerged each working day from the diary pages I was reading. Sometimes I wondered whether I would survive her, for every time I saw her she seemed to kill me a little more.

The director of the nursing home, a geriatric specialist, told me that intellectual women always have a difficult old age because they scorn the homely activities which interest other women, and, true to form, Mother refused for months to take any part in the many occupational-therapy programs which were offered. Finally, however, she did a large pastel of autumn trees and the following spring it won a prize at the annual Rockland County Senior Citizens Arts and Crafts Show. "They gave me a piece of fruitwood with some words on it," she grunted, and handed me a walnut plaque with an inscribed brass plate. The words read: "In recognition of distinguished creative achievement in the years past eighty." I took it home and showed it to Lem.

"My God," he said, "Nani's done it again."

. . .

On March 30 my Uncle Elliott Field died. He had shared none of the eccentricity and unconventionality of his three older sisters and his life had centered around his devoted children, Henry, Barbara, and Don and their families, the Lions Club, the Episcopal Church, and barber-shop quartets; he was a dear and gentle man and I mourned for him. I thought of how his three strong and dominating older sisters had condescended to him all his life because he was not aggressive, and it occurred to me that perhaps his ordinary, happy life had been the serenest of rebukes to all their condescension. "Elliott is the most successful of us all," Mother used to say, and she sometimes believed it.

That spring, while I waited for the reaction of a new publisher to some sample chapters of a book about my parents, I attacked the jungle growth in the long-neglected garden. All day I cut and hacked and sawed and pruned and chopped; on weekends Lem and I would haul the branches into the meadow, make bonfires and march around them, shouting the words of Omar Khayyám: "Come, fill the Cup, and in the fire of Spring/ The Winter garment of Repentance fling." But I brooded about my parents as I worked. In their determination to make the place "the microcosm in the macrocosm," and "the golden land where it is always afternoon," did they give too much creative energy to the garden, the house, and the total *ambiance* at the expense of the books they could have written? My mother's diaries were full of her longing to write, but instead of writing she was always prowling around junk shops for antique treasures, planning and giving wonderful singing parties, or stirring up those vats of spiced grapes whose smell perfumes the memory of my childhood. And my father, who at one time had six publishers begging him for his autobiography, preferred to spend his free hours laying bricks or making a great chestnut table for the grape arbor. Had they made the right choice? It took me a long time to discover that the word "creativity" has many meanings, and to understand that creating an *ambiance* may be even more important than creating a book.

. . .

What a mishmash of relationships life is. One afternoon that spring a lawyer I had met at a Westchester party came to see me; I was considerably surprised when he told me very smoothly that despite the fact of his indissoluble marriage he was looking for a mistress, and thought that I was eminently suited to fill the role, particularly since I was a widow with a son away at school all day. Despite my astonishment—for I had long since concluded that no one would ever again find me desirable—I rallied, and we discussed his proposal with cool impersonality. Finally, I told him I would think it over, and sent him away.

I was torn between the naïve little girl I often felt I was, and the experienced woman of the world I thought I should be. He had a superficial brightness and a kind of slick worldliness which I have never admired, and he did not arouse even a spark of affection in my sentimental heart. On the other hand, it had been almost two years since the last time with Rod and I thought that perhaps my continued depression might be due to this, rather than to loneliness and Viet Nam. Besides, he wasn't physically unattractive and anyway, I told myself, it was high time I got over the nonsense of wanting *love*. So, rather in the mood of someone who takes a new vitamin for her health, I said yes and we went ahead. But it was a mistake, as I should have known it would be from my similar experiment with loveless sex in Japan many years before. Some people, I gather, seem to find this kind of activity pleasurable, but after a few encounters with the prosaic lawyer I came to the conclusion that for me, at least, physical satisfaction could not outweigh a bitter sense of moral degradation; without love the act seems only meaningless and slightly comic. However, I was female enough to feel complimented by his vociferous protests against my adamant farewell, as I did when he telephoned—in vain—six years later.

Early in May, the editor to whom I had sent the sample chapters returned them, saying that my focus was fuzzy. An assignment from *Woman's Day* in June was consoling, and I was relieved and happy when the article I wrote was accepted and a fat check arrived. Lem said, "Mother, you're happy because you were afraid you had forgotten how to write, and this shows you haven't." But I felt I was happy because the check permitted me to indulge a dream of his, and therefore of mine.

Lem, who was still seeing Dr. Chaplan once a month, had

made considerable progress. He had completed a year of school, and although he was never fond of studying he was on the honor roll. He still had no friends of his own age and no social life, but he had made friends with Mark Thomas, who was two years younger and who lived in Sneden's and also went to Rockland Country Day; Mark's parents, British-born Ann and David Thomas, became our good friends and took care of Lem whenever I went away on assignment. But it was clear that Lem was a loner, as the vast, lonely oil paintings he had begun to paint seemed to indicate. He hated mobs and cities, he was passionate about golf, and because golf had originated in Scotland he was almost mystically thrilled at the discovery that he had had a Scottish great-grandmother. What else was there to do for vacation except go to Scotland? So we went.

We hired a car and drove up the west coast from Glasgow, stopping each day to picnic beside placid lochs or roaring burns. One night we stayed at the romantic Kingshouse Hotel, on the edge of Rannoch Moor, where in 1692 the Argylls, the Campbells, and the soldiers of the English plotted the appalling Glencoe massacre of the Clan MacDonald. The next day, driving down into the dark defile where the helpless men, women, and children were slaughtered by those who had been guests in their homes, Lem and I both felt our MacDonald blood pound with ancient rage and sensed an atmosphere of horror which would linger there forever, despite the placid sheep safely grazing on the mountainsides.

After many enchanted days, highlands, and glens, we came at last to the objective of the trip: the Royal and Ancient Golf Course of Saint Andrews, where it all began. Lem was tremendously proud to be there and very excited, but as I watched his hesitant walk toward the first tee I realized that he was also scared. Then a middle-aged Scotsman approached, took a long, shrewd look at Lem, and smiled. "Your first time, Lad?" he asked. "It can be a bit tricky until you get to know it—I'd be glad for the company if you'd like to play around with me." And off they went. Bless that Scotsman, wherever he is. And bless all men who are kind to lonely boys.

We lingered in Saint Andrews for several days, for Lem was enamored of the golf course and I of the medieval town by the edge of the sea, where it seemed to me that everything was in the comfortably right scale for the individual human being, as it is not in the skyscraper canyons of New York. Then we drove to Edinburgh, where we met Eric's sister, Marjorie—who had been a devoted aunt to Lem—and began with her a meandering drive south, which took us through the Lake Country, Wales (where in a copy of *The Times* of London I learned of the death of the *Herald Tribune*, and wept), the Cotswolds, and finally to London. Lem, the most stubborn of fifteen-year-old males, was convinced that London would be just like New York, which he hated; to my fury he refused to go anywhere (except the Battersea Fun Park and Madame Tussaud's waxwork museum) or even to look at the lions in Trafalgar Square. All he wanted to do, he insisted, was to watch cricket matches on the television set in the elegant apartment loaned to us by vacationing Fay and Alan Campbell-Johnson, old friends from my India days.

One day we went to Patrixbourne to visit Jim and Rose Marie Foottit, and I was happy that despite Lem's peculiarities they seemed to like him. Another day, the happiest of them all, we went to Surrey to see Ian and his wife, who took us on an excursion to Brighton. "Regency camp!" Lem exclaimed as he viewed the crazy, wonderful jumble of *chinoiserie* and Egypt which is the Pavilion. Ian and he became instant friends at that moment, and for the rest of the day and evening the hours were filled with laughter and affection; I had so much wanted them to like each other, and I found the twinkling, teasing rapport they developed in the space of a few hours almost unbearably moving.

That night, back in London, with only one day left before we had to fly home, Lem said, "I think I was mistaken, and I would now like to see London." For ten hours the next day we saw the changing of the guard, Trafalgar Square, the Strand, Fleet Street, Saint Paul's, the Bank of England, the Tower, Greenwich and the Thames by boat, Big Ben, and Westminster Abbey. "Very interesting," said Lem, as we collapsed back at the flat. "Too bad we didn't see more."

At home again, we curled back into our lives, Lem with school, piano lessons, and bowling, I with planting 300 daffodil bulbs and beginning to work on a new, nostalgic book so intently that once again I had to struggle with the writing versus housework clash, and reflected that I was continually having to climb out of the deep well of the past, dripping with memories, and put my feet on the dry shores of reality. There was a heavy snow at Christmas, much simple festivity with and without Eric, and many signs that Lem's hidden sweetness was beginning to emerge. On New Year's Day 1967, which was also his grandmother's eighty-ninth birthday, Lem played for her the first movement of the "Moonlight Sonata," putting into it all his gentleness and strength. She cried, and so did all the other old ladies at the nursing home.

In January, he stayed with the Thomases while I went on a swing across the country on another story for *Woman's Day*. The trip took me to Berkeley, where my Aunt Sara now lived, having found it impossible to stay alone at Los Gatos. She was very fragile, confined to a wheelchair, but still full of the old love, the old communion, the old understanding of my own groping creative urges. We talked of Los Gatos, the white petunias on the terraces in the moonlight, the white Japanese poppies in the oxblood Chinese vase, of Erskine blowing his Tirolean horn in the courtyard. "If you write about it, it won't all be lost, will it?" she asked wistfully. I felt an immense desire to reach out and pull her away from the river of time on which she traveled, to wrench her back and keep her from the inevitable rapids, the inevitable waterfall, the Niagara of death. And I knew that my longing was futile, and that no one can stop the flow of the river or the course of all of us who float upon it.

Back home again I wrote the article, and settled down to my own book. A January entry in my journal described something of my mood that winter:

A day of semi-work, but quiet. Lem, newly interested in photography, taking pictures of the cats. Mozart on the record-player Reading the *Times* while Lem does his homework and his remark when he comes downstairs: "My, but it looks good to see you sitting there." Lem reading the introduction to *Tortilla Flat* aloud while I worked on my hooked rug—and then practicing the piano while I completed hooking a green leaf.

I begin to have true desires again. I want to write. I want to bring back the garden, the meadow. I want to finish my hooked rug. But most of all, I want to see Lem a little further on the road to self-confidence and joy. I want him to *live*. And to know that I love him truly and forever, from all dimensions of space and time.

But more and more I began to be depressed by the new atmosphere which had taken over the literary world in which I had
been raised. For several years I had been so absorbed in personal
life and my own intellectual and emotional pursuits that I had
paid scant attention to new books, art, magazines, films, and theater. Now at last I had time to look, and I shriveled inwardly at
what I saw. I went a few times with Lem to plays and movies, as
I had gone so often with my parents, and always we left silently,
unhappy with violence and vulgarity (except for *A Man for All
Seasons,* about which Lem said: "Sir Thomas More is the only
character in plays or movies I've *ever* been able to identify
with").

All contemporary writing seemed aimed either at the mass, or
else at what seemed to me to be a small, sick, basically homosexual intelligentsia—sour, bitter, angry and pervaded by malice.
The most significant books were being written by Jews and Negroes, with whose problems I deeply sympathized but had little
in common. There seemed to be no longer any liking for the virtues I had always admired: honesty, grace, simplicity, understate-
ment, and compassion. I thought I was alone in this conclusion
until I read a book review by Eliot Fremont-Smith which began:
"Grace, good humor, good manners, a sense of proportion about
past and future and ideas and men—these are not much in vogue
these days." I realized then that I was totally and completely a
WASP, as much conditioned by my background and education as
any James Baldwin, Saul Bellow, or Philip Roth, and decided
that I would only betray myself if I tried to become tough and
pornographic. Marya Mannes, a woman I much admire, wrote a
line I also admire: "Our generation was caught between the puri-
tans and the pornographers." So be it.

The young people I saw in those years also puzzled me. I had
always been friendly with several of the children of my friends,
and enjoyed seeing them and listening to their problems. But now
when they came to visit, these people in their early twenties, they
seemed different, full of misery and despair, lacking in conviction
that there was any reasonable way to get through life. "The only
answer to life that I know of," I would tell them, "is guts and
gulp and one foot in front of the other and keep on going." And
then they would ask "Why?"

Meantime, Lem went his own inner-directed way. He no longer

needed to see Dr. Chaplan, and he had made three good friends at school—bright boys who like him rejected the social standards of their classmates, preferred Beethoven to Rock, short hair to long, and chess to marijuana. Because he spent more time at photography than homework his marks were not as good as they could have been, but they were all right. As far as I could make out he never spoke to a girl, but looking at frowsy bunches of them on Nyack's Main Street, in dirty sneakers, torn blue jeans, and tattered shirts, I couldn't blame him. "Oh, Lem," I exclaimed one day, in a sudden burst of unusual honesty, "I wish there were a girl for you all pink and clean and pretty, with roses in her hair!" Lem laughed at this impossible vision, and then sighed. "So do I," he said wistfully.

Photography had now become his dominant passion, and every afternoon he prowled the early spring garden, taking close-ups with my old Rolliflex of snowdrops, winter aconites, and little green spears emerging from the latest snowfall. Nat Fein, an old friend and a Pulitzer-prize-winning photographer from the *Herald Tribune*, lived nearby and dropped in frequently for long conversations with Lem about the techniques of the craft. Nat understood Lem's longing for a really good 35-mm. camera and appeared one night with a $700 Yashica Pentamatic and a variety of powerful lenses, which he said I could have for $500. I said no, quite out of the question. Too indulgent. Nat said, "He's a fine boy, a good boy. I think he's going to *be* somebody. He deserves this." Lem said nothing, but just looked at me. I felt the old familiar hunch which had never betrayed me, and also rationalized that this might spur him to go out into the world, rather than circling around home base forever. So then I said, "Yes," and Lem went into a state of acute and joyous shock.

I, too, received a shock that spring, but one of a different kind. In February an editor, to whom I had sent the revised chapters of my book, took me to lunch and led me to believe he was offering me a contract with a large advance. There followed three months of silence, during which I could never reach him, and then in mid-May a telegram telling me that the editorial board had approved the book but that the owner of the publishing house had rejected it, along with several others. Contrary to my usual pattern I did not cry or get drunk, but set the book aside for the summer, the editor forever, and went on with plans to drive across the country with Lem after school was out. Psychologically, I had been preparing him to drive ever since he was two years old; now that I had been actively teaching him to drive for the past year, I found that this earlier conditioning plus his natural motor ability had produced a sure, safe driver with whom I could confidently change places at the wheel during our cross-country drive.

In the past three years I had put 40,000 miles on Rod's old Buick station wagon and it was in no condition for a 9000-mile trip. Early in June we bought a new, two-door Buick Special, a sensible blue car that suited my brain but not my heart. "But Lem promised to buy me a bright red convertible when I'm seventy," I wrote happily in my journal. Lem was always good at presents—he gave me an apple tree and a cherry tree when I was fifty.

We more or less followed the route of *Travels with Charley*, by John Steinbeck, to whose books Lem had become passionately devoted, a northern route which took us to Niagara Falls, the Michigan lakes, the Wisconsin Dells, the great stretches of Minnesota and Montana, Glacier National Park, Idaho forests, Washington wheatlands, and, finally, the long Pacific rollers on the Oregon shore. We also, for much of the way, followed the route of Lewis and Clark, and took turns reading to each other from Bernard De Voto's *The Course of Empire*. We picnicked every day, saw beavers and mountain goats, prairie dogs, coyotes, deer, bear, sea lions, and eagles, and were very happy.

In Berkeley we stayed with my cousin Kay, and I tried to show Lem something of the San Francisco I loved. But he was as grudging about looking at the city as he had been about London and preferred to spend his time wandering the beautiful Berkeley hills and visiting with his Great-Aunts, Sara and Marion. "I'm glad we stayed with my relatives," he said firmly as we started south to Carmel. "I *like* my relatives." They, too, seemed to have approved of him, and since there had been little affection on either side in the past, I was profoundly grateful for the changes that time and growth can make.

Then came stars and fog at Carmel, Yosemite waterfalls, Nevada sagebrush, the Grand Canyon, and the smaller but lovelier Canyon de Chelley, and then the Colorado mountains, where Lem dreamed of buying property—he said, smiling, that he would spend his days putting up "No trespassing" signs and photographing bees. I had intended to drive the more dangerous mountain roads, but to my dismay I discovered that I had lost my nerve for cliffs; the only thing to do, I found as we approached each terrifying precipice, was to take a drink, bury my face in a pillow, and let Lem do the driving.

Thus we were able to survive and eventually to come home safely to the little house.

❧20❧

That fall of 1967 Lem turned our small garden house into a dark-room, and after a cursory brush with homework each evening would disappear for hours of printing and enlarging. I was lonely in the house, but the pictures he was producing were compensation, for they seemed to capture not just the image of a tree or rock, or of our yellow cat, Chini, but the mysterious essence of tree-ness, rock-ness and cat-ness. "But what are my pictures compared to this?" he asked, when on Christmas Night we read aloud Dylan Thomas's *A Child's Christmas in Wales,* and he sensed that Dylan was expressing in words a quality of experience that Lem sought to capture in his photographs.

Because we had been together for such a long time, Lem and I could almost read each other's minds, and often communicated in a kind of verbal shorthand. Once, about a year after Rod's death, we were driving somewhere in the car and suddenly, with no prior reference, I asked Lem, "Do you think it would have worked?" He was silent for several moments. Then, "No," he said. I thought for five more miles. "I'm afraid you're right," I sighed.

Sometimes it was a private kind of humor we shared. "It's been a long time since anyone called me 'Bright Eyes,'" he mourned, remembering the nickname his grandmother had given him. "Well," I snapped, "it's been *years* since anybody called me 'Pretty Legs'!" And we both collapsed with laughter.

We were both a little afraid of the close relationship which had been forced on us by our relative isolation from normal society, and for this reason as well as because of our WASP tendency to understate, we were restrained in our expressions of mutual affection. But there had been a homemade valentine in the refrigerator the previous February, and another under my pillow. Lem believed that Mother's Day was nothing but a commercial holiday and therefore refused to commemorate it, but after he had gone to bed one May Sunday, he called downstairs: "Mother—even though I don't believe in Mother's Day or do anything about it, I want you to know I *appreciate* you." The next day I found a vase of white lilacs in my room.

And one day that spring, after several weeks of gloomy taciturnity and irritable criticisms, he brought tears to my eyes with an astonishing burst of volubility and perception. "Mother," he said, suddenly, "I never realized before what it must be like for you to be alone in the house day after day, with the telephone never ringing. I thought you were silly to want the radio on, but now I understand. Why, nobody from Sneden's ever comes to see you, except maybe once a month or so, do they? And all day long alone, day after day, with no friends . . . It must be awful!"

I reminded him, of course, that I did have many friends who truly loved me, but that unfortunately they all seemed to live somewhere else; that while it was true that I had more acquaintances in Sneden's than friends, it was also a notoriously difficult community in which to be accepted, particularly for a woman who was all three of the suburban pariahs: divorcee, widow, and professional career woman. In any case, I added, Sneden's had never been a "drop in and gossip" kind of place. Besides, I asked, didn't I frequently ask people out from New York for Sunday lunch? But the loneliness was, in fact, quite as awful as Lem thought it must be—except when I was working. So, I worked.

The spring of 1968 drifted in, with snowdrops and crocuses for Lem to photograph, but also with the assassination of Martin Luther King. I felt—as I did two months later when Robert Kennedy was killed—that ugliness, unreason, and violence stalked the world, and wondered where we could flee to, so that Lem's rare and lovely vision of the natural world could be cherished and allowed to grow in peace as it should grow. One Sunday late in April I came home from Quaker Meeting, which I had begun to attend, and found him sitting in a canvas chair directly under one of the pink and white flowering Japanese crab apples, staring up into the blossoms in tranced absorption. Suddenly, I remembered a little piece I had written ten years earlier for the *Ladies'*

Home Journal. It was called "When Did I Love Him Most?" and ended with the words: "Now, now, *now*." Yes, I thought, circling quietly around him, at seventeen as at seven, always right *now*.

The end of the school year neared. Lem took the Scholastic Aptitude Test (a preliminary to college application) and passed with a very high rating. He also took the National Merit Scholarship tests and received one of the seven "Letters of Commendation" in Rockland County. At the final banquet for juniors and seniors, he was named captain of the baseball team for the following year, presented with a special award for sportsmanship, and was referred to by the athletic coach as "Mr. Baseball himself." But the empty days loomed ahead—and what was a lonely seventeen-year-old to do with himself? He was still too lacking in self-confidence to look for a regular job, and although he cut lawns for various neighbors, that activity seemed unappealing as the sole one for a summer. The passion for golf had given place to tennis and each day he would sit for hours by the tennis court with his racket, but the men always showed up in pairs, no other Sneden's boys were interested in the game, and I wasn't a good enough player to be worth his consideration.

One Sunday in mid-June Lem pointed out an advertisement in the Sunday paper for an Australian-run tennis camp near Saratoga. "That's where I'd like to go, if it weren't so expensive," he said. I looked at the ad and gulped. "You're so right," I said. "Four hundred dollars for only three weeks is too rich for *our* blood." The subject was dropped, but after he went to bed that night I began to think. This was the first time in his whole life that he had voluntarily suggested going away from home and from me, I realized. Somehow it seemed a milestone, marking his full recovery from the phobic days of 1965. And he needed so much to be happy, and to be encouraged to move out into the world! But I would have to dip again into the savings account to pay for it. . . .

Two days later we loaded Lem's suitcase, filled with new white tennis clothes, into the car and drove three hours north to the Aussie Tennis Camp in Schuylerville, New York. Lem looked at the lovely old buildings (which are a boarding school during the rest of the year), the tennis courts and gardens near the slow-flowing river, and was introduced to the courteous Harvard boys who were the tennis instructors. "I want to come back next year, too," Lem said firmly as he walked with me back to the car.

. . .

Those three weeks were the first time I had been completely alone since the days when Rod was in the hospital and Lem still at Hackley. But I was not lonely, for in April I had acquired what Quakers call "a concern," and by mid-summer it had become almost obsessive. The concern was Muriel Snow, a childless widow who lived across the meadow from me, and who did not know that she was dying of cancer.

Even in the days before I knew her well, I think I recognized —without knowing that I recognized—a special quality about her. I noted her narrow little figure, brisking along the road to the post office in an expensive camel's hair coat, alligator shoes, a Cossack hat cocked at a rakish angle above her long and narrow face with its large gray eyes, a face reminiscent both of Virginia Woolf and a thoroughbred horse, and I sensed, even then, the *élan,* the breeding, the self-containment, and the uncomplaining loneliness which later I came to know so well. I remembered Homer, her husband, a tiny, tight-coiled man, with slick black hair parted in the middle, and a bow tie, and how after I returned to Sneden's in 1952 we waved amiably from garden to garden but that was all, for the gulf between people who grew up in the 1920s and those who matured in the 1930s seemed unbridgeable and not worth trying to bridge. When Homer died a year or so afterward I was briefly sorry, but incurious.

Twice, during the first year of our return in 1965, Muriel had asked me over for a drink; both times we drank too much and I was aware of her appalling loneliness and frightened by it, terrified that liquor might become my ultimate answer as perhaps it was hers. For this reason I did not go again; in any case, I had no desire to associate with other widows and particularly with one I considered dull. So the months drifted into years, and I was only peripherally aware of Muriel trotting along to her part-time job at the local gift shop. A wave, a smile, and on my part a twinge of soon-forgotten guilt. Am I my brother's keeper?

"Did you know that Muriel is in the hospital for an operation?" my neighbor Blythe Finke asked one March morning in the spring of 1968. "I don't know what—exploratory, I guess."

There were two operations and she was in the hospital for a month; then in a nursing home for two weeks.

Late in April she came home. The house had been polished and cleaned by neighbors, and a pewter pitcher, filled with early white lilacs, rested on a pine table. The refrigerator was filled with bowls of Vichyssoise, *crème brûlée*, wine jelly, and other enriching exotica—Muriel had never weighed more than a whisper, and now she was down to eighty-seven pounds. Old friends she had known most of her life hovered about like plump and anxious mourning doves. How could I, a heretofore disinterested slight acquaintance, be of any help? Rather casually, I offered to bring her mail every morning in the course of my regular walk. Thus, in a simple gesture of neighborliness, began a relationship which by the end of the summer was to possess me utterly.

When I came she would be dressed and sitting straight as a small ruler . on the living-room couch, conscientiously eating breakfast from a tray arranged with almost spinsterly precision. One morning she invited me to sit down and have a cigarette, and, after that, shared cigarettes and coffee became part of every morning. Oddly enough, I enjoyed these visits although our conversation was often desultory and sometimes we simply sat in sunlit silence, looking out of the picture window at the little lawn and the trees beyond, while Muriel's old Siamese cat purred asthmatically on the yellow rug at our feet, and the blossoms of white lilacs dropped silently on the polished leaves of the little pine table. Finally, stirring herself, Muriel would pick up the week's Double-Crostic.

"What's a thirteen-letter word for the goal of Buddhism?"

"Enlightenment?" It fitted and I felt triumphant. I have never been any good at Double-Crostics, but Muriel, I discovered, could solve them with comparative ease. She also, I found, took care of the bookkeeping at the gift shop, where she had worked until her operation—and unlike mine, her checkbook always balanced.

We talked often in those early days of the progress of her recovery. Because I had had a small operation I was full of what I thought was the wisdom of experience. Postoperative depression? Well, that will be gone in a week or two. Weight? With all the fattening food the neighbors kept bringing over she was sure to start gaining soon. Pain? Well, that was only natural. Twinges in the back? That was simple—what she needed was to walk more. All very cheerful, very reassuring. "But God damn it!" her deep, fog-horn voice would mutter.

As May glimmered by and the early roses of June appeared, I began to watch her more closely, and to visit her two or three times a day. I saw that her dresses hung more loosely than they had a month before, that she seemed to be eating less than she had earlier, that her hands shook almost uncontrollably and that she had taken to drinking her coffee through a bent glass straw, that she winced whenever she shifted position on the couch. Her own doctor, a local man, went away for the summer—without having come to see her or leaving a replacement. She went to see the surgeon and he told her she had developed a diverticulosis of the intestine, which was slowing her recovery. He gave her some pills "to melt it," but they didn't seem to do much good.

Late in June, cutting across the daisied meadow to my own house, I talked with Blythe Finke (who with her husband, John, had bought "Margaret's House"). Although Muriel was well out of earshot, we found ourselves whispering. "It must be cancer," she said. "There's no other answer." I looked at her and realized that I agreed, although until that moment I had not really thought about the possibility. But what was there to do? we wondered as the bumblebees buzzed in the clover around our ankles. Muriel's doctor seemed to have deserted her, and she was alone in the house. Nor was there any money—we both knew now that she lived the life of a gallant lady on nothing but social security and Medicare. The camel's hair coat and the alligator shoes had once belonged to wealthier friends, the antiques came from New England ancestors, a live-in companion would be out of the question. And so we whispered and worried, while all around us summer moved toward its zenith.

Between concern for Muriel, visits to my mother, and work on my book, the three weeks without Lem went by quickly. On July 7 I drove up to retrieve him, and as he ran toward me from the courts I thought he looked taller, thinner, browner, rosier, and in his tennis shorts and shirt one of the handsomest and healthiest young men I had ever seen. Before we left, the director told me that he wanted Lem to come back as a salaried counselor the following year and not just because of the strong game he had developed. "He's extremely popular, and he's very good with younger children," he said. "Also, he has the most highly developed sense of justice I've ever encountered in a boy." I knew about the justice and of Lem's tenderness toward children, but the news of his popularity stunned me, for never before had it been a word which could be applied to him, any more than it could be to me.

"I didn't miss you as much as I had expected I would," I told Lem as we drove away.

"I didn't miss you at *all*," he said flatly, and added that he might have, if he hadn't been so happy. He was ecstatic at the prospect of returning next year for the entire summer.

There were other benefits from that expensive investment. One was that the tennis-playing men of Sneden's soon discovered that Lem's game was the equal of theirs and sometimes better, so that he no longer sat lonely and ignored beside the court and in fact spent most of the rest of the summer playing on it. But there were even more important second and third developments.

A week after he had come home, a long thin box arrived for him in the mail. As he had never before received any personal mail except at Christmas and his birthday, I was surprised, but gave it to him without comment and he disappeared with it into his darkroom "studio." That night at two minutes to ten he said goodnight, carried a brass Russian candlestick up to his room, and closed the door; the next morning I discovered a tall red candle in the candlestick, burned down half an inch. That afternoon he went off on a mysterious shopping errand, returned to ask for brown wrapping paper, and made an unexplained trip to the post office. Every night after that his room glowed with candlelight for five minutes before he went to sleep.

Then the letters to him began arriving, lavender, pink, or pale blue envelopes, inscribed in a round, schoolgirlish hand, and bearing a return address in Massachusetts of someone I shall call Linda Adams. I remembered that there had been a fifteen-year-old girl at camp who had taught Lem some lines of Shelley which he liked to quote and whose photograph, young and smiling as a new daisy, he had shown me among others he had taken. He grabbed each letter when it came, and went off to his studio where, after a while, I could hear his typewriter pounding for hours. It was clear from all this, and from his bouncing joy, that he was in love for the first time; I was tremendously curious as well as very happy about this new development, but, remembering my father's references to "the secret arcanum of the soul," refrained from any questions.

One day I noticed that Lem's hair was beginning to look more like a poodle's than a dachshund's. "I've decided to let it grow," he told me briefly, and as the unshorn weeks went on I discovered to my amazement that the developing ringlets were very becoming. He suddenly insisted on switching from the heavy horn-rimmed eyeglasses he wore to a kind with thin metal frames, called "granny glasses." He bought some folk-rock records, and instead of echoing to the sounds of Mozart and Beethoven at a modest volume, the little house shook with Peter, Paul, and Mary at top volume, while Lem sat on the piano stool beside the phonograph, snapping his fingers to their rhythms. I was dazed by all these changes, but also profoundly relieved that Lem had at last found a way to join his own generation, presumably through the gentle influence of young Linda Adams. I wanted to hug her for accomplishing what I had never been able to do.

Early in September he took another step forward. From his lawn-cutting and the money he had earned from developing and printing other people's negatives, he had bought himself a new camera, a Crown Graphic. Like his idol Eliot Porter, he explained, he was now beginning to specialize in close-up studies of natural forms, and, in order to avoid distortion, needed a camera with a larger negative than the 35-mm. Yashica provided. To test the camera, he decided (with my permission) to go on a five-day camping trip in the Adirondacks—the first time he had ever gone off overnight alone in the car. After he had loaded the sleeping bag, the boxful of canned food, and the cameras into the car, he lingered for a moment, not quite knowing how to say good-by on this significant occasion.

"Well . . . feed my bird," he said finally, reverting to *Amahl and the Night Visitors.*

"Yes, I promise," I said.

"Watch the cat!"

"Yes, I promise."

"I shall miss you very much," he quoted, and drove off.

It was the first time in his life that I had not known where he was sleeping at night, and I was moderately relieved when he returned in three days rather than the five he had planned. "I have discovered that man needs companionship," he reported gruffly.

. . .

Muriel grew worse. In desperation I called on our neighbor Dr. Cushman Haagensen, one of America's leading cancer specialists and always a good friend to anyone in the community who needed help. Cushman understood Muriel's deep hatred of hospitals, but insisted that she should not be alone during the day; through the generosity of one of her nephews, we were able to hire a wonderful woman named Dorothy Dietz, who came every morning at nine and stayed until six. But, for two months night nurses were a perpetual problem and, near the end, Blythe Finke and I took turns staying with Muriel in the interim hours between nurses and sometimes at night when no one else could be found. Other friends would have helped, of course, but Muriel could not bear to let them see how much she had changed; the only people she could tolerate in the final weeks were Blythe and me, the nurses, and Cushman, who came every day and sometimes oftener and kept her relatively free of pain.

That was a strange September, it seems to me now in recollection. I would spend an evening watching television in the dimly lit living room with Muriel, who was now down to eighty-one pounds and who seemed to consist of nothing but bones, courage, and a fierce determination to get well. Then I would walk back across the dark meadow, thinking of my own fierce determination to help her die at home as gallantly and painlessly as possible, and blink as I entered our brilliantly lighted house to the roar of "Please, Mrs. Robinson" and the sound of Lem's snapping fingers and tapping feet. He was so vital, so young, so strong, flashing, flexing, yearning, stretching toward manhood that the contrast with dying Muriel always astonished me.

The behavior of birds was unusual that September, although perhaps I imagine this. But something about them led me to write in my journal:

What really captures my attention are the birds which shimmer and dart in and out of the grape arbor, voracious for the grapes, spitting the skins on the flagstones so that the arbor is purple-stained and littered and rolling with bunches the eager birds have knocked against. I lie in the hammock and watch them crashing among the leaves, watch them flickering in the crab-apple tree, yanking at the little yellow fruits, watch them lighting on the stone birdbath, sipping, flirting with the water, dipping and shaking. And this is happiness.

One other thing happened which seemed of no significance at the time. One day at the tennis court, Lem introduced me to Dr. Daniel Stern, a psychiatrist at the Columbia Presbyterian Medical Center's Psychiatric Institute, who had recently moved to Sneden's with his wife and two children. Aside from the fact that Dr. Stern was a handsome man in his early thirties with black hair and mustache and flashing dark eyes, I had no particular reason to remember the introduction—except that as we shook hands I suddenly thought: my life is going to have something to do with this man. I had never had a similar experience in meeting anyone else (although I have had other episodes of precognition), so I dismissed the thought as mere wistful thinking.

Lem began his senior year at school, and the serious choice of a college was upon us. He wanted a small, coeducational, photogenic college in the country, he said, with a liberal-arts program and a good darkroom. We made appointments and at the end of October drove to Colby in Maine, Middlebury in Vermont, and then down to spend a day at Swarthmore. I had not urged him to choose my old college and had rather thought he would reject it simply because I had gone there, but he could think of nowhere else after that happy day on the campus, the football game at which he cheered for "our" side, and a highly successful interview with the assistant dean of admissions. And the unique beauty of the place impressed him as much as it always impressed me.

Muriel had grown much worse during our absence, and it was clear that she was near death. One night early in November we couldn't find a night nurse, so I stayed with her on the twin bed next to the hospital-style bed Cushman had procured. She was heavily sedated, quite delirious, and also restless, often needing to be turned, to be lifted onto the commode beside her bed or for a massage of her poor, withered legs with the still pretty little white feet. As I did these things through the long, dark hours I suddenly thought: I am ministering unto the body of Christ. This astonished me, for I do not often think in this vein.

She dozed, and I watched a petal drop from the red rose I had brought her the day before. The silence was so deep that it seemed to me the petal actually made a "clunking" noise as it fell into the dim lamplight on the top of her dressing table. Then Muriel roused and began talking to herself. "I'll never go there any more . . ." she muttered. She sat upright in bed and shouted, "The Bowery! The Bowery!" So I sat up too, and together, at the top of our lungs, we sang "The Bowery" all the way through. She sank back on her pillows, but a few moments later she began shouting again. "Die Die Die Die Die Die Die Die Help Me Die!" she screamed. I held her hand and she slept for an hour, while I thought about how strange it was to be up all night after so many years. I remembered the Victory in Europe night in San Francisco, Dixie Tighe's deathwatch in Japan, the night before Lem was born, the night after Liaquat Ali Khan's assassination. There must also have been nights of love, I reflected as I stared at Muriel's gaunt face on the pillow, but I don't remember them.

Muriel died peacefully two days later. A few days afterward, Cushman Haagensen stopped his car when he saw me on my morning walk. We looked at each other silently. "You have a halo over your head," I said finally. He smiled and shrugged. "You were very good," he said. "You made the difference." Coming from Cushman, who was known to be a terror to nurses and young doctors, this was such high praise that after he drove off I simply stood where I was, staring after him. So you don't have to be just one thing, like a writer, I thought. You can be other things too. It was the first time such a thought had ever crossed my mind.

. . .

Lem's eighteenth birthday was duly celebrated with a new tripod and a good wrist watch, and a superb light meter from his father, who had recently retired and who had moved with his wife to the Windward Islands. As November went on, the psychic drain I had felt from the long months of Muriel's illness was replaced by another feeling, which I tried to describe in my journal:

I have been so close to the country all year, to the slow growing and the greening and the coming of the browns and the reds of autumn that I feel magnetized to the earth, almost as if we were one. As if my hands had been for many months on its pulse and that by staying, by being close, I have grown and changed with the earth.

Like Muriel, I realize with some surprise but also with a sense of surety. By being so close, day after day with, in effect, my hand on her pulse, I have come close to some reality which would have escaped me if my life had been more distracted, more diversified. The two are connected—the closeness, the growth, the decay, the slow inevitabilities. It seems almost a mystic revelation, whose import I don't yet quite understand. But I think it has something to do with what I learned in India: that everything is part of the whole.

Still, I was in no way prepared when on Sunday, November 24, Lem suddenly said, "I'm sick," and went heavily to sleep.

❧ 21 ❧

Monday morning he said his teeth hurt. I made an emergency appointment with his dentist, but the dentist saw nothing wrong and suggested he see a physician. When we came home, Lem fell instantly asleep, and slept so deeply all afternoon and evening that I couldn't bear to wake him. I couldn't believe that there was anything seriously wrong, but I was uneasy enough to write in my journal that night that I felt "as if a strong young hemlock had suddenly fallen."

The next morning he showed me some minute red spots all over his legs and said he felt no better. At 1 p.m. I took him to our local doctor in Nyack, E. Deland Battles, Jr., whom I trust and like. When Lem emerged he said the doctor had been noncommittal but wanted him to have a blood test at Nyack Hospital. We had the blood test and went home to await the doctor's phone call. At 4:30 he telephoned and said that Lem was to go into the hospital immediately and that a bed was waiting. He would see me there at 6 p.m., he said. He sounded serious and I decided, for no reason I can remember, that Lem had mononucleosis.

While I packed a bag for him, Lem sat at the piano and played the first movement of the "Moonlight Sonata" with a surge of passionate love and strength that I had never heard before. Then he went upstairs to get the only book he wanted to take with him, Mark Twain's *The Mysterious Stranger* (which tells, among other things, of the death of an adolescent boy).

We drove to the hospital, and by 5:30 Lem was in a bed in a room with two other patients. At 6 Dr. Battles appeared at the door, said a cheery hello to Lem, and asked me to come out into the lobby. We sat down face to face, and I saw that his eyes were full of pain.

"I have to do the hardest thing a doctor is ever required to do," he said. "And that is to tell a mother that her child has a fatal illness. I must tell you that the blood test indicates that Lem has a very severe case of leukemia, that there is no known cure for this disease, and that he will die within a few weeks. If it is any consolation, it will be a relatively painless death."

I could feel all the blood draining from my face. "How long?" I managed to ask. "Around four weeks," he said. There would be more tests in the morning, he said as we stood up, but he did not think there would be any change in the diagnosis.

The most difficult thing I have ever had to do in my life was to go back to Lem and say a cheerful goodnight. He was ferociously curious about the nature of his illness and I said the doctor didn't know yet. I went down stony-faced in the elevator, and as I walked along the main corridor, trying not to have hysterics in public, I saw a door marked "Chapel." Almost blindly I went into the empty room and threw myself on my knees. I don't know how long I sobbed out my prayers to an unknown God, but when I emerged I was composed enough to drive home.

At home I telephoned Cushman Haagensen. He said it was much too early for a firm diagnosis of leukemia, and that he would arrange immediately for a bed at Columbia Presbyterian Medical Center—which I learned later is one of the four greatest cancer treatment centers in America. The rest of the evening is hazy, but I remember taking a tranquilizer and going to see my friends Mary and Jo Chamberlin because they had a Merck's *Medical Manual*—which it turned out I couldn't bear to read. At midnight I walked down to the river, planning my eventual suicide.

The tests on Wednesday morning only reconfirmed the original diagnosis. That afternoon I drove Lem to Presbyterian. I had not told him what he probably had, but by that time he realized that it must be serious.

"Well, if anything happens to me, please see that my photographs get to the world," he said lightly as we turned onto the Parkway.

A little later, in a very bantering tone of voice, he spoke again, addressing me with a word I had never heard him use. "I say, Mater," he drawled, "it seems to me that life has given you quite a lot of hard blows." It was difficult not to choke up, but I could not burden him with my own agony; during all the weeks he was in the hospital I never allowed myself to cry—because I knew that his perceptive eyes of love would instantly note the slightest sign of swollen eyes. Even so, when he looked at me two weeks later he said compassionately, "Mother, you've aged since I've been in the hospital."

Lem was given a private room on a ward floor, a narrow, gloomy room which gradually became brightened with get-well cards scotch-taped to the walls and brilliant abstract paintings by Harold Goldstein, his school's art teacher, whom Lem much admired. There was also, as the weeks went by, a clutter of plants, flowers, record-player, records, tv set, books, and later a Hansel and Gretel house made of cookies and candies.

The day after Lem went to Presbyterian was Thanksgiving. That morning I had a visit from Dr. Donald F. Tapley, a neighbor who was also, it developed, Lem's attending physician. A tall, blond man in his forties, he retains a somewhat clipped British accent from his Canadian background, and an air of remoteness which had always somewhat intimidated me. Our closest contact, heretofore, had been the fact that Lem sometimes cut the lawns of the elegant Victorian house where Dr. Tapley lives with his wife and his three beautiful young daughters.

Further tests had reconfirmed the diagnosis of leukemia, he told me. There was no cure, he said, but sometimes it was possible to achieve a "remission" by the use of certain new drugs which they would try on Lem. But he held out little hope, for the leukemia was acute and, in fact, the worst the hospital had ever seen.

"Aren't there sometimes miracles?" I asked desperately.

"Yes . . . sometimes. Very rarely."

"Of course it would be impossible for me to go on living if Lem dies," I said, feeling very controlled and matter of fact.

"In that case, you would do no credit to Lem," said Donald icily. A curious sentence, really, but possibly the most important ten words anyone has ever said to me.

After that I spent the hours of 2 p.m. to 9 p.m. every day with Lem, finding in myself some reserves of strength I never knew I had, so that it was possible to enter his room each afternoon with an air of calm confidence which I did not feel anywhere else. I would return home exhausted every night, profoundly grateful for the food I always found on my front porch; the entire town had been electrified by compassion, and it was a rare night when I didn't find a casserole or a roast chicken awaiting my return, and a warm, encouraging note from Blythe Finke, Ann Thomas, or other neighbors.

Lem nearly died those first two days, I later learned, but blood and platelet (a component of the blood) transfusions pulled him through. The platelets made his joints hurt and he complained once—the only time during all the weeks—of the pain. "I know better than to ask myself such a silly question," he said, "but sometimes I just can't help wondering what I ever did to deserve such pain."

The next three weeks, during the two-week course of the new drugs and the week following, Lem lost twenty pounds but seemed to grow better. Eric and his wife, Margie, whom I had telephoned, flew up from Grenada and Lem enjoyed their daily visits. One day early in December the hematologist said to me: "I think there is a reasonable chance of getting him into a meaning-ful remission." I knew that a remission could last anywhere from a week to, at the most, eighteen years, and that during any remis-sion a complete cure might be discovered; leukemia is closer to a breakthrough than other cancers. I rushed away to the ladies' room to weep with joy, and actually wrote the words I had just heard in pencil on the wall, just to *see* them. (Later I tried to rub them out, but I couldn't. Perhaps they are still there.)

One afternoon when I arrived at the hospital I heard the sound of the hospital radio on the wall above Lem's bed, and just as my hand touched the door I heard the word "leukemia." My hand dropped to my side and I stood there, frozen, listening to a round-table discussion of the disease which described Lem's symptoms in detail and held out little hope of recovery; it would have been useless to interrupt, for the program had evidently been going on for some time. When I walked in he snapped off the radio and looked at me quietly.

"I have leukemia, don't I?" he asked.

"Yes," I said, for I had never lied to him, and, in any case, it would now have been useless. "But you are in one of the greatest hospitals in the world, you have some of the greatest doctors, and there are new drug treatments that have been successful which they are using. There is every hope for your recovery."

"I see," he said. "Well, I'm glad to know the truth at last."

We began to talk of getting home for Christmas, and Eric and Margie were so encouraged by Lem's improvement that they returned to Grenada. I marveled that Eric could leave without a word of kindness to me, or a question about the medical expenses, but I was grateful for Lem's sake that he had come. The night Eric left, Lem told me of his father's final phone call. "Eric just won't say he loves me," he reported. "He telephoned to say good-by and ended by saying 'Well, cheers and good luck.' And I said, 'Good-by, Eric, I love you.' And he choked up and said, 'Thank you,' before he hung up."

Lem was not well enough to come home for Christmas, but I brought in the manger of his childhood and decorated the room with some of his favorite ornaments. And on the day before Christmas I dragged into his room a red corduroy boot as big as I was, containing presents from at least ninety neighbors, which had been collected by Ann Thomas. That night, Christmas Eve, he was allowed to get out of bed and stand beside me in the doorway to watch a procession of pretty student nurses wind by, each carrying a lighted candle and singing "Silent Night." He was taller than I was now, and I remember that I felt a great surge of pride that this tall, slim young man, standing so straight by my side, was my son.

The next day I gave him my special present. A year before he had said to me: "Mother, I wish you'd write down the words of all the lullabies you sang to me when I was a baby and a little boy. I want to make sure that . . . well, excuse me, but in case you're not around . . . I could sing them to my own children." I hadn't done it, so this Christmastime I bought a blank book with a lovely cover and every night when I came home from the hospital I wrote in it the words of lullabies, and on the opening page the words of the little Quaker prayer: "Jesus tender shepherd hear me, bless thy little lamb tonight. . . ." He looked at it silently on Christmas morning, murmured a thank you, and I saw that there were tears in his eyes.

We opened presents from the big red boot almost all day, marveling at the generosity and ingenuity of our neighbors. Lem particularly loved a medieval flute and oboe record which had been given to him by Dr. Stern, his erstwhile tennis opponent about whom I had had such a strong presentiment; we played the record several times, lighted the three little candles in front of the manger, and listened to "Sheep May Safely Graze." "It wasn't such a bad Christmas after all," Lem said sleepily, as I kissed him goodnight.

Dan Stern had started to visit Lem every day and gradually he began ministering also to me. He prescribed a stronger tranquilizer than the one I had been taking, and started me on an antidepressant which he told me would take two weeks to become effective. This was just as well, because after Christmas everything went downhill.

The first course of drugs did not, after all, have any appreciable effect. They tried a second. No good. They asked my permission to try a drug which had not yet been licensed and I gave it. No good. They consulted with other specialists all over the country. Nothing. Blood and platelet transfusions became a daily event. Lem grew very tired, very quiet. Once he asked me with a shy little laugh, "I say, I'm not on the brink of extinction, am I?" Of course not, I told him firmly, and I think that is the only time in his whole life that I ever lied to him.

Several times I looked up from reading or knitting to find him staring at me, his large hazel eyes grave and full of wonder— once our eyes locked in what seemed an eternity of silent communion. Every twilight I would go to the window and look toward the southern sky until I could say, "Your special star is out, darling." Several times as I awaited the star, his deep, already masculine voice would break the silence with the words, "I love you, Mother. I love you very much." And when I left at night he would say gently "Be careful driving home, Mother. Be *very* careful." Often he spoke of his father and speculated on business affairs which might bring Eric back to New York. But more and more as the days went on he just wanted to lie quietly and have his hands held, his beautiful hands which seemed more wasted hour by hour.

By Wednesday, January 8, 1969, Lem was running a temperature which sometimes reached 106 degrees, and even the ice mattress on which he lay could not bring it down to much below 102 degrees. That afternoon, Donald Tapley came into the little waiting room where I was having a cigarette and said, "I think you should call his father and ask him to come back." I telephoned Eric, in Grenada; he caught a 7:30 plane the next morning, and was in the hospital by mid-afternoon on Thursday.

He stayed with Lem for two hours, while I chain-smoked in the waiting room. After he left I went in to Lem, who said in a wondering voice, "My father held my hand for the whole time he was here. I never knew he was so compassionate." Later he added, "My father said he loved me three times. That is the first time he ever said those words to me."

The next day, Friday the 10th, he dozed almost all day. My cousin Kay's daughter, Sara Caldwell, came up to the hospital to be with me, and because she was coming out to the country for dinner I left a little earlier than usual, around 8:30. Before I left I kissed Lem's forehead and he squeezed my hand with great strength. I was uneasy about leaving, but the nurse on duty said she thought he would be all right for the night.

Five minutes after we arrived home in Sneden's the phone rang. It was the nurse and she thought it advisable for me to return to the hospital. I called Eric, who was staying with relatives in town, and Dan Stern, who had promised to come. Sara and I made it back to the hospital in twenty minutes.

Lem was comatose and obviously near death. I sat beside him, held his beautiful right hand and covered it with hot tears, and pleaded to a nonexistent God for my treasure . . . my life . . . my beloved son. Lem knew nothing and felt nothing and I could not follow him, much as I longed to do so; as I could not help him any longer I was overwhelmed by the feeling that no woman who loved a son as much as I loved Lem should have to sit beside him and actually watch him die. So I stumbled across the hall to the waiting room and sat in a dark corner, hunched and frozen.

Eric arrived, went in to Lem, came back to me. I don't know how much time went by—it was past visiting hours and the corridors were very quiet. Eric went back to Lem's room. A few minutes later he came out and said huskily, "It's all over." It was 10:20 p.m.

Donald Tapley arrived. Dan Stern arrived. The nurse said we could take a farewell look at Lem. Eric went, and said when he came out that "the boy never looked more beautiful." I didn't go. I was still frozen, partly due to tranquilizers but also due to my determination not to scream the way I had heard so many women scream during my six weeks at the hospital. I signed an autopsy permission and a cremation order. A flock of sorrowing nurses arrived and packed all the possessions from Lem's room into brown-paper bags. We all carried them down to my car. Eric refused any tranquilizers or sleeping pills, and went home alone on the subway. Dan drove my car to Sneden's, leaving his own in the city to be picked up later.

Donald and Dan came into the house with Sara and me. We made strong drinks and lighted the living-room fire. Donald began to talk about Lem, of his courage, his style, his uniqueness. "He has left a glow in the sky behind him," he said. I asked him if he would repeat some of these thoughts at the memorial service.

There must have been 300 people in the Quaker Meeting House by the time we arrived on Sunday afternoon. There were friends from Boston, Washington, New York, and, because of Eric, from the United Nations. The entire school body of Rockland Country Day seemed to be there, and almost all of our Sneden's and Palisades neighbors. Eric was sitting on a front bench near the door, with his wife and her family, and he half stood up as I came in with Sara and her mother, Kay, who happened to be in the East. I was told later that I swooped him up with a queenly gesture and led him firmly forward to sit with us on the front benches, at right-angles to the glowing fireplace.

After a brief silence, Lorraine Sharpless, a leading member of the Meeting, rose and explained that Friends worshiped in silence, but that anyone might speak if he felt moved to do so. Then a deep silence settled over the Meeting, broken only by the sound of the crackling logs in the fireplace. Finally, one woman voiced gentle praise of Lem, and another spoke of the Meeting's love for me. More silence.

Nicholas Van Dyke, the young minister of the Palisades Presbyterian Church, who had helped so many people in the community, had moved to Princeton, but he had come up for the weekend to be with me. Now he rose in the Meeting and read, as I had asked him to do, the 104th Psalm; this has always been my favorite psalm, for it is an exultant celebration of life, of beauty, and of the interrelationships in the world which make everything part of the whole or, if one wills, of God. It is a total defiance of death, and I could think of nothing more appropriate to Lem and his life.

After a short silence, Donald rose and spoke. This is what he said:

Margaret asked me to say something here and I said I could not, but I know I have to. I knew Lem Britter as a doctor at the Presbyterian Hospital, where he lived alone and isolated from his friends in a small bare room. I came to know him well. I know things about Lem that his friends do not.

Lemuel Parton Blakeney Britter entered this world on November 5, 1950, and left it last Friday. He was born in India. I did not know him then but I read his mother's book about that time. When Margaret was carrying Lem she asked herself many questions, as I suppose all women do. But she asked one question which others do not ask: "Will he have an old soul or a new soul?"

I can tell you that Lem had an old soul. A new soul could not have left the world with such grace.

Lem Britter was in the hospital for forty-five days and I think he knew from the first he had leukemia. He never asked me and I never told him, but I knew that he knew from the nature of the questions he asked of the orderlies and the nurses. He never asked me. We spoke in our own special code.

In the last ten days or two weeks of his life, certainly in the last four or five days, he knew he was dying.

There was something very special about Lem. All of us, the doctors, the nurses, the aides, were struck by this and we asked ourselves what it was. It was not his courage in facing death. There are, as we see them in hospitals, many examples of courage in facing death. What was special about Lem? We talked about it and what we decided was that he had a style, beyond courage.

I would like his friends to know of this and I shall give you an example of it.

It was my custom to visit Lem late every afternoon. He would never ask me about himself but only ask in our casual code "How'm I doing?" I would always answer "Fine. Goodnight, Lem. See you tomorrow." And he would say "Goodnight. See you tomorrow." His last evening he was so ill we were at our wits' end. His fever was so ferocious that I thought he might not live through the night. For several days he had not asked me the code question: "How'm I doing?" That night he asked it. I was caught off guard and answered, "Fine, Lem. We'll lick that fever. Goodnight, see you tomorrow."

He did not answer. We had always spoken the truth to each other, respecting the code. Now I knew that he knew I had broken it.

I left, realizing that he was the better man. Then I went back. I told him how we all felt about him—that he was "great stuff," and how much we all loved and admired him.

Then he said "Thank you for asking my father to come." We had tried to keep this from him and present it casually. I knew that he knew. I said "Goodnight, Lem." And then he said "Goodnight."

That was Lem Britter's style.

After that no one could say anything more and the Meeting ended. Everything ended.

❧22❧

Except it doesn't end, of course. Or anyway, it doesn't end if one makes the choice of life over death. It seems to me that this choice is the individual's ultimate right, and so there were many times in the following years when I wavered between the two options. Some nights, alone and swept by storms of grief, I would stare at Lem's .22, and twice I loaded it and held the muzzle in my mouth. Several times I poured sleeping pills into my hand, and waited to find out what I would decide. But each time I would hear Donald's icy sentence: "In that case, you would do no credit to Lem" and recall Blythe Finke's little note: "Your courage gives courage to us all." Then I would put the gun or the pills away until the next time of temptation.

Does one live by slogans? So often, when I had relived the night of Lem's death for the uncontrollable twentieth or fiftieth time, I was overwhelmed by a desire to go where Lem was, wherever that might be. But each time I heard the voice of my little Quaker grandmother: "Thee must await God's time." I knew then, as I still know, that this is true, although why it is I do not know. Perhaps it is merely a disguise for the instinct of self-preservation, for certainly I cannot believe in a personal God who plans our individual fate any more than I can believe in the power of prayer, after those six imploring weeks when I wept my supplications at the feet of Buddha, Allah, Jehovah, Jesus, Mary, and God, God, God. No longer, either, do I flirt with superstition or magic, for I know now that there is no truth in them. All I have faith in is the belief that there are great immutable laws which make everything part of the whole, and that we must live out our lives within the rhythm of these laws. "No one can dance the tango perfectly, but all of us must dance it the best way we can" my Spanish housekeeper used to say. Lord David Cecil, in his interpretation of Joseph Conrad's view of life, said it in another way and one which to me is profoundly meaningful:

What one lives for may be uncertain, but how one lives is not. . . . Man should live nobly though he does not see any practical reason for it, simply because in the mysterious, inexplicable mixture of beauty and ugliness, virtue and baseness, in which he finds himself, he must want to be on the side of the beautiful and virtuous.

In my struggle to do this I often fail, but I have also been strengthened by the discovery that Lem's life and death taught me what is truly important, so that I no longer need to fear those things I used to fear. I no longer care what other people think of me, and therefore am free to be as honest to myself as I am capable of being. I no longer worry about being hopelessly out of step with current intellectual and literary movements, and simply accept myself as someone who is absorbed in unfashionable thoughts about love, truth, and the continuity of time. I have lost my fear of being ridiculous, as I no doubt am when I bellow, "When General MacArthur at Last Returned" as I search for Japanese beetles in the rose garden. And I smile now when I think of my own eventual death, for it means that wherever Lem is, I will be with him.

In February 1968 I recorded one of our typical conversations in my journal:

I weep at the horror of Viet Nam, which I heard all day on radio.

We eat dinner. We watch an episode of *Star Trek,* a science fiction fantasy. Commercial comes on. "While we watched that, one hundred people died of starvation," Lem says.

We watch another act of *Star Trek.* Commercial comes on. "We could join the Peace Corps," I say. "Next November you'll be old enough, and I'd be allowed, too." "It wouldn't do any good," Lem says.

Another episode. Another commercial. "Art does good," I say. "Study does good. It helps to know *why.*"

On the screen people fight and kill. "Love is the way," I say. "Yes," says Lem.

No longer do I ask the eternal "Why?" But it has been some comfort to me to reflect that while the scientists say they do not yet know the cause of leukemia, I know there nevertheless is a cause, and that Lem died for a scientific reason and not because of some unbearable coincidence, like a whistling boy on a country road cut down by a drunken driver.

I have found some other comforts in these years without him. I find now that I often look at the world about me in a way that he taught me to see, and as I study the pattern of raindrops on an oak leaf or observe the back-lighting of sunlight on the soft pink fuzz of a raspberry stem, I feel that he is looking out through my eyes. Or I watch my old yellow cat, Chini, sitting in a square of sun on the kitchen table, as she stares through the window at the chickadees on the bird-feeder, swishing her tail and growling with frustration. And my throat fills with loving laughter which sounds like his. Often I am flooded with joy at the memory of him, and of gratitude that he existed and was the person he was.

. . .

My mother poisoned her middle age with constant brooding on old age and death, and I think I have learned a lesson from her example: do what is intelligent and possible to provide for the future, and then stop thinking about it and take joy in each day. I try to do this and not to reflect too often that basically it is a very lonely road and that I must walk it by myself. Still, there are friends who have stepped out of the forests of their lives and walked with me for a while. The first of these is my beautiful cousin Sara Caldwell, who lived with me for many weeks after Lem died, who commuted—sometimes with difficulty—to her job in New York, and who has continued to visit me. Dan Stern came to see me every day at first, then twice a week for a year, every week for another year, and at least once a month since then; with his blessed antidepressants and tranquilizers and his wise understanding he led me back to life again. Those two were the constants. Together in the September following Lem's death, we three walked into the woods Lem had loved and on a bluff overlooking the Hudson River buried his ashes under a great oak tree. Every year I go there on his birthday in November to plant three daffodils, and again at the end of April to look at his favorite flowers celebrating with their beauty the place where he lies.

Of the many who have helped me there are two I especially

cherish—one a man, the other a little boy. The man is someone who has loved me for many years and who miraculously continues to do so. He lives in a far city and we can only be together three or four times a year, but his letters, his phone calls, and, above all, the knowledge of his steady, unchanging love nourish the roots of my entire being.

The boy is Bartholomew Lawrence Hyde and he was born on January 10, 1966—the same day which was to become the anniversary of Lem's death—to Gail Wrenn Hyde, whose father had been my boss at *The New Yorker*, and to Joe Hyde, whose grandmother was Mary Tonetti and whom I have known since he was a baby. The Hydes live in the "Big House" just across the lane from me, and their two older children, Annie and Philip, have been in and out of my home for years. But it is golden-haired Barry who has become my most frequent visitor and also my official godchild.

Our friendship began the December after Lem died, when three-year-old Barry began to come over to play a Santa Claus game with me, alternating the roles of gift-giving Saint Nick and snoring sleeper. One day, he looked at a photograph of Lem and said, "You loved him very much, didn't you?" I said, "Yes, I did."

"Would you like me to get you another boy?" he asked. "I know a store where they sell boys and I could get you one. I'll get you a baby boy."

"Well, that would be fine," I told him, "but babies are pretty hard to take care of, you know."

"Oh, that's all right, Margaret," he said earnestly. "I'll get you one with all his teeth in." I began to love him seriously from that moment.

Barry has stayed with me several times when his mother was away, and I have rejoiced in the presence of a small boy in the house, the clutter of pans and sieves in the bathtub, the noise and the singing, the peanut-butter and jelly sandwiches, the twinkling jokes. In summers he helps in the garden and we study insects and leaves and flowers; in winters, we toast marshmallows at the fireplace, drink cambric tea, and read *Winnie the Pooh* or *The Wizard of Oz* aloud. I do not confuse him with Lem, for Barry is very much his own self, a vibrant child whose friendship I am grateful to have, not only for its own sake but because he leads me toward the future, and reminds me—as my son's presence once did—that the child is more important than the adult. Only by this reminder can we be truly prepared for our own death.

. . .

I have traveled a lot during these last three years. To California, to share my grief with Aunt Sara and Aunt Marion, both of whom had lost children. To Boston, to work on editing Dr. Paul Dudley White's autobiography—a "busy work" which Helen Everitt had suggested. And when I was home, back and forth to my mother's nursing home. I did not tell her of Lem's death because I knew that she would suddenly remember her dearly loved grandson, whom she had now forgotten, and that her flashing sorrow would be a knife in her old heart. There was little to talk of now, so we would just sit quietly, holding hands, saying from time to time "I love you, I love you." It seemed miraculous to me that after all our years of jealous hostility the dross was gone and only the gold of love remained.

Although her memory had virtually disappeared, she still retained flashes of her old, irreverent, humor.

"How old am I?" she asked me that spring of 1969.

"You're ninety-one," I said, scarcely able to believe it myself.

"Ninety-one!" she exclaimed. "No *wonder* I keep urinating!"

She marveled another time when she was told her actual age. "What was I *doing* all those years?" she asked. "Why, I must have been skipping rope for generations!"

"Tell me," she asked one day, "have you seen Mother lately? The Mother who took care of us all?"

"She died a long time ago, darling. In 1926."

"Oh . . . she did?" Silence. Then, timidly, "And Father? Where is Father?"

"He died more than fifty years ago, darling." She was quiet, thinking over what I had said.

"When there is nothing to mark the events of the day," she slowly explained, "the years and their events also become nothing. Everything merges on a flat plain and only a few individuals loom against the horizon." I stroked her hand.

"Tell me," she said, "is there anyone left of my father and mother's generation?"

"No," I said.

Her eyes became almost opaque as she stared at air, at nothing, and then full of bewilderment back at me.

"How . . . strange," she said finally. "The generations come and they are strong and they live and stand against the sky and then they just . . . fall into an abyss and disappear. And then another and another . . . Is there nothing to tell us what it all *means*? Is life meaningless? Is it all meaningless?"

Her hands fell into her lap and she looked at me, her vivid eyes full of wonder.

"What does life mean?" she asked. I was silent.

July 1 a nurse called from the hospital to tell me that Mother had pneumonia and was not expected to live. It was an end which she had long desired, yet as I sat beside her bed for the next two days, the tears streamed from my eyes in a great flooding which I could not control. My mother, my mother, my *mother*. I held her hand and said her name, and I thought perhaps her eyes flickered. "I love you," I said. "I love you." She died on July 3, 1969.

Recently, pawing around her hundreds of letters to me, I found one she wrote me when I was in college in the mid-thirties. For all its sentimentality, one paragraph seems to me to be a fitting epitaph:

Darling, I believe that life is worth having experienced. It holds moments of rare happiness, hours and hours of gentle peace, much pain, and if one is imaginative and vicarious, much more pain. Yet . . . it is good to live and "it doth not yet appear what we shall be," for man stands on his hind legs and his face lifts to the stars. No other animal does.

The next summer I buried her ashes in the garden, near to those of my father.

. . .

There were two other deaths that terrible year of 1969. In January, only a few days after Lem's, I learned that my dear English friend Rose Marie Foottit had thrown herself under the wheels of a train. And on October 30, Helen Everitt was found dead of a heart attack in her bed, her arms around a pillow, smiling. Sweet, sweet Helen . . . O Christ, why must we love people so much? I miss her always; her style, her courage, her perception, her love.

In the spring of 1970 I finished the Dr. White book, sent it off, and began to plan a fall trip to England. It had been four years since I had been there, since I had seen Ian . . . Ian.

Never in my sleeping life had I dreamed of Ian. But one dawn that year, I did. I saw him standing some distance away from me in the middle of a narrow lane in an English village, between rows of thatched cottages. He was rosy and rotund as usual, and he was smiling at me. I cried out, as I would have in reality, "Ian! Ian!" I reached out my arms, as I would have longed to do in reality, and began to run toward him.

As I approached he slipped around the corner of the last cottage on the left, and I lost sight of him. I reached the corner at last, looked around it, and gasped, for the person I saw there was tall, pale, and black-haired instead of gray. But he, too, smiled at me. "Don't be afraid," he said. "I am still Ian. I have gone through a change and I seem different. But I am not. I am still the same person. I am still Ian." He said the last sentence with great emphasis and a look almost of compassion.

Then I woke, found that I remembered the dream in every detail, and realized as I made coffee, dressed, and went out to get the morning paper that it haunted me. As I sat in the big chair by the fireplace, with *The New York Times* on my lap, I stared vacantly at the headlines but my mind was full of Ian and the old, old love. I tried to concentrate on the paper, but fragments of the poems he had read to me on our last night together in San Francisco drifted through my memory like wry ghosts. . . . "O my luve is like a red, red rose . . ." "When you are old and gray and full of sleep . . ."

Impatient with myself, I opened the paper at random. And there, smiling at me from the obituary page, was Ian's photograph. He had been a well-known man in Great Britain and there was a long, appreciative obituary. He had died the morning before, of a heart attack.

I have wrestled with an explanation of that dream for a long time now. At the dawn I dreamed it, Ian had already been dead for more than eighteen hours; the English papers carrying his obituary were long since on the streets, and so, too, were the early and late editions of *The New York Times*. As telepathy has been proved a valid phenomenon, it seems to me that one or several of the five or six people who knew about the importance of Ian in my life might have read about his death and thought of me —thoughts which communicated themselves to my sleeping mind.

But how then to explain that very personal message? "I seem different . . . but I am still Ian." How could a simple, telepathic thought of sympathy have taken that consoling form?

A psychologist friend of mine who has a way of stepping on my fancies has a possible explanation: "The telepathic knowledge of his death was communicated to your sleeping mind by someone," she says. "Then your unconscious, unable to accept the flat fact of annihilation, translated the news into terms which you could accept. That's all." Well, perhaps. But only perhaps. Life would be unbearable, I think, unless we continued to believe in the possibility of that which we cannot yet understand, that central mystery which we can only know "in God's time." When I was four, my mother prayed that for me there would always be some landscapes over which the fogs hang; her prayer was granted.

. . .

So I did not see the living Ian when I went to England in September, but I saw his wife and we wept together. I visited Jim Foottit in Patrixbourne, and he showed me Rose Marie's grave under the copper beech at the end of the lawn. I am happy I had that week with him, full of good talk and great music, for Jim died the following August and today lies beside Rose Marie under the copper beech. I mourn for them, and I mourn for lovely Patrixbourne, which I will never see again.

From Kent I slowly made my way across Southern England to the desolately beautiful coast of North Cornwall and a remote little hamlet called Morwenstow, where I found a thirteenth-century inn so delightful that I stayed for two weeks. Each day I walked for miles through heather and gorse on high moors, gazing at the sea's horizon, or climbed down deep glens and walked under venerable trees beside roaring brooks. Each night I drank my warm whisky in the friendly pub, listened to the laughter, and made friends. And as time went on I felt in myself that a vast healing was beginning to take place.

At home again I found that the healing had progressed to the point where I was able, at long last, to read once more the pages I had written about my parents' lives and then, very gingerly and only at Lucy Freeman's urging, to consider the possibility that it might be necessary to relive my own life before I attempted the vicarious experience of reliving theirs.

I began this book in the spring of 1971 and was absorbed with it during most of the year. In the summer I took a little time out to play in a Sneden's croquet tournament, in the course of which I discovered to my great surprise, that I enjoyed winning. (How life continually opens up new vistas of the self!) I also took a little time out for twilight daydreaming, for I had fallen rather gently in love—hopelessly, as usual. But it was a pleasant affliction while it lasted and at least it indicated to me that there was still life in a heart I had thought dead. And from it I derived one consoling thought: the fact that I have fallen in love so many times does not necessarily mean that I am fickle, but only that there are a great many lovable men in the world.

In September, Bob Lubar, who was now managing editor of *Fortune,* and his wife, Pat, suggested that I join them on an island-drifting trip in Greece. I was tired of writing and felt I was going stale. Dan Stern advised me to go, and so did my editor. I had traveled happily with the Lubars in Ceylon, India, and New England. So I agreed to meet them in Athens on October 21.

On October 14, I flew off for five days on my own in Venice, which I had never seen. I had expected it to be pretty, but depressing in its widely publicized decay, and I was unprepared for what happened to me. I was shaken, shattered, and overwhelmed as I had not been by any other city in the world. I felt as someone might who saw Helen of Troy for the first time; the recognition of beauty was instant and so, too, was the conviction that there can be no other beauty as great. I was possessed by a strength of emotion I had thought I was no longer capable of feeling, and suffused by a fragile happiness I had never expected to find again. None of my friends had ever reported a similar reaction to Venice, and I was bewildered at the violence of my love until I came upon a fine English book called *The Companion Guide to Venice,* by Hugh Honour, in which he quotes Henry James as follows:

Almost everyone interesting, appealing, melancholy, memorable, odd, seems at one time or another, after many days and much life, to have gravitated to Venice by a happy instinct, settling in it and treating it, cherishing it, as a sort of repository of consolations . . . the deposed, the defeated, the disenchanted, or even only the bored, have seemed to find there something that no other place could give.

One day I went to the enchanted island of Torcello and on the *vaporetto* coming back I fell into conversation with an old Englishman with an aristocratic accent and dark, intelligent eyes. I told him that the beauty of Venice constantly made me want to cry. "But my child," he said gently, "beauty *should* make you want to cry. It is the only possible reaction."

So I spent my days wiping away the occasional tears of joy as I wandered the winding streets (feeling again in scale with architecture, as I had at Saint Andrews), drifted through museums and churches, or sat over a *cappuccino* at an outdoor *caffè*, watching the changing sunset light on the gold mosaics of San Marco. When the time came to leave I felt like someone torn from a new and passionate love affair, but I also felt a little foolish, as I might had I suddenly developed an infatuation for Rudolf Valentino. Still, I have never been much interested in contemporaneity —and I have been studying Italian ever since I came home.

I met Bob and Pat in Athens and we set off by Greek steamer on a three-week trip which took us to Mykonos, Santorini, Rhodes, and Crete. The islands were all wonderful and it was a great trip, but I did not find what I had really come to find. I had thought that wandering the ancient ruins where Socrates had taught, or gazing at Homer's wine-dark sea, surely some illumination would come to me, some revelation which would explain the purpose and meaning of life. But none came, even when I went alone to Delphi and sat on that magnificent mountainside staring at the Temple of Apollo, god of light and truth.

On the plane coming home I tried to decide which particular experience in Greece had most impressed me, and decided that it was the gradual way in which all three of us had learned to pay attention to the regularity of heavenly bodies. While traveling on the ships or staying on the islands we began to observe sunset: when it occurred, and how many minutes later than the day before the sun dropped below the sea's horizon. We began to note the evening star, Hesperus, and how it came out each evening in almost the same place the sun had been. We began to observe the moon: when it was new, how many days it took to become full, how it waned. I think we noted these phenomena because of the gaunt Greek landscape, where there is horizon everywhere, but also we had the time to notice, and to come to understand how important it is to be aware of the ageless circlings-around of the universe, in which we humans have so small a place.

John Muir, too, felt this great sense of cosmic order, and as I wander now across the beautiful body of the world, or work in my garden, I think often of some words he wrote:

How deeply with beauty is beauty overlaid! The ground covered with crystals, the crystals with mosses and lichens and low-spreading grasses and flowers . . . these with larger plants, leaf over leaf, with ever-changing color; the broad palm of the firs outspread over these; the azure dome over all like a bellflower, and star above star.

So there is progress. But it is not steady and there are frequent relapses when I wake in the morning weeping for Lem and must practice stringent self-discipline. And sometimes during the long, lonely days I feel that I am living a kind of dream, acting out the part of a museum curator and head gardener, keeping things in order until "they" return; the grapes are rich and full, the flag-stones are swept—so why don't the laughing people arrive for the party, as they used to? And surely when "they" return, my mother and father will approve of what I have done; Rod will be proud of the way I have coped; Lem will pat me on the back and say laconically, "You didn't do too badly, Mother." But when? When? If I worked harder, pulled more weeds, polished the furniture more ferociously, would they come sooner? I know this is wrong, perhaps bordering on insanity, but I also know that I must be patient with myself, and accept the silence of the house, with its voices echoing only in my memory.

Now that there are no actual possibilities left, and no moral dilemmas, I find it easier to daydream than I did in other years: I am, for instance, floating in our pool near the end of summer (we have somehow acquired a pool). My husband Ian comes out of the house, bearing a sheaf of manuscript, his eyeglasses at the end of his nose.

"My dear, would you just take a look at this last bit?" he asks.

"Of course, darling," I say, emerging gracefully from the pool and taking the manuscript in my slim brown hands. "Oh yes, you have it perfectly!" I exclaim. "Oh, very good, very good indeed! But . . . just perhaps *here*? A less pejorative word? Ancillary, perhaps?" "You're right," he says, "the perfect word. What would I do without you?"

"I've been meaning to ask you to look at my own latest chapter, beloved," I say, "and perhaps you can do it while I am poaching the salmon in *court bouillon*. As you know, we are having our favorite guests for dinner under the grape arbor: Charlie Campbell and Dorothy, Jack Winocour, Bob Waithman, Arthur Webb, Paul Scott-Rankin, and Sylvia Porter. We will probably sing 'On Ilkney Moor Bart'at.'"

"Splendid!" he exclaims. "I shall go chill the champagne." Just then Lem, tall and handsome, arrives from the tennis camp where he has been a counselor all summer. With him is a slim, pretty girl in tennis whites with a daisy in her hair. She smiles shyly and shakes hands.

"Mother," says Lem, his arms around both our shoulders and smiling warmly at Ian, whom he adores, "this is Linda Adams from camp. She'll be a sophomore this year at Swarthmore, where I, of course, am a senior." The two young people gaze at each other dreamily and Ian, catching my eye, winks.

Usually I end up crying, or giggling at my own absurdities. Then I make myself go plan a party for real people.

. . .

Now I have almost finished this reliving of the past, and I am ready to move into the unknown future. I don't know whether I have rebuilt the part of me that burned to the ground, and I have not found any real answers to the meaning of life, or discovered exactly why my own life went the way it did go. But I have learned that you pay for love with loss, rather like a deal with the devil except that I believe that this one is with God. Perhaps it would be better if we were given a choice at the beginning of life between loving and suffering loss or never loving at all, but we aren't and we can't, for our capacity to love depends on how much love our parents poured into us before we were able to choose at all. But even if the choice had been mine, and I had been able to avoid anguish, I would still accept all the love I was given, and be grateful.

I am amused by people who say to me: "Oh, you've had such a terrible life!" I've had a great life and I'm not sure that it might not always be in the past tense, even now. Every day of my life I thank God for the miracle of having been born. I have seen moons and suns rise, palm trees against Ceylon skies, and skunk cabbages emerging in spring in swamps among hazel bushes. I have watched birds and clouds, and a red leaf floating on the brown waters of a brook. I have listened to Beethoven and Mozart and read Shakespeare's sonnets. I have felt the joyous movement of my body cutting through surf in Hawaii, serving an ace in tennis, or rippling in the orgasms of love. I have smelled the brown earth of spring, plum pudding with burning brandy, and the happy sweat of my own body. I have felt the softness of milkweed fuzz, of my cat's belly, of the back of a baby's neck. I have crunched on the cold, crisp apples of October, tasted raspberries picked from my own bushes on hot August mornings, and in December licked upon snow laced with maple syrup. I have loved and I have been loved.

Above all, I have borne a child and raised a child. I created life and I cherished that life. I took part in the mystery of continuity, and I know that the love which is at the center of the mystery can never be lost. It exists forever. I have been blessed.

Sneden's Landing, November 5, 1972